LAWYER LINCOLN

LAWYER LINCOLN

Albert A. Woldman

Carroll & Graf Publishers, Inc.
New York

Copyright © 1936 by Albert A. Woldman

First Carroll & Graf edition October 1994

Carroll & Graf Publishers, Inc.
260 Fifth Avenue
New York, NY 10001

Library of Congress Cataloging-in-Publication Data
Woldman, Albert A. (Albert Alexander), 1897–1971.
    Lawyer Lincoln / Albert A. Woldman.—1st Carroll & Graf ed.
    p.   cm.
    Originally published: Houghton Mifflin, 1936.
    Includes index.
    ISBN 0-7867-0156-0 : $12.95
    1. Lincoln, Abraham, 1809–1865—Career in law.
  2. Lawyers—United States— Biography. I. Title.
  E457.2.W85 1994
  973.7'092—dc20
  [B]   94-28128
                                                                  CIP

Manufactured in the United States of America

PREFACE

MORE has been written about Abraham Lincoln than about any other character in the history of the world with the exception of Jesus of Nazareth and possibly Napoleon.

Then, why another Lincoln biography? Why a book dealing with the immortal Emancipator's career as a lawyer and the legal and constitutional problems that confronted him as Civil War President?

Because 1937 marks the centennial of Lincoln's admission to the bar.

Because Lincoln is the law profession's noblest contribution to American civilization.

Because, without his twenty-three years of experience at the bar, he might never have become President of the United States.

Because no other chief magistrate of this Nation was ever confronted with so many grave legal and constitutional problems demanding summary solution.

Because Lincoln's training at the bar prepared, molded, and qualified him for his mighty task and enabled him to meet the unprecedented constitutional questions created by the crisis.

And yet, Lincoln's biographers, with few exceptions, have seen fit to give his law career but passing comment. For the most part they fill the few pages devoted to his life in the courts and in his law office with mythical anecdotes that depict him as a Don Quixote of the judicial circuit searching for causes of injustice to combat. They encircle his head with a halo as they strip him of all practicality, acumen, and shrewdness, and portray him as an oafish country lawyer, perversely honest, who eschewed the technicalities of the law, who refused cases where there was the least doubt as to his prospective client's innocence, and who was naïve almost to the point of simplicity when it came to charging fees for his services.

Too long has the general conception of Lincoln the lawyer been formulated by this silly twaddle.

In the present day economic crisis, replete with its difficult constitutional problems, jurists and statesmen frequently cite Lincoln as their guide and authority.

It is well that his constitutional interpretations, his understanding of the broad principles of law and justice, and his fine legal conscience and reasoning power are causing jurists like Lord Shaw of Dunfermline, a leading English legal authority, to rank Lincoln, with Papinianus, Grotius, and Lord Mansfield, among the greatest lawyers of history.

Bar associations, civic and patriotic groups, and men and women of all walks of life will desire to commemorate the centennial of Lincoln's admission to the bar as one of the most momentous events in all his epoch-making career.

For these and other reasons, we believe this book to be a timely and necessary addition to the vast store of Lincolniana. We trust that the new material and new treatment and new interpretation of old material will give the world a better understanding of the shrewd and practical leader of the Illinois bar who became the Nation's leader in its hour of greatest trial.

CONTENTS

LAWYER LINCOLN

I. AN UNFAMILIAR STORY

SHORTLY after Abraham Lincoln passed into history, a sorrowing nation came to the realization of a startling fact: it hardly knew its martyred leader.

Only four years and two months before the hand of the mad assassin removed Lincoln from the scene of action, he had arrived in Washington virtually unknown to the country at large. For about fifteen hundred days he governed practically as a dictator. In this short period he quelled the rebellion that threatened the nation's life, preserved the Union, extirpated slavery, and altered the destiny of the human race. And then, like a comet that flashes across a troubled sky and vanishes from the sight of men, he was gone.

In reverent devotion his grateful countrymen began to weave around the memory of this superbly human man of the people a gossamer garment of appreciation and veneration, spun out of the filaments of wonder and hero-worship.

One short turn of the kaleidoscope finds the chosen leader of a stricken nation canonized by the very men who only a brief time before jeered, doubted, and fought him.

Now Lincoln's countrymen saw only the humble child of the backwoods, born in wretched poverty—without a worldly advantage—and they marveled that, when late in life he was entrusted with the destiny of a nation in a crisis affecting the fate of human freedom, he was pre-eminently ready.

They remembered the unpolished rustic, with less than one year of actual schooling, growing to young manhood amid the primitive wilds of the frontier—amid surroundings such as ordinarily crush every aspiration to mental achievement—and yet they saw the day arrive when men of deep learning and statesmen of vast experience eagerly listened to his counsel and willingly followed his leadership.

They recalled how the graceless courtroom advocate and awkward political debater, untrained in the art of oratory, became one of the most gifted pleaders of all ages.

They beheld the simple, unassuming, self-styled "mast-fed" lawyer develop into the great interpreter of the American Constitution.

Reverently they acclaimed him as the liberator of the slaves and the deliverer of their country.

Dazzled by the luster of his achievements, they who had mistrusted and reviled him while he lived now began to wonder whether, after all, Abraham Lincoln had not been more than a mere mortal. With a weird sense of something supernatural they wondered whether the obscure country lawyer had not in reality been a heaven-born genius or a prophet chosen by God for a special task.

But those who really knew Abraham Lincoln, and could retrace the plodding steps by which he had made his upward climb, found nothing mysterious about his attainments. They knew how the shrewd lawyer, devoid of academic learning, had trained himself for his career. They recalled how his practical experiences— his training as a surveyor, legislator, political stump-speaker, and congressman—all contributed something essential to his unique mental makeup, and how his long arduous practice for nearly a quarter of a century at the bar of Illinois constituted his principal preparation for his future task.

For law, with its sphere varied as life and as broad as the activities of government itself, was indeed Lincoln's chief schoolmaster.

No other pursuit could have given him a better background of life and conditions and manners of mankind. None could better develop those forces of intellect and character he was to display in the great crisis. As Edmund Burke declared in one of his great speeches commenting on the power of the colonial lawyers at the time of the Revolution: "This study of law renders men acute, inquisitive, dextrous, prompt in attack, ready in defense, full of resources. No other profession is more closely connected with actual life than the law. It concerns the highest of all temporal interests of man—property, reputation, the peace of all families, the arbitrations and peace of nations, liberty, life even, and the very foundations of society."

The law taught Lincoln more than merely the technical knowledge of rules of practice, of demurrers, of pleas in abatement and pleas in bar. It proved for him a study of human institutions and of history itself. For, as the laws of a country mark its history and its progress, its statutes and judicial reports were for Lincoln fountains of knowledge respecting the progress of Anglo-Saxon society from feudalism down to his own day. In the study and practice of law, the untutored Lincoln found the facts necessary to understand not only men—as they have been and as they are—but also the processes through which men have passed in their progress towards a higher development.

For nearly a quarter of a century, Lincoln's association and forensic combats with the giants of the early Illinois bar—a coterie of brilliant lawyers distinguished in law, politics, and eloquence—broadened his faculties for the practical game of life. In the daily matching of wits with these able barristers, the bookless man found the technical schooling he lacked as a youth. In the forums of justice, with his soul on fire with the spirit of freedom, he established and defended the rights of men. Through the instrumentality of the law he fought for civil liberty and human rights as he was to fight on a scale far more vast when later called to the Nation's chief magistracy.

The study of law by Lincoln made this product of the prairies a student of government and constantly brought him into direct contact with its working features. It taught him to promulgate laws and to enforce them, and taught him the principles of international law. His study of the common law, with its repeated blows leveled at the feudal system, subconsciously laid in the brain of the future Emancipator the foundation of the principles of civil and religious liberty!

Yet Lincoln's twenty-three years of professional activities, which enabled his genius to take root and flourish, have remained but a meaningless and colorless background to the stirring story of his last four years. Too long has this all-important period of training been permitted to remain an unfamiliar story.

Lincoln came on the scene when the all-consuming issue of the day was the conflict between slavery and freedom. It was an issue replete with questions of constitutional law. Slavery was fixed in the law of the land and confessed in the Constitution. Like other forms of special privilege, slavery lay snugly entrenched behind an entanglement of constitutional guarantees, legal technicalities, and statutory limitations.

The Supreme Court of the United States by its fateful pronouncement in the Dred Scott case compressed the whole question into a problem of legal and constitutional interpretations. Epitomized, the issue became: Is the Dred Scott decision good law?

Then followed the most vital issue of all—the assumed right of State secession. Almost in its entirety it was a legal and constitutional proposition. Briefly, the question was: Can a State lawfully withdraw from the Union? The disputes between slavery and freedom, secession and union were but conflicts of contrary doctrines of constitutional law.

In rapid succession came a formidable series of unprecedented legal and constitutional questions requiring interpretation and immediate decision and action.

In the career of no other President was the legal phase as prominent and important as in the life of Lincoln. No other chief magistrate of this Nation has ever been confronted with more grave legal and constitutional problems demanding summary solution. None experienced greater need of a comprehensive legal training and understanding of the broad principles of law and justice, combined with a reasoning power to find the legal way out of the maze of constitutional entanglements and technicalities that threatened to thwart every effort of Lincoln during the terrible crisis.

The emergency that confronted Lincoln demanded a leader possessed of a legal conscience—a man imbued with the supremacy of the law as embodied in the Constitution; who by wise and sane interpretation could give to the Constitution an elasticity and adaptability necessary to cope with the unparalleled situation and yet act at all times within its provisions.

Abraham Lincoln, without special training for high executive office, was qualified to assume his stupendous obligations because the problems that confronted him as President, in a general sense, were not unlike those he had tackled for nearly a quarter of a century as a lawyer—only on a scale far more vast.

No picture of Lincoln, therefore, is complete without the detailed background created by his experience at the bar. Nowhere are his individuality, characteristics, and idiosyncrasies more marked than in the law office and courtroom. Nowhere are his humanity, reasoning, logic, and eloquence more impressive. Even in petty and trivial cases, otherwise dull and uninteresting, can be found touches of his characteristic love of justice, honesty, humility, and forbearance. They are replete with his moral courage, humaneness, modesty, sympathy, tact and adroitness, wit, humor, and power of satire. Here can be found his human weaknesses as well as the elements of his greatness. Even in his pleadings and briefs, technical and seemingly unimportant, are characteristic specimens of his method of reasoning and style of expression.

To understand Lincoln, the adroit stump-speaker of the Douglas debates; the fearless critic intelligently taking issue with the Supreme Court of the United States over the Dred Scott decision; the logician calmly analyzing the constitutional status of slavery before a learned audience at Cooper Institute, requires an analysis of his law career.

To comprehend Lincoln the cautious President, sanely and coolly counseling his perplexed countrymen from ways of danger to safety as they undergo their greatest trial, makes essential a knowledge of Lincoln the lawyer as he advised his litigious neighbors of Sangamon County.

To vision Lincoln, the defender of the Constitution, successfully combating the legal sophism of the Southern leaders claiming secession to be a constitutional right of the individual States; to perceive the interpreter of the Constitution rising to a level with Marshall and Webster as he makes momentous and unprecedented decisions affecting the very life of that instrument and the government created by it; to understand Lincoln the preserver of the Union and author of the Emancipation Proclamation—one must know the Lincoln who spent twenty-three of his fifty-six years in law offices, in the courts, and on the judicial circuits. In no other way can his seemingly inexplicable genius become comprehensible.

II. THE BOOK OF LAW

A BARREL of junk—contents unknown—purchased by Abraham Lincoln for fifty cents, shaped his career and changed the course of history.

Shaped his career—for weeks later when this barrel was emptied, it disgorged on the floor of Lincoln's store a much-worn edition of Blackstone's *Commentaries*. So assiduously did Lincoln read the elementary principles of law explained therein, and so impressed became his naturally analytical mind with the logic and reasoning of the great English jurist, that from the chance finding of this book of law arose one of the most momentous decisions in all of Lincoln's epoch-making career—the resolve to make law his life's calling.

Changed the course of history—for it is highly improbable that this otherwise unlearned and intellectually undeveloped product of the Illinois prairies could ever have become available for the Presidency of the United States without the twenty-three years of training he eventually received at the bar.

Well may we wonder what change in the course of history might have resulted if, instead of entering the law profession, Lincoln had chosen some other line of endeavor.

After toiling as a farm laborer, hostler, boatman, and store clerk, he thought seriously of becoming a blacksmith. He changed his mind, however, when presented the opportunity to purchase a country store on credit. Failing in this enterprise, he later became a land surveyor. What if he had decided to remain permanently in any one of these trades? What would have happened if he had entered the pulpit, medicine, journalism, or some other learned profession instead of the law? Would the course of history have run the same? Or would he have lived his days in almost unrecognizable obscurity and then have gone down to his grave "unwept, unhonored, and unsung"? Well may we wonder! For it is impossible to study the life of Lincoln without observing that his training and experience as a lawyer influenced nearly every important and outstanding event of his public career.

Unquestionably Lincoln possessed some natural aptitude for the law, for certainly he inherited none. Himself the son of a carpenter, his forefathers for six generations include a weaver, two blacksmiths, and three farmers; and as Lincoln said, "There is no smell of royalty in that"—nor, it might be added, is there any groundwork for a successful career at the bar.

The accidental discovery of Blackstone's *Commentaries* having focused his attention on the law, as an ambitious young man he undoubtedly regarded a legal career as a stepping-stone toward improving his standards of living and as a means of earning a decent livelihood. He early acquired a bent for the open forum and politics, and law and politics mixed well. He observed that in his community the leading men were lawyers. He may have been impressed by the high regard that the bench and bar then commanded. For De Tocqueville, writing his *Democracy in America* at about the time Lincoln began his studies, recognized and gave voice to the fact that "in America lawyers form the highest political class and the most cultivated circle of society."

Undoubtedly all these influences bore some weight in the choice of Lincoln's career. How he prepared for it and practiced it, and how it fitted him to do his work in life, is one of the most fascinating adventures in life ever recorded.

At the early age of eighteen years, Abe Lincoln received his first glimpse into the great world of jurisprudence in a most practical fashion.

In the spring of 1827, the lanky, rawboned youth, grown to six feet, four inches in height, was hauled before Squire Samuel Pate, a justice of the peace near Lewisport, Kentucky, for operating a ferryboat without a license. Abe had built a scow and was delivering travelers to steamers passing along the Ohio River. John T. Dill and his brother Lin, Kentucky ferrymen, claiming the exclusive right to carry passengers across the river at this point, were eager to end this unlicensed competition. By a ruse they induced Lincoln to accompany them to Squire Pate's home, where they swore to a warrant charging Abe with violating the "Act Respecting the Establishment of Ferries"; and the trial of the Commonwealth of Kentucky *vs.* Abraham Lincoln soon began.

The Dill brothers testified that they had seen Abe Lincoln transport a passenger from the Indiana shore to a steamer which had stopped in midstream, and contended that this competition constituted an infringement upon their license.

The gawky young boatman, awed by the proceedings and somewhat scared, readily admitted that when the Dill ferry was not available he carried passengers in his scow from the Indiana shore to steamboats in the middle of the river. But he pleaded that he had no idea that he was violating the law. Moreover, the resourceful future lawyer had a question to ask: Even if it were true that Mr. Dill held the exclusive license to transport passengers *across* the river, how did the carrying of people who missed the Dill ferry *to* passing steamers in midstream constitute a violation of this right?

The Dill brothers protested that this was mere quibbling, but Squire Pate thought there was much merit to the question.

He took down the statute-book and read the pertinent provisions again.

He observed that the statute concerned itself with *trans-river* craft exclusively, and specifically prohibited the unlicensed conveying of persons *over* any river or creek where public ferries exist. The evidence, he realized, was not that Lincoln had carried passengers *over* or *across* the river but only *to* passing steamers in midstream. This was not an offense within the contemplation of the statute, Squire Pate reasoned; and despite the angry protests of the Kentucky ferrymen, he dismissed the warrant.

Young Lincoln was deeply impressed by the proceedings and the reasoning of this officer of law and justice.

He walked over and thanked Squire Pate. The justice of the peace graciously suggested that a young man should know the laws governing his business. "Read up a bit on the law," he advised.

As Lincoln sculled over to the Indiana shore there remained in his subconscious mind the indelible impression of the operation of the machinery of law and justice and its logic, reasoning, and common sense. Squire Pate had invited him to visit his court again on "law days." It ought to be worth his while to do so, Abe was thinking.

Thereafter, when his farmhand and boating duties would allow, Abe would paddle across the waters of the Ohio and attend the sessions of Squire Pate's court. More often he attended "court" in the Indiana towns of Boonville and Rockport.

Not long after Abe's trial at Squire Pate's, young Lincoln was doing some work for David Turnham, a prosperous farmer who lived near Grandview on the Ohio. Turnham was also a constable connected with the township justice of the peace court, and as an officer of the law found it necessary to own a copy of the *Revised Laws of Indiana*. Abe saw this formidable compendium, and recalled Squire Pate's advice to read up on the law. Eagerly he browsed through its five-hundred-odd pages. Something in its dry-as-dust contents fascinated him. He asked Turnham for permission to take the volume home. In his leisure moments the almost illiterate youth, with a hungry desire to improve himself, avidly read this first law book to come into his hands. About four fifths of the five hundred pages were filled with the matter-of-fact enactments of the Indiana Legislature—laws defining the machinery of civil government, crimes and punishments, rights and remedies, courts and procedure, and the like. But easier to read and of greater interest to Abe were the Declaration of Independence, the Constitutions of the United States and Indiana, and the Ordinance of 1787 for the Northwest Territory, all of which were published in a sort of prefix to the state code.

In the immortal Declaration Abe read that "all men are created equal."

In the Ordinance of 1787, for the governing of the Northwest Territory, he saw the significant article, "There shall be neither slavery nor involuntary servitude in the said Territory, otherwise than in the punishment of crime whereof the party shall be convicted."

And the Indiana Constitution contained this expression of the disapproval of slavery: "As the holding of any part of the human creation is slavery ... and can only originate in usurpation and tyranny, no alteration of this constitution shall ever take place so as to introduce slavery ... in this state."

Here was Lincoln's first contact with the legal and constitutional aspects of slavery that were to absorb so great a part of his life. Here was his first study of the Declaration of Independence and the American Constitution, from which so many of his future political sentiments were to be drawn.

It was also about this time that Lincoln wrote a composition on the necessity of preserving the Constitution and perpetuating the Union. He showed it to William Wood, a neighbor, who was so impressed that when John Pitcher, a circuit lawyer, came to his home, he asked him to read the essay. "The world couldn't beat it," Mr. Pitcher exclaimed enthusiastically upon completing it.

Abe eagerly went to visit this new admirer at his home in Rockport, Spencer County, where Mr. Pitcher became a prosecutor and later a judge. "The things I want to know are in books," Abe told the circuit lawyer during the course of a heart-to-heart conversation. "My best friend is the man who'll get me a book I ain't read."

"I understood he wanted to become a lawyer and I tried to encourage him," said Mr. Pitcher years later. But Abe realized that the few dollars he was earning by working for neighboring farmers were more important to the Lincoln family just then.

Some twelve or fourteen miles distant from the Lincoln cabin in Gentryville stood the tiny village of Boonville, the seat of Warwick County. When not prevented by farmhand duties, Abe

Lincoln would go to the circuit court that convened here twice a year. Here Abe saw the itinerant judge, accompanied by a cavalcade of circuit lawyers, arrive to attend to the trials at law of the district.

In the drab and colorless lives of Lincoln's neighbors, the solemn court sessions were gala occasions, the greatest performance in the range of their experience. The courtroom was the theater, recreation center, and lecture-room to which folks for miles around flocked for entertainment and intellectual stimulation. Flushed with a holiday spirit, entire families would pack their lunches and make the long trip to the courthouse in wagons and buggies to hear the great lawyers "plead." Often they camped in the nearby groves throughout the sessions. At these trials appreciative capacity audiences witnessed the enactment of real dramas of life, sometimes trivial and humorous but more often serious and pathetic, portraying every form of human pettiness, misery, despair, and misfortune. But always these dramas had the same theme—the search for justice.

The crowd enjoyed the forensic display of the lawyers, and it is little wonder that the youthful Lincoln rarely missed a court session at Boonville. How the proceedings must have appealed to the budding ambition within him.

One day while attending a murder trial at Boonville, Abe Lincoln became enthralled by the argument, learning, and pleading of John A. Brackenridge, the attorney for the defense. What eloquence! thought the impressionable youth. He listened as though his own life depended on the lawyer's skill to sway the jury to his client's cause. It was the most magnificent appeal he had ever heard.

"I felt," he told Mr. Brackenridge in the White House many years later, "that if I could ever make as good a speech as that my soul would be satisfied."

But on this day he could not repress his enthusiasm, and hardly had the jury returned its verdict when Lincoln, gigantic in size, gawky, and solemn visaged, pushed his way through the crowd and extended his huge, toil-worn hand to congratulate the gifted orator. That the lawyer saw fit to ignore the proffered hand of a shabby youth made little difference to Lincoln, for he had been too profoundly impressed by what he had seen and heard. Even then he may have mentally visioned the day of the not so far distant future when he too with the skill of a Brackenridge would stand before a jury as a champion of justice and equity.[1]

It would not have been difficult for him to prepare himself for the bar, for the only qualification then existing for admission to the practice of law in Indiana demanded that the applicant must have a good character. But whatever his desires along this line may have been, they were suddenly thwarted when his family again was uprooted by his father's wanderlust, and the Lincolns in March, 1830, moved to Decatur, Illinois.

About a year later, at the age of twenty-two, Abe became a resident of the little village of New Salem. Here Lincoln was to follow the temporary occupations of clerk, storekeeper, postmaster, and surveyor. New Salem was to be his alma mater in the preparation for his life career.

Here Abe met Bowling Green, the justice of the peace; Dr. Allen, the physician; William Graham Greene, his fellow clerk, who had been a student at Illinois College; and Jack Kelso, the village idler and poet, who taught him to love the beauties in the writings of Burns and Shakespeare. Here the capable schoolmaster, Mentor Graham, advised him to study grammar, saying: "If you are going before the public, you ought to do it." Lincoln walked six miles in the country to borrow *Kirkhams' Grammar* from a friendly farmer. Every leisure moment he spent in its study. When in doubt he consulted the faithful Mr. Graham. The mastery of the book was the first step in his search for the power of clear expression that was to give his speeches a permanent place in literature.

Lincoln joined a literary and debating club that met once a week in the Rutledge Tavern, where he had a chance to "practice polemics," as he expressed it. He soon gained a reputation as a

---

[1] A Herndon and Weik manuscript refers to the tradition that Lincoln may have borrowed law books from the library of John A. Brackenridge of Boonville, Indiana, stating that "when Lincoln caught sight of the several hundred volumes he was astonished at such a collection."

strong speaker and able debator. In 1832, he felt himself fit for public service and became a candidate for a seat in the state legislature. He made the campaign, but met defeat—the only time he was to lose in a popular election.

Later he enlisted in the Black Hawk War. Here he met and won the friendship of Major John T. Stuart, who was to serve with him in the state legislature, encourage his law studies, and become his first law partner. When he came back from the war, he founded a partnership with William F. Berry in the merchandising business; they purchased three stores by issuing their notes therefor. The venture proved disastrous, and burdened Lincoln with a "national debt" of eleven hundred dollars that was to take him many years to pay.

But a most important event occurred during his career as a merchant-prince—the event destined to shape his career and change the course of history. It was in 1832, when Lincoln was twenty-three years old, that a man came to the store and offered to sell him an old barrel with its contents unknown. The incident is best described in Lincoln's own words as he related it to Alban Jasper Conant, the artist, who painted his portrait in Springfield in 1860:

"One day a man who was migrating to the West drove up in front of my store with a wagon which contained his family and household plunder. He asked me if I would buy an old barrel for which he had no room in his wagon, and which contained nothing of special value. I did not want it, but to oblige him I bought it, and paid him, I think, half a dollar for it. Without further examination I put it away in the store and forgot all about it. Some time after in overhauling things, I came upon the barrel and emptying it on the floor to see what it contained I found at the bottom of the rubbish a complete edition of 'Blackstone's Commentaries.' "[1]

Out of the misty clouds of Mount Sinai, Moses, the Hebrew lawgiver and liberator of his race, received from Providence the Ten Commandments.

And now, just at the right moment—out of the mysterious

---

[1] A. J. Conant, 'My Aquaintance with Abraham Lincoln,' in *Liber Scriptorum*, p. 172; *McClure's Magazine*, March 1909, p. 514.

barrel of rubbish that Providence through a migrating pioneer brought to New Salem, appeared this prized book of law—the one book of all others needed to awaken the inborn ambition of this future lawgiver and liberator of another enslaved race.

"I began to read those famous works," Lincoln continues in his account of this fortunate discovery, "and I had plenty of time; for during the long summer days when the farmers were busy with their crops, my customers were few and far between. The more I read the more intensely interested I became. Never in my whole life was my mind so thoroughly absorbed. I read until I devoured them."[1]

---

[1] Another version of Lincoln's providential acquisition of Blackstone's *Commentaries* is contained in *Lives and Speeches of Abraham Lincoln and Hannibal Hamlin*, a campaign biography of 1860, by William Dean Howells, which Lincoln himself is said to have corrected. It states that while living at New Salem he (Lincoln) "bought an old copy of Blackstone one day at auction in Springfield and on his return to New Salem, attacked the work with characteristic study."

See also Bulletin No. 35 of the Abraham Lincoln Association (June, 1934), p. 8.

III. PREPARATION FOR THE BAR

STRETCHED under an ancient shade tree that stood just outside the door of his store, his long bare feet resting high on the bark of the tree, Abe Lincoln read aloud from his law book. "Municipal law," he recited, "is a rule of civil conduct prescribed by the supreme power in a state, commanding what is right and prohibiting what is wrong."

The primary and principal objects of the law, he read in the *Commentaries,* are rights and wrongs. Rights are divided into rights of persons and rights of things. Rights of persons include the rights of personal security or the legal enjoyment of life, limbs, body, health, and reputation; personal liberty; and the right to acquire property. Wrongs are simply violations of rights, and are divided into private wrongs and public wrongs.

To the few straggling customers who came to his store, Abe Lincoln could explain by referring to the pages of his Blackstone how absolute rights of individuals can be preserved through the writ of habeas corpus. He could discuss the merits of different forms of government—democracy, aristocracy, and monarchy. He could answer: Can slavery subsist anywhere consistently with reason and the principles of natural law?

He became familiar with crimes and punishments and with domestic relations of husband and wife, parent and child, guardian and ward, and master and servant. He read of the history and purposes of the common law and the struggle for Anglo-Saxon liberty, the formulation of the Magna Charta, trial by jury, the Petition of Rights, the Bill of Rights, and the development of that system of jurisprudence which has ever been a bulwark of defense against oppression and injustice.

In the Indiana *Revised Statutes* he had read laws and documents which were confined exclusively to American institutions. Now he was drinking from the very well-head of these institutions.

There was a popular saying that three books—the Bible, Shakespeare, and Blackstone, embodying the best in religion, philosophy, literature and law—constituted a sufficient library. Now the unschooled pioneer youth was adding a comprehensive study of the commentaries of the famous English jurist to his knowledge of the Bible and the writings of the immortal bard of Avon. With tireless industry and ever-widening horizon he explored the abundant stores of legal learning that chance had brought to his door.

The stern need of earning a living made Lincoln's reading of the law as sporadic and haphazard as his earlier schooling. He could not leave his odd jobs long enough to adopt a systematic mode of study by which other law students were preparing for the bar.

Generally speaking, lawyers were then educated by the apprentice method. After the usual common-school training and a smattering of Latin, if possible, the prospective lawyer would make arrangements with an established, successful lawyer to enter his office and read law under his direction for three or four years.

The lawyer gave the student what attention he could. Some preceptors assigned regular lessons and prescribed readings based on Blackstone, Kent, Greenleaf, and Chitty, and questioned and examined the applicant in the fundamentals of law and preparation of court papers. Quite often, however, the mentor was too busy to give the reader any attention and the student was left to get along as best he could. After the fundamental law books were mastered, the student would devote his time to the special fields of law—chancery pleading, evidence, vendors and purchasers, bailments, criminal law, and the like. A form book and law dictionary would make him familiar with legal forms and phrases. This apprentice method of study ordinarily made the student a virtual counterpart of the lawyer under whom he read.

But Lincoln, driven by the need of applying himself to the job offering him an immediate means of making a livelihood, could not adopt so systematic a mode of study. In 1833 he received an appointment as deputy to the county surveyor. With the help of his faithful schoolmaster friend, Mentor Graham, he studied arithmetic and treatises on surveying, and in a few weeks became proficient enough to satisfy his superior officer. He eventually laid out several towns in Illinois.

A certain candidate for the office of clerk of court in one of the pioneer settlements of Indiana boasted of his superior qualifications by declaring that he had been sued on every section of the statute and that he was, therefore, very familiar with the law, while his opponent had never been sued and consequently was ignorant of the law. Lincoln received his first practical experience at the bar in a like manner—as a litigant rather than as a lawyer. While still an assistant surveyor, four lawsuits naming him as defendant were filed. The first of these vexatious actions arose on a note for $104.87 ½ given by Lincoln and Nelson Alley as an accommodation to the creditors of Captain Bogue in his ill-fated venture of piloting the steamer *Talisman* up the Sangamon River to prove the navigability of that stream.[1]

In the second action filed against Lincoln, his friends David Rutledge and William Green were named as co-defendants. The plaintiffs sought judgment on a bond for one hundred and fifty dollars, signed jointly by the three defendants. The bond, securing the conveyance of a lot on Main Street in the town of New Salem, was in Lincoln's handwriting, and was probably the first

[1] Sangamon County Circuit Court, Judgment Docket A, Record B, p. 225.

legal instrument ever drafted by him. This case was settled out of court.[1]

The next lawsuit against Lincoln was far more vexing. It was the first to arise out of the failure of the Berry and Lincoln store. Peter Van Bergen, holding a note for one hundred and fifty-four dollars due as a balance on an account for groceries, instituted suit in the Sangamon County Circuit Court against the struggling young man. When the helpless Lincoln was unable to satisfy the judgment, an execution was issued and the sheriff of Sangamon County levied upon and took possession of Lincoln's horse and surveying instruments, practically depriving him of his means of earning a livelihood. Fortunately a friend, "Uncle Jimmie" Short, who "liked Abe Lincoln," bought the horse and instruments at the sheriff's sale and returned them to their owner. Lincoln never forgot his benefactor. He repaid the money from his subsequent earnings as a lawyer, and years later, as President of the United States, appointed his friend in need as an Indian agent in California.

Still another lawsuit arose to annoy the impecunious deputy surveyor. Hardly had the Van Bergen case ended when Thomas Watkins of Menard County sued Lincoln to recover a balance of ten dollars due on the purchase price of the horse almost lost in the previous case. Lincoln somehow raised the money and satisfied the claim out of court.[2]

Undaunted by these troubles, the ambitious Lincoln in 1834 found time to turn from his surveying long enough to make a successful campaign for the legislature. He was elected by the largest vote ever cast for any candidate in the district, and eventually was elected for three more successive terms. Thus the fall of 1834 saw the stock of Abraham Lincoln going up, as he held three public offices—postmaster, assistant county surveyor, and membership in the lower house of the General Assembly. However, the emoluments from all three offices failed to enrich his purse, and necessity forced him to borrow money to purchase clothes for his new dignity.

[1] Townsend, *Lincoln the Litigant*, p. 62.
[2] Townsend, *Lincoln the Litigant*, pp. 68-71.

The campaign of 1834 assumed importance, not so much for Lincoln's success at the polls as for the fact that it led to the final determination to make law his life career. In his travels over the district he frequently met Major John T. Stuart, with whom he had served two years before in the Black Hawk War. Major Stuart, a well-established lawyer at Springfield, was now Lincoln's fellow candidate on the Whig ticket for a seat in the legislature. In a conversation, the deputy surveyor confided to him his ambition to study law, and Stuart encouraged him and offered him free use of his library at Springfield. The spark ignited by the chance finding of Blackstone's *Commentaries*, and then left smoldering, now burst forth into a bright, all-consuming flame.

Law now became the greatest absorbing interest of Lincoln's life, never again to go out of his mind. As he expressed it, he now "went at it in good earnest." He served no office apprenticeship. His legal education was to be even less formal than his academic training. He became an articled clerk to himself, so to speak. He walked or rode on horseback to Springfield to borrow Major Stuart's books for study.

He borrowed the few law books owned by Squire Bowling Green, at whose home he boarded for a while, and mastered them. Although compelled to continue surveying to pay board and clothing bills, he took advantage of every leisure moment to pursue his studies at home, in the fields, and on the road between New Salem and Springfield. Persons who in later years recalled Lincoln's studious habits in New Salem often observed him reading his law books while walking between New Salem and Springfield, and "so intense was his application and so absorbed was he in his study that he would often pass his best friends without observing them." Some, noticing his sunken cheeks and bleary, red eyes, said Lincoln was going crazy with hard study. Sometimes he read forty pages or more on a trip between two towns. Often persons saw him wandering at random across fields repeating aloud salient points of what he read.

In season and out he added to his legal knowledge. From a form book he learned to draw up deeds, mortgages, leases, contracts, and bills of sale. Soon he felt that he could make some practical application of this training and offered his services in drafting such legal instruments for his friends and neighbors.

"In 1834," says Daniel Green Burner, "my father Isaac Green Burner sold out to Henry Onstott and he wanted a deed written. I knew how handy Lincoln was that way and suggested that we get him. We found him sitting on a stump. 'All right,' said he, when informed what we wanted. 'If you will bring me a pen and ink and a piece of paper I will write it here.' I brought him these articles and picking up a shingle and putting it on his knee for a desk, he wrote out the deed."

He drafted a will for Joshua Short of Sangamon County. The instrument, which bears Lincoln's signature as an attesting witness, is an early characteristic specimen of his simple yet classic style of expression.

He continued the habit formed at Boonville, and frequently attended the trials at the justice of the peace court of his friend Bowling Green. As there was no practicing attorney residing in New Salem, the friendly squire permitted him to act as sort of "next friend" to parties and plead the cases of his neighbors. His knowledge of the *Revised Laws of Illinois*[1] sufficed to enable him to handle these cases capably and impressively. The justice of the peace seemed deeply impressed by the legal knowledge and reasoning of the embryonic practitioner. Weighing three hundred pounds and "given to mirth," Squire Green especially enjoyed Lincoln's droll stories and ludicrous tales. This unofficial practice proved a valuable experience to Lincoln, despite the fact that the justice of the peace often overrode both law and evidence to arrive at his common-sense decisions. Squire Green is reported to have decided a hog case known as Ferguson *vs.* Kelso by declaring that the plaintiff's witnesses were "damned liars," the court being well acquainted with the shoat in question and knowing it to belong to Jack Kelso.

One day Lincoln left his surveying to go to the justice of the

---

[1] Tradition has it that during the winter of 1830–31, while visiting the home of Major Warnick, sheriff of Macon County, Lincoln "got his first look at a law book"—a volume of the *Statutes of Illinois* owned by Warnick.

peace court of Squire Berry at Concord and plead a bastardy case for a young unmarried mother. The man's character, Lincoln argued, was like a piece of white cloth, which though soiled could again be made clean by washing and hanging in the sun to dry. But the character of the girl, who was probably less to blame than the man, was like a broken and shattered bottle or glass vase, which could never be restored and made whole again.

Of course, Lincoln, without a license to practice law, received no fees for "pettyfogging," as he called it, before Squires Green and Berry, nor for his services in drafting legal instruments for his neighbors.

However, this practical experience in the justice of the peace courts proved very valuable training. It was the only apprenticeship to the law that Lincoln could afford. He continued to borrow books and continued to study. No one examined him. He simply read on until he completed the prescribed texts. The number of books he read, while not large, constituted the necessary volumes for preparation for the bar. He never regarded this method as ideal, and was often to refer to himself as a "mast-fed lawyer."

We get some idea of how Lincoln pursued his law studies from letters he wrote in later years to students who asked his advice regarding the best method of preparing for the bar. To one young man he wrote:

"If you are resolutely determined to make a lawyer of yourself, the thing is more than half done already. It is but a small matter whether you read with anybody or not. I did not read with anyone. Get the books and read and study them till you understand them in their principal features; and that is the main thing. It is of no consequence to be in a large town while you are reading. I read at New Salem, which never had three hundred people living in it. The books, and your capacity for understanding them, are just the same in all places. Always bear in mind that your own resolution to succeed is more important than any other one thing."[1]

---

[1] Tracy, *Uncollected Letters of Abraham Lincoln* (hereafter cited as *Uncollected Letters*), p. 61.

To another student's inquiry as to the "best method of obtaining a thorough knowledge of the law," Lincoln advised: "The mode is very simple, though laborious and tedious. It is only to get the books and read and study them carefully. Begin with Blackstone's Commentaries and after reading it through, say twice, take up Chitty's Pleadings, Greenleaf's Evidence and Story's Equity, etc., in succession. Work, work, work, is the main thing."

When Lincoln completed the standard texts that law students of the period usually read in order to qualify for the practice of law, he was not required to pass any examination. Not until March, 1841—about four years after Lincoln's admission to the bar—did the Supreme Court adopt the rule requiring all applicants for admission to the bar to appear for examination in open court.

In the absence of any record of formal examination, much confusion and controversy exists over the exact date of his admission to the bar. In the records of the Circuit Court of Sangamon County, dated March 24, 1836, is found this entry: "It is ordered by the court that it be certified that Abraham Lincoln is a person of good moral character." This was but a preliminary formality, complying with a statute enacted in 1833, under which the only requirement for the granting of a license to practice was a certificate procured from the court of some county certifying to the applicant's good moral character. On September 9, 1836, a license to practice law was issued to Lincoln by two of the justices of the Supreme Court, and a number of biographers designate this as the date of his formal admission to the bar. Manifestly this is incorrect, for the statute made necessary not only the securing of the license, but also the additional step of appearing before the clerk of the Supreme Court for enrollment. It was weeks later before Lincoln presented himself to the clerk and took the oath to support the Constitution of the United States and of Illinois. After this formality, the license, with the oath endorsed thereon, was duly presented to the clerk, and on March 1, 1837, the name of Abraham Lincoln was formally enrolled as an attorney or counselor, licensed to practice law in all the courts of the State of Illinois.

Thus did the backwoodsman, farm-laborer, clerk, flatboat hand, storekeeper, captain, postmaster, and deputy surveyor become "the Hon. A. Lincoln, Esquire, Attorney and Counselor at Law."

IV. LINCOLN'S FIRST LAW PARTNERSHIP

BARELY a month after he became a full-fledged practitioner, Abe Lincoln sadly bade adieu to his friends of New Salem, mounted a nag borrowed from Bowling Green, and rode forth to Springfield. He had made a momentous decision. He had sold his compass, chain, marking pins, and Jacob's staff to start a new career, a new life. He had abandoned a sure means of earning a livelihood for a vague uncertainty. In his pockets were the proceeds of the sale of his surveying instruments—about seven dollars; in his bulging saddle-bags were his portable belongings; in his mind lingered the staggering burden of the thousand-dollar balance still due on his "national debt."

As a member of the legislature he had been instrumental in the passage of the act which removed the state capital from Vandalia to Springfield. Many citizens of the latter town who attended sessions when the bill was discussed, and heard Lincoln argue in their behalf, were pleased with his efforts and impressed with his ability. They urged him to launch his new career in

25

their city. As the new state capital, it was bound to become a place of great importance, they pointed out to him.

So he came to Springfield to take "pot luck," he told Joshua Speed, the storekeeper who invited him to share his lodgings above the store. After carrying his saddle-bags upstairs, Lincoln announced tersely, "Well, Speed, I'm moved." Thus began his residence in the new capital of Illinois.

A few days later, the Sangamon *Journal* of April 15, 1837, published this notice:

"John T. Stuart and A. Lincoln, Attorneys and Counselors at law, will practice conjointly in the courts of this judicial circuit. Office, No. 4 Hoffman Row, upstairs."

Major John Todd Stuart, a cousin of Mary Todd, the future Mrs. Lincoln, was planning for his congressional campaign against the young but formidable Stephen A. Douglas. So that he could devote sufficient time to this canvass, he had offered Lincoln a partnership in his established law practice. It was a great opportunity for the novice, and he accepted eagerly.

This partnership formally commenced April 27, and was to continue for about four years. The office of the new firm, says Herndon, "was in the upper story of a building opposite the northwest corner of the present courthouse square. In the room underneath, the county court was held. The furniture was in keeping with the pretensions of the firm—a small lounge or bed, a chair containing a buffalo robe . . . a hard wooden bench, a feeble attempt at a bookcase, and a table which answered for a desk."[1]

This association with Stuart was a stroke of good luck for the twenty-eight-year-old Lincoln. It was the turning-point in his life, the start on the high road of ambition and achievement. And it was a proud moment for the young barrister. On the flyleaf of his *Webster's Dictionary* he wrote, "A. Lincoln, Esq. Attorney and Counselor-at-Law," as if to see how his new title appeared on paper. But yesterday an obscure deputy surveyor, engrossed in petty tasks with hardly a chance for advancement; today, the

[1] Herndon and Weik, *Herndon's Lincoln, the True Story of a Great Life* (hereafter cited as *Lincoln*), 1, 184.

partner of the leader of the Whig Party of the State and one of the ablest and most prominent lawyers of Illinois.

Stuart was a man of dignified and commanding presence. Handsome, polished, and courtly in his manners, he was a marked contrast to his junior partner, who was still careless in his dress and general appearance. Lincoln's deportment was unassuming. He had not outgrown his backwoods rusticity of manner and the unpolished characteristics of his earlier days. Tall and lanky, he still wore very plain clothing of homespun Kentucky jeans. Little wonder, then, that John W. Baddeley, who had retained Stuart to defend a case for him, refused to accept the ungainly Lincoln as a substitute. The skeptical client dismissed Stuart's partner and employed James A. McDougall instead.

Stuart was too absorbed in his political future to give the law his undivided time. The responsibility of managing the partnership business and conducting its cases, therefore, devolved largely upon the newly-enrolled lawyer. It became Lincoln's duty to prepare the pleadings and briefs in long hand, attend to trial work, and make the entries in the firm account book, in which he signalized Stuart's departure for Washington after his success at the polls by the entry, "Commencement of Lincoln's administration 1839, November 2." Realizing that Lincoln's knowledge of law was still elementary, Stuart must have counted heavily on the common sense and oratorical ability of his junior partner.

Fortunately for the novice, comprehensive knowledge of the law was not required of him. Litigation was then very simple as compared with that of present times. The judicial system, like the country, was still in its infancy, with no voluminous collection of precedents to master and no array of authorities to cite. There were then few adjudicated cases by the Illinois Supreme Court.[1]

[1] The first two volumes of State Reports did not appear until 1839, Lincoln's first case in the Supreme Court, Scammon vs. Cline, decided in 1840, appearing in the third volume. Today (1936) there are 340 volumes of Illinois Supreme Court Reports in addition to hundreds of Appellate Court Reports, to say nothing of the thousands of reported cases of the lower courts, and

Lawsuits were yet extremely simple and involved small sums of money. Technical training was not yet essential for a lawyer. Railroads, corporations, trusts, big business, and inherited wealth that have revolutionized our economic, social, and political life did not trouble the profession with their countless abstruse and subtle legal problems.

The fundamental principles of Blackstone and Chitty, together with a fine intellect, ability to marshal facts, power of reasoning, common sense, force of character, tenacity of purpose, ready wit, and a gift of gab, were more than sufficient to make Lincoln a worthy assistant to Stuart.

He tried his cases on principle rather than on precedent. He based his arguments on the solid foundation of right and justice rather than on previously adjudicated cases. He appealed to the faculty by which we distinguish truth from falsehood and right from wrong to carry conviction of the righteousness of his client's cause.

He had little opportunity to distinguish himself by any exhibit of legal skill in these early days. Business conditions in general were bad on account of the financial crash of 1837, which left the entire country in a state of bankruptcy. Though the masses of people were poor and heavily involved in debt, the situation afforded a great deal of work for the lawyers. A vast system of public improvements was abandoned in an uncompleted state. Contractors, unable to collect for their labor and materials, were forced to suspend payment to their creditors. Merchants did likewise. Many suits for the collection of debts and actions to set aside fraudulent conveyances were thus created. Some sought relief in the two-thirds law, and others, hopelessly insolvent, found refuge in bankruptcy.[1]

The depression engendered bitter feelings, and many actions

endless codes, digests, texts, and reports of the courts of the United States and of the forty-eight individual States, to keep the modern lawyer buried in his office digging up precedents and analogous cases.

[1]James C. Conkling, *Recollections of the Bench and Bar of Central Illinois*, Fergus Historical Series, Chicago Bar Association Lectures, p. 39.

for slander, trespass, and assault and battery arose from these quarrels to give employment to the lawyers.

Lincoln's early cases were generally of this character—petty and uninteresting. There were actions arising out of neighborhood quarrels, differences about a yoke of oxen, disputes about a cooking-stove, litigation involving damage to growing crops by trespassing cattle, injuries inflicted upon the cattle by vicious watchdogs, replevin suits to recover possession of cattle, horses and sheep running at large, a goodly number of libel and slander suits intended to vindicate the honesty and integrity of aggrieved parties, cases for debt, a few divorces, and the like.

Lincoln's first case—of interest solely because it *was* his first case—was Hawthorne vs. Wooldridge. On July 1, 1836, months before Lincoln had become a licensed practitioner, Stuart had filed the action in the Circuit Court of Sangamon County, over which Judge Stephen T. Logan, destined to become Lincoln's second law partner, then presided.

"The court was in session and a case was then in progress," wrote a lawyer from the East, after a visit to the Sangamon courthouse some months before the filing of this case. "Judge Logan was on the bench, and Mr. Douglas—the 'Little Giant,' as he was afterwards called—on the floor. To us, just from the city of New York with the sleek lawyers and the prim and dignified judges, and audiences to correspond, there was a contrast so great, that it was almost impossible to repress a burst of laughter. Upon the bench was seated the judge, with his chair tilted back and his heels as high as his head, and in his mouth a veritable corn-cob pipe; his hair standing nine ways for Sunday, while his clothing was more like that worn by a woodchopper than anybody else. There was a railing that divided the audience; outside of which smoking and chewing and spitting tobacco seemed to be the principal employment."[1]

In such surroundings Lincoln made his debut as a lawyer; for before the case of Hawthorne vs. Wooldridge came up for trial he became Stuart's partner, and the latter, busy with his campaign for Congress, turned the case over to the novice to try as he

[1] R. H. Beach, *History of Sangamon County* (1881), p. 183.

deemed best. It was typical of the petty litigation of the period, involving a dispute about the use of two yoke of oxen for breaking up some prairie-sod ground. There were also charges of assault and battery and other claims and counter-claims.[1]

It is significant that Lincoln's first case never came to trial but was settled out of court. In New Salem, disputing neighbors had learned to leave their differences for settlement to him as arbitrator. Lawyer Lincoln's office early became a court of conciliation. Thus in a country where folks were litigious, at a time when every dollar was needed for livelihood and for reduction of his burdensome "national debt," Lincoln discouraged litigation, turned away business, and tried to keep people out of court. He persuaded his clients to compromise their differences with their adversaries whenever they could do so with honor.

Accustomed to open-air life, Lincoln at times found clerical work and the drudgery connected with the preparation of pleadings in a dusty, stuffy office rather tedious. Herndon later said of Lincoln that he never was an office lawyer and that he cared little for method, system, and office efficiency. Soon the firm papers became scattered hither and yon. Notes he carried in his vest pockets or threw into a drawer. His usual receptacle for carrying papers was his hat. On March 15, 1838, we find him apologizing to Levi Davis, a lawyer of Vandalia, for failure to reply to his letter of the "2nd inst." "We have been in a great state of confusion here ever since the receipt of your letter," he writes. "We beg your pardon for our neglect in this business. If it had been important to you or your client we would have done better."[2]

Nor was Stuart any more methodical. Most of his time and thought were given to his political career, and Lincoln was often obliged to write him concerning deeds and legal papers that the senior partner had filed away but which could not be found when clients called for them. In one letter Lincoln wrote:

"A d———d hawk-billed Yankee is here besetting me at

[1] Weik, *The Real Lincoln*, p. 134; Herndon and Weik, *Lincoln*, 1, 182.
[2] Tracy, *Uncollected Letters*, pp. 2–3.

every turn I take, saying that Robert Kinzie never received the
eighty dollars to which he was entitled. Can you tell me anything
about the matter? Again, old Mr. Wright, who lives up South
Fork somewhere, is teasing me continually about some deeds
which he says he left with you, but which I can find nothing of.
Can you tell me where they are?''

Whenever the junior partner could escape from the drudgery
of the office, he went to Speed's store, a meeting-place for a
congenial crowd of lawyers, politicians, and men without any
occupation at all.

In these informal gatherings Lincoln was a star actor. His
knowledge of the current problems of his community and State,
coupled with a ready wit and inexhaustible supply of anecdotes,
delighted his hearers and made him ever welcome.

Law was then, as it is now, the principal avenue to public life.
Every lawyer was necessarily a politician, and solicited office to
augment his slender income. It behooved him to make himself
felt on important public questions of the day. The lawyer, who
was an effective stump-speaker, often was retained as a likely
victor in a lawsuit to be argued. Lincoln, Herndon, James Matheny, Noah Rickard, Evan Butler, Milton Hay, Newton Francis,
and other young men who congregated in Speed's store organized
a society to encourage public speaking, debating, and literary
efforts.

Lincoln never missed an opportunity to make a public address.
He joined the Young Men's Lyceum of Springfield, which held
public meetings. Late in 1837, before a large assemblage he
delivered his first noteworthy oration, a carefully prepared speech
on "The Perpetuation of Our Free Institutions," inspired by the
recent killing of the defiant Abolitionist Elijah P. Lovejoy, at
Alton, only sixty miles from Springfield, and by the subsequent
burning of a negro by a St. Louis mob. A plea for law and order
was its message, and so great an impression did it make upon his
audience that the Lyceum delegated James Matheny to procure a
copy of the address for publication. Obedience to law as the
quintessence of patriotism and the highest attribute of American
citizenship was the burden of this address. To Lincoln it became

an absorbing topic. He condemned mob violence, the increasing disregard for law, the substitution of "wild and furious passions in lieu" of the sober judgments of courts.

The address created for the twenty-eight-year-old orator a reputation that soon extended far beyond the limits of Springfield.

The courthouses of Illinois were then popular rendezvous for the people of the neighborhood. There they flocked by the scores for the entertainment and mental stimulation they were certain to receive from the eloquence of the members of the bar. Lincoln soon became a star courtroom attraction. Especially fortunate was a lawyer retained in a case involving a political and legal controversy of general interest, for it was certain to gain him prominence among the masses and give him an opportunity to display his ability.

Such a case soon came to Lincoln. It created a sensation, and advertised him throughout the State as a shrewd practitioner and a tireless fighter.

Mary Anderson, a widow, and her son Richard retained Stuart & Lincoln to recover for them a tract of land which they claimed belonged to them as the heirs of Joseph Anderson, the deceased husband and father. Lincoln found that General James Adams, a prominent politician and now a candidate for the office of judge of the probate court, claimed title to the land through deeds of record purporting to have been executed in his favor by Mr. Anderson. Upon close examination of the records and documents, Lincoln became suspicious of their genuineness. An assignment by Anderson to Adams of a judgment, dated several months before the judgment, appeared to the young lawyer as a deliberate forgery on the part of the politician.

Associating himself with Stephen T. Logan, the recognized leader of the county bar and later his partner, Lincoln instituted proceedings in behalf of the widow for recovery of title to the land. Adams vehemently denied the charges of fraud, and characterized the action against him as a political conspiracy.

Then followed a curious newspaper warfare with seemingly endless charges and countercharges, with Lincoln using the columns of the Sangamon *Journal*, and General Adams the Springfield *Republican*, until the Lincoln-Adams quarrel became the talk of the State. But Lincoln's bitter attacks won for Adams the sympathy of the voters and he was elected judge by an overwhelming majority. He died shortly afterwards, however, and the case never came to trial.

Lincoln's renown as a lawyer, especially as a jury pleader, spread, and his practice in Springfield as well as on the circuit grew steadily. George Stockton had him sue James Tolby for one hundred dollars damages to a cooking-stove in transit between Beardstown and Springfield. Lincoln claimed that Tolby, having driven a conveyance for hire, "was a common carrier." When a client was being sued by the Hickox brothers for "good merchantable, superfine flour" sold and delivered, Lincoln brought his storekeeping experience into good use and pleaded that twenty barrels of flour were not as represented but, on the contrary, greatly inferior in quality.

He defended William Fraim for murder and was unsuccessful; the records of Hancock County, where the case was tried, reveal that Lincoln's client was convicted April 25, 1839, and by the court order "hanged by the neck till dead" twenty-three days thereafter.

He filed divorce proceedings for Nancy Green against Aaron Green and succeeded in dissolving the "marriage bond" on the ground of desertion.

The owners of a boat loaded with corn retained him to bring an action against some fish-trappers for obstructing the navigation of the Sangamon River and damaging the boat and its cargo.

He procured a judgment against David Prickett for $513.49, in favor of the surviving partners of the firm of A. & A.W. Kern & Co.

When Harvey Ross came to procure the testimony of a witness to prove his title to a farm at Macomb he found the court adjourned for the summer. But Lincoln, whom he had retained as legal counsel, induced the witness to accompany him and Mr. Ross to Judge Thomas's cornfield, where they found the jurist, sleeves rolled up, helping some laborers raise logs to build a corncrib and hogpen. Here Judge Thomas wiped the perspiration from his face, swore in the witness, and held a "shirt-sleeve court in a cornfield." The judge was convinced by the testimony that Ross should have clear title to the land, and signed the desired papers. In return for the judge's kindness in holding the impromptu court session, Lincoln and Ross pitched in and helped roll the logs and build the corncrib and hogpen. Because Harvey's father, Cassian M. Ross, former postmaster at Havana, had been friendly to Lincoln when he held a similar post at New Salem, the lawyer refused to accept any fee from the son.

"I guess I will not charge anything for that," he said. "I will let it go on the old score."[1]

Lincoln filed suit in behalf of William Edwards against Oliver Hazzard Perry Rush to recover damages in the sum of one thousand dollars for slanderous words spoken by Rush charging the plaintiff with stealing money. For Manly F. Cannon he brought an action against Matthew P. Kenney for one hundred dollars for wrongfully taking his sorrel horse and disposing of it.

He sued for divorce in behalf of Eliza A. Lloyd, who charged that her husband, Peter Lloyd, after one year of married life, left her "in a helpless condition with a newborn infant . . . and never furnished her or her child with support." He secured a divorce for Ann McDaniel from her husband Patrick McDaniel because he deserted her and their three children, "never in any way contributing to their support."

These cases were typical of Lincoln's early law practice.

During his partnership with Stuart, in 1840, Lincoln was retained in his first case before the Supreme Court of Illinois. It was the action of Scammon vs. Cline.[2] He had been a member of the bar but three years. Yet U. L. Loop, original counsel for Cline, thought enough of Lincoln's ability to retain him, of all the attorneys available, to be associated with him in the appeal

---

[1] Onstot, *Pioneers of Menard and Mason Counties*, pp. 41–44.
[2] 3 Ill. 456.

to the Supreme Court. In the years to follow, Lincoln was to be employed by other counsel in numerous other cases before the State Supreme Court, as well as the federal, district, and circuit courts.

From the very outset, the practice of Stuart & Lincoln was extensive. In fact, they had more cases of record in the Circuit Court of Sangamon County than any other lawyer or firm of lawyers. Thus the docket of the July, 1837, term shows twenty-six law and chancery cases filed by Lincoln's firm, while Logan & Baker, the nearest competitor, had but eight. During the October, 1837, term, Stuart & Lincoln tried twenty law and five chancery cases. And in practically the same proportions ran their cases during 1838 and 1839.

Despite the extensiveness of their practice, it was not lucrative. The income of the partnership never exceeded sixteen hundred dollars a year. Fees were trifling, and many were traded out for groceries, vegetables, poultry, produce, and even clothes. Luckily for Lincoln, board and lodging cost him little.

Whenever he received a fee he divided it immediately with his partner. In case of the partner's absence he wrapped his share in a piece of paper marked "Stuart's half," to be paid to the partner at the first opportunity. "I have received five dollars from Deed of Macon, five from Lewis Keeling, five from Andrew Finley, one-half of which belongs to Stuart and has not been entered on the books," was one of his typical memoranda.

Another entry read: "Dec. 6, 1841. Received of A. H. Keller $12.50, the balance of his note to Stuart & Lincoln, and for one-half of which I am to account to Stuart."

Despite Lincoln's dislike for clerical work he attempted to keep an account book of the firm's income, probably to be able to show Stuart the earnings of the partnership during the latter's absence. He apparently did not continue this provident habit long, for the account book shows few entries during 1837 and 1838. They are all in Lincoln's handwriting, and are interesting in that they throw light upon the character of his early practice and the fees charged.

One entry reads: "Lincoln rec'd of Z. Peter $2.81 ¼ which is taken in full of all balances due up to this date." Other fees ranged from two and a half dollars to fifty dollars, with five dollars as the most popular fee. One for fifty dollars charged to Wiley & Wood "to defense of chancery case of Ely" shows a "credit by coat to Stuart, $15.00."[1]

But not all of Lincoln's early fees were trifling. Stuart & Lincoln charged a farmer a fee of five hundred dollars in one case. The client executed his notes for that amount and secured their payment by a mortgage on his farm.[2]

Not only Stuart's time, but Lincoln's as well, although to a lesser degree, was taken up with politics. His political activities were instrumental in advertising him extensively as a lawyer.

Elected for the fourth consecutive term to the Illinois legislature in 1840, he withdrew from further contests for the office. He was popular enough with his constituents to hold the office longer if he had wished, but he felt that he had received all the honor and distinction the position had to offer. The eight years spent as a member of the General Assembly were unimportant and uneventful. Lincoln was an average member of the legislature in so far as noteworthy achievements were concerned. The chief value of this experience to the young barrister was the opportunity it gave him to meet the coterie of legal lights who also were members of the legislature.

Thus did Lincoln spend the four years of his partnership with Stuart. They were busy, formative years, a sort of practical postgraduate course to fill up the gaps in his limited theoretical education as a law student. In the trial of every conceivable variety of cases, before justices of the peace, on the circuit, in the State Supreme Court, and in the district courts of the United States— because of Stuart's absence—he had to do his own thinking. He had to stand on his own feet. It filled him with confidence and self-reliance, and taught him to plan in his own way the solutions

---

[1] Weik, *The Real Lincoln*, pp. 142–43.
[2] Stringer, *History of Logan County, Illinois*, p. 213.

to the various legal problems that confronted him. His alone was the responsibility. Seldom did he seek advice, and when he received it, he carefully weighed it and then in the end reached his own conclusions.

V. LOGAN, A CONSTRUCTIVE INFLUENCE

WHEN Stuart was elected to Congress for a second term, Lincoln realized that the senior partner's long absence from Springfield made a continuance of the partnership a practical impossibility.

And withal, Lincoln was then a very unhappy man. He was betrothed to Mary Todd, a refined and well-educated young lady of Lexington, Kentucky. But he had formed grave doubts as to their mutual compatibility. Crushed with the great mental strain of uncertainty and self-torment, he wrote to Stuart:

"I am now the most miserable man living. If what I feel were equally distributed to the whole human family, there would not be one cheerful face on earth. Whether I shall ever be better, I cannot tell; I awfully forebode I shall not. To remain as I am is impossible. I must die or be better, as it appears to me. I fear I shall be unable to attend to any business here and a change of scene might help me. If I could be myself I would rather remain at home with Judge Logan."

He did "become himself" again, for in the spring of 1841 the partnership of Stuart and Lincoln was dissolved; and on April

14, at the request of Stephen T. Logan, the firm with the alliterative name of Logan & Lincoln replaced it. Truly a significant mark of the well-founded confidence of that prominent lawyer in the ability of the thirty-two-year-old Lincoln!

Independent and self-reliant to an extraordinary degree, Lincoln nevertheless felt keenly the deficiencies of his own legal education when pitted against the leaders of the Illinois bar. It was then that he needed the advice and guidance of an older and more experienced man. Judge Logan stood out as a truly great advocate—the greatest natural lawyer of his day, according to David Davis, later justice of the Supreme Court of the United States. He stood at the very head of the Illinois bar. In his office many leading lawyers were developed, including four future United States senators and three governors of States. Powerful was his influence as a preceptor, and great his faculty for recognizing latent ability. From the viewpoint of Lincoln's advancement in the law, the association with Judge Logan was indeed fortunate.

Judge Logan had found ample opportunity to recognize the qualifications of Lincoln. As judge of the circuit court, he had made the order admitting Lincoln to the bar; he had signed the journal entry which terminated Lincoln's first case, Hawthorne vs. Wooldridge; he had met the novice in a number of legal battles in the justice of the peace and circuit courts, and the Supreme Court, and had found the novice worthy of his steel. In fact, in all three cases in which Lincoln opposed Judge Logan in the Supreme Court, the younger man emerged the victor.[1]

Stephen T. Logan was about ten years older than Lincoln. He had come to the Springfield bar from Kentucky in 1833, with no mean reputation as a lawyer. For ten years previously he had practiced his profession in his native State. And though he came to compete with such giants as Douglas, Stuart, Baker, Bledsoe, McDougall, Strong, Edwards, Lamborn, and many others then

---

[1] Cannon vs. Kinney, 4 Ill. 9; Bailey vs. Cromwell, 4 Ill. 71; Elkin *et al* vs. The People, 4 Ill. 207.

rising into eminence, yet all soon recognized his masterly ability and willingly accorded him the leadership.

From 1835 to 1837 he served as circuit judge, and resigned the office, then paying seven hundred and fifty dollars a year, to build up what became for some years to come probably the largest private law practice at the Illinois bar. He could be found on one side or another of nearly every leading case that went to the State Supreme Court.

He was a small thin man, with a little, wrinkled, wizened face, set off by an immense head of hair which might be called frowsy, and Elihu B. Washburne also recalls that "he was dressed in linsey woolsey and wore heavy shoes. His shirt was of unbleached cotton and unstarched and he never incumbered himself with a cravat. His voice was shrill, sharp, and unpleasant, and he had not a single grace of oratory; but when he spoke he always had interested and attentive listeners. Underneath this curious and grotesque exterior there was a gigantic intellect."

Stephen T. Logan was perhaps the most constructive influence in Lincoln's life. Stuart had been indifferent to Lincoln's carelessness, lack of method, and slipshodness. Placing politics above law, Stuart had been inclined to rely on his own native wit and ability, rather than on study and preparation, to win cases. He trusted to the spur of the moment; and the junior partner had adopted the same haphazard methods.

But Judge Logan was different. Unlike many lawyers of the day, he did not regard the law as merely a stepping-stone to political preferment. In fact he lacked the elements of a successful politician and needed an orator like Lincoln to assist him. But to an eminent degree he possessed the true qualities of a great advocate. Well grounded in the law as a science, he was devoted equally to its philosophy and art, re-reading Blackstone every year. He pursued the practice for its own sake, and deservedly had the reputation of being the best *nisi prius* lawyer in the State.

Methodical, industrious, particular, painstaking, and precise, Logan could not tolerate Lincoln's disorderly ways. He immediately exercised influences that were of great worth in inculcating a habit of closer application and deeper study of the principles underlying a lawsuit. He compelled the junior partner to study the authorities and prepare each case carefully in advance. Attention to details, thoroughness, and exactitude became more prominent in his practice. The younger man appreciated the soundness of judgment, accuracy of learning, and brilliancy of legal conceptions of his senior associate. He observed the intuitive vision with which Logan could see the strong point in his own case or the weak one of his opponent; how logically and tersely he stated his points to the court; and how with the same terse logic, the same hugging of the point of his case "but adding a mesmeric force often overwhelming," he argued his cause to the jury.

Association with so able a lawyer inevitably produced a speedy and beneficial effect upon Lincoln. It stimulated him to unusual endeavors, and soon he began to adopt the methods of Judge Logan. He studied his cases with greater care and diligence. He examined the law both of his side and that of his opponent. We have his own statement for the fact that he was never thereafter surprised by the strength of an opponent's case. By analyzing it he often found it weaker than he first feared. This ability to foresee and comprehend an adversary's contention was to stand him in good stead in the momentous days to come, memorably so in his now historic debates with Douglas, where he so mastered the arguments of his adversary that frequently he was able to turn the contentions of his great rival to his own advantage. He began to comprehend a case in all its fullness of circumstances. He became a formidable adversary not only in pleading to the jury but in the presentation of legal arguments as well. Judge Logan had expected little from his new partner other than that he would be a great help in pleading before juries, but he was pleasantly surprised to find Lincoln develop into an able all-round lawyer.

The partnership of Logan and Lincoln became known as one of the leading firms in the State. Springfield, as the seat of the legislature, Circuit, Supreme, and United States District Courts, was the capital of all things legal. From all over the States came retainers. Logan & Lincoln fairly monopolized the sessions of the Supreme Court. At the December term of 1841, the junior partner alone argued fourteen appeals before that high tribunal, losing only four. Not even the renowned Logan surpassed this record. During the terms of 1842–43, the firm argued twenty-four cases in the Supreme Court and was successful in all but seven. All in all, Lincoln personally participated in thirty-nine Supreme Court cases during his partnership with Judge Logan.

Some of these actions became landmarks in Illinois jurisprudence, settling the law regarding the points involved, in some instances, until this very day. One of the cases which must have given Lincoln great satisfaction was the litigation in which Thomas Margrave sued William G. Grable for damages for the seduction of his daughter. The Supreme Court ruling in this action, which followed the contentions of Lincoln, who was acting as counsel for the father, became a guide in the assessment of damages in a large number of subsequent seduction cases.[1]

The fee Lincoln requested for arguing this important case before the State's highest tribunal is a unique item in itself. July 14, 1842, he wrote to Samuel D. Marshall of Shawneetown, who had represented Margrave in the circuit court: "As to the fee, if you are agreed, let it be as follows. Give me credit for two years subscription to your paper and send me five dollars, in good money or the equivalent of it in our Illinois money."

Lincoln's later letter acknowledging the receipt of the five-dollar fee ends up with: "Nothing new here, except my marrying, which to me, is a matter of profound wonder."

Just seven days before, he had taken the "awful plunge" and married Mary Todd at the residence of Ninian W. Edwards. The Reverend Charles Dresser of the Episcopal Church officiated.

Owing to Mrs. Lincoln's disagreeable temper, their married life was not entirely happy. One can, therefore, readily understand the significance of the notation Lincoln penned on the back of a pleading in the divorce case of George Miller vs. Elizabeth Miller. "A pitiful story of marital discord," was his

[1] Grable vs. Margrave, 4 Ill. 372.

suggestive memorandum. Logan and Lincoln represented the husband. The junior partner, married but a short time, seemed to impart his heartfelt sympathy for the client, as he penned the petition. Writing in an unconstrained manner with his usual artless grace, he pours forth the marital woes of an unhappily married pair.

During the summer of 1841, Logan and Lincoln were associated with Edward D. Baker in the defense of three brothers accused of murder. It was a most unusual case. It created a great deal of excitement in the community and caused Lincoln much personal concern.

It appeared that Archibald Fisher, last seen accompanying William Trailor and Henry Trailor, on a visit to a third brother, Archibald Trailor, in Springfield, suddenly and mysteriously disappeared. The brothers were heavily in debt. Fisher was known to have had a considerable amount of money on his person. Suspicion naturally was cast on the brothers, and subsequently they were arrested. While in custody, the police procured from Henry, who was somewhat weak-minded, a confession that his brothers William and Archibald had killed Fisher. He guessed the body could be found in Spring Creek, between Beardstown Road and Hickox's mill, he told the officers. Feeling in the community ran high. There was even wild talk of lynching.

"Away the people swept like a herd of buffalo, and cut down Hickox's mill-dam *nolens volens*, to draw the water out of the pond, and then went up and down and down and up the creek, fishing and raking, and ducking, and diving for two days, and after all, no dead body found," Lincoln wrote in a letter to his friend Joshua F. Speed.

At the arraignment, Lincoln and his associates could only raise a doubt. By the testimony of a Dr. Gilmore and other reputable persons they brought into evidence the fact that two or three years previously the missing man had suffered a serious injury to his head from the bursting of a gun, since when he had been subject to bad health and occasional aberration of mind. The doctor testified that on other occasions Fisher had wandered away in a state of derangement and was unheard of for weeks at a time. Was it not possible that this had occurred again? The police then bent their efforts to proving or disproving this theory, and were amazed to learn that Fisher, in a demented condition, had indeed wandered away to Warren and was safe and sound. Of course the defendants were discharged, "while Henry still protested that no power on earth could ever show Fisher alive," and "Hart, the little drayman said, it was too damned bad to have so much trouble, and no hanging after all."[1]

Although Lincoln had put his very heart into this case, and even defrayed part of the expenses from his own pocket, the Trailor brothers failed to pay his modest fee, and four years later he was forced to sue James D. Smith, executor of the will of William Trailor, deceased, for one hundred dollars "For defending Trailor against an indictment for murder."

Certain real estate came into the possession of Rowland and Smith Company, Louisville merchants, in satisfaction of a judgment procured by Lincoln. When the Kentucky firm wrote to Logan and Lincoln to manage the property for them, the junior partner replied: "As to real estate we cannot attend to it. We are not real estate agents, we are lawyers. We recommend that you give the charge of it to Mr. Isaac S. Britton, a trustworthy man, and one whom the Lord made on purpose for such business."[2]

The practice of the firm of Logan & Lincoln was large, and although Logan received the lion's share of the income, Lincoln for the first time soon was able to make more than a bare living. In May, 1844, he was able to purchase for fifteen hundred dollars a home from the Reverend Charles Dresser on the northeast corner of Jackson and Eighth Streets, Springfield. Here, sixteen years later, amid the thunderous cheers of his fellow townsmen, he was to receive the notification of his nomination to the Presidency of the United States.

[1] Nicolay and Hay, *Complete Works of Abraham Lincoln* (hereafter cited as *Works*), I, 168–75; Lamon, *The Life of Abraham Lincoln from his Birth to his Inauguration as President* (hereafter cited as *Life of Lincoln*), pp. 317–19; Gibson W. Harris in Columbia (Ky.) *Spectator*, January 27, 1905.

[2] Herndon and Weik, *Lincoln*, I, 251.

Various reasons have been given for the termination of the Logan-Lincoln partnership. Perhaps the conflicting ambitions of both men to go to Congress brought them to the parting of the ways. Unsatisfactory financial arrangements by which Logan retained the greater share of the firm income might have been the cause; or the fact that Lincoln, naturally easy-going and independent, chafed under the restraints imposed upon him by the senior partner and could not at all times accommodate himself to Logan's methods. Herndon, who was then studying law in the office of Logan & Lincoln, observed that "on occasions Lincoln would forget Logan's training and go back to his old careless methods of trying cases. He would then trust to his general knowledge of the law and the inspiration of the surroundings to overcome the judge or jury."

However, there is no reason to doubt Logan's statement regarding the dissolution of their association. He told Herndon: "Our partnership continued perhaps three years. I then told him that I wished to take my son David with me who had meanwhile grown up, and Lincoln was perhaps by that time willing to begin on his own account. So we talked the matter over and dissolved the partnership amicably and in friendship."

Logan and Lincoln had but little in common. Two such conflicting, ambitious, and independent personalities could not exist together indefinitely in one small office, and the partnership came to an end.

September 20, 1843, is the commonly given date of the termination of the partnership. This, however, in the light of facts now known, appears to be erroneous. Although it is difficult to fix the exact date of the dissolution of the firm of Logan & Lincoln, there are many facts to indicate that the association continued to the autumn and probably the winter of 1844, or even to the beginning of 1845.

Lincoln in a letter to D. M. Irwin in 1850, itemizing his bill for professional services performed on behalf of the heirs of one Payne, writes:

To Logan & Lincoln   Dr
1844 To attending to Ejectment suit against Hall in
Sangamon Circuit Court. $20.00

Same
To A. Lincoln   Dr
1845–46 To attending same suit in Supreme Court $10.00

Same
To Lincoln & Herndon   Dr
1846–7–8–9&50 To attending to Chancery suit between
same parties in Sangamon Circuit
Court. $10.00
                                               $40.00

"Above is the bill as you requested me to send you. Logan
only attended the first trial in the circuit court—I alone—that is
without any partner attended the case in the Supreme Court. In
the Chancery case Mr. Herndon was my partner—I mention all
this to explain the three separate bills."[1]

In a letter dated September 13, 1853, Lincoln writes George
B. Kinkead of Lexington, Kentucky: "I can prove . . . by Stephen
T. Logan of Springfield, Ill. that he and I were partners from the
spring of 1841 to the autumn of 1844."[2]

But whatever the exact date of the dissolution of this partnership, the fact remains that Lincoln left Logan with an established
reputation. The raw novice whom Stuart started in the practice
of law some seven years before was now one of the outstanding
leaders of the Illinois bar.

Pitted against lawyers of unusual ability and power, he had
come to be regarded as a dangerous adversary in every type of
case and in every court. Before a jury he had grown to have but
few peers. He had learned to refrain from covering up a defi-
ciency in the knowledge of law with florid rhetoric and flighty
appeal. He had formed those habits of close application and se-

[1] *Journal of Illinois Historical Society* (June, 1916), IX, 209.
[2] Lamon, *Life of Lincoln*, p. 345.

vere intellectual labor which are indispensable to permanent success at the bar. He had learned the value of study, thoroughness, painstaking attention to details, and exactitude.

The years spent as Logan's associate were indeed constructive years. They were years of education, training, and discipline. The benefits were to last Lincoln all his days.

VI. LINCOLN & HERNDON

IMMEDIATELY after the firm of Logan & Lincoln was dissolved, a shingle bearing the legend "Lincoln & Herndon" appeared in the dingy stairway of a building opposite the courthouse square in Springfield. It was to remain hanging for twenty-two years while the first-named grew into national prominence, became the leader and deliverer of his country, the liberator of the slaves, and a martyr canonized by mankind.

Lincoln had known William Henry Herndon long and intimately. They had first met in 1832 when William's cousin, Rowan Herndon, pilot of the *Talisman,* had chosen Abe Lincoln as his assistant to navigate the steamer through the Sangamon River from near Springfield to the Illinois River.

After this chance meeting on the banks of the Sangamon, Herndon often saw Lincoln in New Salem and in Springfield, where Herndon attended school and worked at odd times in Joshua Speed's store. Later he attended Illinois College at Jacksonville. When the Abolitionist editor, Elijah Lovejoy, was shot by a mob at Alton while defending his press, the students at the college were aroused to a fever heat.

Edward Beecher, brother of Harriet Beecher Stowe, author of *Uncle Tom's Cabin,* and of the Reverend Henry Ward Beecher,

48

eminent clergyman, was president of the institution. He had been one of Lovejoy's staunchest supporters, and now the college, ablaze with righteous anger, became the center of Abolition sentiment. Indignant students and faculty joined in denouncing the outrage. William, in a fiery speech to his fellow students, accused the institution of slavery with the direct responsibility for the brutal crime, and bitterly denounced the attempts to gag the press by mob rule.

Archer C. Herndon, William's father, was strongly pro-slavery and when he heard of his son's speech he declared that he would have no share in the education of a "damned Abolitionist pup" and ordered him to leave college at once and return to Springfield. If he thought he was thus saving his son from further infection with the poison of Abolitionism, he was mistaken, "as it was too late," Herndon wrote. "My soul had absorbed too much of what my father believed was rank poison." From then on, the destruction of slavery became to him his most absorbing political objective.

He was nineteen years of age when he returned to Springfield. He induced Speed to re-employ him as a clerk in his store. He slept in a large room above the establishment, also used as sleeping-quarters by Speed, Lincoln, and Charles R. Hurst. The future partners saw much of each other, and a degree of intimacy neighboring on brotherly affection developed between them. "There was something in his tall and angular frame, his ill-fitting garments, honest face and lively humor that imprinted his individuality on my affection and regard," Herndon said of his friend and idol. Both joined a debating and literary society which met in Speed's room or in a lawyer's office. They were also members of the Young Men's Lyceum, where Lincoln delivered his famous address on "The Perpetuation of Our Free Institutions."

After Lincoln became associated with Judge Logan, he invited Herndon to study law in their office; and even before the latter received a license to practice law, Lincoln one day, greatly agitated, informed him of his determination to leave Logan, and invited the young man to become his partner. This occurred in the autumn of 1844. Not until December 9 of that year was Herndon admitted to the bar.

What a strange thing for Lincoln to do—to leave the association of one of the ablest lawyers in the whole mid-West and then ally himself with an inexperienced novice! There were undoubtedly a dozen well-trained and successful attorneys in Springfield who would gladly have accepted the opportunity to form a partnership with him. But it was apparent that he desired just such an associate as Herndon—a young man whom he could train according to his own methods. He longed for independence from the restraint of a peer or superior. He wished to be his own master.

There are many indications that throughout his partnership with Logan the judge kept the reins of authority in his hands, and that Lincoln chafed under the restraint. With a junior, the condition would be reversed. Lincoln was politically ambitious. Logan, himself desirous of a seat in Congress, preferred that Lincoln devote more of his time to law. With young Herndon it would be different. What he lacked in experience as a lawyer would be more than compensated by his political sagacity.

He was then in his twenty-fifth year, nine years Lincoln's junior, a fine-appearing young man; five feet, six inches tall, handsome, energetic, and an all-around good fellow. He had a knack of winning friends, and had already become uncommonly strong and influential in molding the political opinions of the young men of Springfield. He was a leader in the ranks of the young Whigs, and Lincoln felt his aggressiveness would be a great help to him in the political arena as well as in the law office and in the courts of justice.

"I confess I was surprised when he invited me to become his partner," Herndon later wrote. "I was young in the practice and was painfully aware of my want of ability and experience; but when he remarked in his earnest honest way, 'Billy, I can trust you, if you can trust me.' I felt relieved and accepted his generous proposal. It has always been a matter of pride with me during our long partnership, continuing on until it was dissolved by the

bullet of the assassin Booth, we never had any personal controversy or disagreement."[1]

Unlike in temperaments, habits, and natures, it is a mystery
how two such conflicting personalities managed to get along for
so many years in harmonious friendship. It was a curious alliance. Lincoln always called his junior "Billy," while the latter
addressed him as "Mr. Lincoln." The senior associate was a
conservative, while Herndon was a radical and militant enthusi-
ast. Lincoln was a total abstainer, while Herndon all through his
career was a victim of the drink habit. Lincoln hated slavery but
believed that by confining it to the States where it already had
a foothold it would gradually disappear in the natural course of
events; Herndon, an agitator and abolitionist, was intent upon the
immediate destruction of the institution. "Choke down slavery"
was his constant cry.

And yet they possessed much in common. They respected each
other as comrades, and Billy almost worshiped his friend as a
hero. They helped each other by their fellowship and contact.
Herndon's self-effacement in his senior's behalf was nobly self-
sacrificing. He was his man Friday. If such a thing be possible,
he was more ambitious politically for Lincoln than Lincoln himself. So despite the dissimilarities in their thoughts, habits, and
temperaments, they were mutually helpful and formed a well-
nigh perfect combination both from a business and a political
standpoint. Lincoln, by nature so secretive and reticent, poured
out his soul to Billy, and though Herndon was far from being a
Boswell, the world is indebted to him for its intimate knowledge
of many facts of his partner's life and character that otherwise
would have been irretrievably lost.[2]

"No father or brother I ever knew exerted a more complete
control over their nearest kin than did this senior partner over
his junior," writes Mr. Rankin. "It was a quaint, peculiar power
that Lincoln exerted; silent, steady, masterful."

Mr. Rankin relates that after Lincoln had collected a large
account for Jacob Bunn, the Springfield banker, and had fixed

[1] Herndon and Weik, *Lincoln*, 1, 252.
[2] Newton, *Lincoln and Herndon*, p. 21.

his fee at one hundred dollars, he requested Mr. Bunn to keep the money for him, "for sometimes I have a sudden need for some cash funds and then I will come in and get it." Several months afterwards Lincoln hurried to Mr. Bunn's place of business and demanded the money. Breathlessly he explained that Billy Herndon and Judge Logan's son, David, and another youth named Ferguson had been arrested for fighting and wrecking the furnishings in a grocery-store where the fray took place. The young men were still in jail, and the irate grocer was intent upon prosecuting them unless the damages, totaling one hundred dollars, were paid at once.

Lincoln collected his hundred dollars and the three youths, whose fathers were among the wealthiest citizens of Springfield, were released through Lincoln's money and timely intervention. "The whole affair," writes Rankin, "remained a secret from respective and respectable sires until many years after."[1]

Herndon, according to his own statement, was little more than an office clerk during the first year of his partnership with Lincoln. He developed into a fair lawyer in time, attending to the routine of the office, trying cases in the justices' courts, and preparing for the next term on circuit. At the outset Lincoln personally handled practically all of the important trial work of the firm. But later Herndon began to bear his full share of the labors of the partnership. It is erroneous, however, to believe that the junior partner took care of all the clerical work and drafted most of the pleadings. On the contrary, not only did Lincoln always handle the bulk of the important litigation, but he also drew up most of the necessary legal documents for his cases.

While Lincoln was associated with Logan, it appears that the judge did not trust him with drawing up the pleadings, as indicated by the fact that nearly all the law papers filed by the firm of Logan & Lincoln in Sangamon County are in the senior partner's handwriting. But with the formation of his alliance with Herndon, Lincoln resumed the task he had begun as Stuart's partner, and drafted practically all the pleadings. Engrossed as he was in the

[1] Rankin, *Intimate Character Sketches of Abe Lincoln*, pp. 64–66.

trial of cases, in riding the circuit, and in his political activities, one marvels how he found the time or inclination to write out these numerous documents—and with such laborious care. His penmanship was always uniform and legible. He was painstaking about punctuation and rules of grammar, and his diction was unusually accurate and apt. Though now and then he misspelled a word, these errors were extraordinarily infrequent for one with such limited formal education.

Lincoln had hoped that Herndon would bring order and system into the office, but soon found the young man had not the slightest conception of system, but did have the legal ability of developing into a good lawyer—"so that he was doubly disappointed." And if Herndon installed no order and office efficiency, Lincoln cared little. Papers and notes that he could not carry in his pockets or tall stovepipe hat he tossed into a drawer. A large envelope on his desk stuffed full of loose papers bore the significant legend, "When you can't find it anywhere else look in this." Soon we find him apologizing to a lawyer in another town for failure to answer a letter. "First, I have been very busy in the United States Court," he wrote, "second, when I received the letter, I put it in my old hat and buying a new one the next day, the old one was set aside, and so the letter was lost sight of for a time." Though he bothered little about order and system in his office, his speeches and writings reveal what extraordinary symmetry, method, and logic prevailed in his mind.

Lincoln and Herndon established their office in a room above the post-office and across the hall from the headquarters of the clerk of the United States District Court. It was a shabby and unpretentious affair.

"The furniture, somewhat dilapidated, consisted of one small desk and a table, a sofa or lounge with a raised head at one hand, and half a dozen plain wooden chairs. The floor was never scrubbed. If cleaned at all it was done by the clerk or law student who occasionally ventured to sweep up the accumulated dirt. Over the desk a few shelves had been enclosed: this was the office bookcase holding a set of Blackstone, Kent's Commentaries, Chitty's Pleadings, and a few other books.'' This description has been left by Gibsen W. Harris, who served as a student and clerk in the Lincoln & Herndon office in 1845.[1]

The most popular article of furniture was the rickety leather-covered sofa. On this Lincoln would throw himself on his arrival at the office, usually about nine in the morning and sometimes as early as seven. Although the couch was of ordinary size, it was too short for him, and he would throw one foot on a chair and the other on the edge of a table. Thus having made himself comfortable he would read the newspaper aloud. This annoyed Herndon, and when once he asked his senior partner why he read aloud, Lincoln replied, ''I catch the idea by two senses; for when I hear what is said and also see it, I remember it better even if I do not understand it better.'' He was an omnivorous reader of newspapers, as they kept him informed of the times and especially of current political events throughout the country. Often he would interrupt his reading to discuss or comment upon a news item of interest. It would remind him of something which ''had happened in Indiana or 'down in Egypt,' '' Herndon said. ''That incident would lead to another and still another and the array of stories would follow each other until a large part of the morning was thus consumed. His narratives were almost invariably so witty and amusing they kept all of us in the office laughing, a result which no one enjoyed more heartily than he.'' And yet at other times, when no pressing matters claimed his attention, he was gloomy, dejected and ''dripping with melancholy.''

Lincoln was always singularly stubborn. He came to conclusions slowly and only after due deliberation. But when he once settled upon a conviction it was extremely difficult to change it. And Herndon confessed that he was ''never conscious of having made much of an impression on Lincoln'' in so far as his opinions were concerned.

When Herndon, the rabid Abolitionist, supplied the office table with the leading anti-slavery papers of the North, and at times would read the Abolitionist views to Lincoln, the latter would

---

[1] Weik, *The Real Lincoln*, p. 106.

not concede Herndon's arguments without hearing the Southern side. "Let us have both sides on our table," Lincoln once declared. "Each is entitled to its day in court." As a result, the office subscribed for some Southern periodicals so that the anti-Abolitionist views might also be understood.

Lincoln, who compared his uncanny memory to a piece of steel—very hard to scratch, but almost impossible to free of any mark once made upon it—listened respectfully to Herndon's reading. One item—a political sermon opposing the extension of slavery, written by Herndon's friend, Theodore Parker, and read aloud by the junior partner in the office some time in 1857—must have made an indelible impression on his steel-like memory, for after listening quietly and attentively he began to discuss its political significance and rhetorical qualities with his partner and two students present in the office. Herndon then gave the pamphlet containing the sermon to Lincoln. Some time later upon examining it he observed that Lincoln had underscored several paragraphs with his pen. One interlineated line read, "Democracy is direct self-government, over all the people, for all the people, by all the people." Another marked sentence was, "Slavery is in flagrant violation of the institutions of America—direct government, over all the people, by all the people, for all the people."

Years later these phrases were to be developed into one of the most quoted sentences of his deathless Gettysburg address, namely, "That government of the people, by the people, and for the people shall not perish from the earth."

Starting anew without any established clientele, Lincoln found his natural following flocking to the office of the firm, keeping the partners busy from the very outset. One gets an idea of the extent of their business from the fact that Lincoln argued twenty-four cases at the December, 1845, term of the Supreme Court during the very first year of the partnership, and sixteen cases during the December, 1846, term. Although their practice was not very lucrative they managed to set aside the sum of $98.64 for more books and furniture. Their fees, though numerous, were small. In a "day book" of the partnership, written mostly in

Lincoln's hand, is a record of the fees collected in one hundred and eighty-two cases in a period of over three years. They total a trifle more than two thousand dollars. Five and ten dollars appear to be the most general fees charged, as in sixty-four cases the former amount was paid, and in sixty-three the latter. Other popular fees varied in amounts from two dollars and fifty cents to twenty-five dollars, while five were as high as fifty dollars and one, a hundred dollars. It was not uncommon for them to handle a case all the way through the State Supreme Court for ten dollars.[1]

Although Logan had always retained for himself the larger share of the partnership income, Lincoln divided his fees equally with his junior associate.

The partners started a firm bank account, but they seldom permitted any balance to accumulate. Fees paid in cash were

---

[1] Following is a page of entries from their account book:

Scott vs. Busher (for Deft)
To attending case in Menard Cir. Court if it ends where it is Paid $20

Negro vs. Robert Smith (for Deft)
To attending case of Negro Bob J. P. $5.00

Stevenson & Wardell vs. Garrett (for Deft)
To attending case in Sup Court Dec Term 1846 $10.00

Roswell Munsill vs. Temple (for Plff in error)
To attending case in Sup Court.
By note $10.00 Note mislaid and cannot be found.
Later—paid cash in full of note.

Mrs. Little vs. Littles estate (for Deft)
To attending to case before J. Probate
Dan & Sam Little bound for this $10.00

(Across the lines of this entry are written "incorrect," and again "not right.")

G.B. Merryman vs. Lake, (for Plff)
To attending to case—Cir Court
½ goes to Logan $10.00

divided immediately. "There you are, that is your half," Lincoln would tell Herndon as he handed him an equal portion of the fee collected. When the fee came in the form of a check or draft it was seldom deposited in the bank and credited to the firm account. Usually the partner receiving it would go at once to the bank, cash the check, return to the office, and divide the proceeds with his associate. No other formal accounting was ever made.

"While Lincoln and I were partners," Herndon wrote, "we kept no books as to our partnership, though we did, of course, keep due accounts of our transactions so far as other interests were involved. Lincoln did the major part of the circuit work, while I remained in Springfield to look after the local end of the business. Occasionally I was out on the circuit with him, but never for long periods. At such times all money paid to either of us was immediately divided. What Lincoln collected on the circuit, when I was back in Springfield, he would bring home with him. If, when he returned, it happened I was not in the office, he would withdraw from his pocketbook my share, wrap the money in a paper with a slip attached, containing my name and a memorandum indicating whence it came and place it in a certain drawer where I would be sure to find it. If, on the other hand, I was in the office when he arrived he would open his pocketbook and make the requisite division. He was so prompt and his rule was so invariable that I ventured once to ask him why he was so timely and particular in the matter. 'Well, Billy,' he answered, 'there are three reasons: first, unless I did so I might forget I had collected the money; secondly, I explain to you how and from whom I received the money, so that you will not be required to dun the man who paid it; thirdly, if I were to die you would have no evidence that I had your money. By marking the money it automatically becomes yours and I have no right in law or morals to retain or use it. I make it a practice never to use another man's money without his consent.' "[1]

Busily occupied with his extensive though not very lucrative law practice, Lincoln did not neglect his political ambitions. In 1842 and again in 1844 he strove to win the Whig congressional

[1] Weik, *The Real Lincoln*, pp. 213–14.

nomination for his district, but first John J. Hardin and then
Edward D. Baker became the party choice and eventually won
their respective elections. Lincoln, however, was undaunted. In
1846 there was to be another contest, and this time he was determined to win. As he rode the circuit he made personal calls on
all the influential Whig leaders, most of whom were fellow lawyers. "If it be consistent with your feelings . . . set a few stakes
for me," he wrote Henry Dummer, Stuart's former partner. "Let
no opportunity of making a mark escape" was the keynote of a
letter to another friend. He wrote more letters—to newspapers,
party workers, and voters. He thought he would have no serious
opposition this time. Hardin had served a term; Baker was now
serving; his party could not refuse him. But he was mistaken.
Hardin, "a man of desperate energy and perseverance and one
that never backs out," again became his adversary. "Turn about
is fair play," Lincoln pleaded, referring to an alleged tacit understanding among Whig leaders in the district that Hardin, Baker,
Lincoln, and Logan in rotation were to be the party nominees
for Congress. Hardin vehemently denied the report that he had
agreed not to oppose Baker in 1844 and Lincoln in 1846. But
later, amid bitter factional feeling, Hardin in disgust withdrew
from the contest, leaving the field clear for Lincoln. At the Whig
convention in Petersburg, May 1, 1846, of which Herndon was
secretary, Lincoln was nominated by acclamation. Three months
later, after a spirited election campaign marked by religious big-
otry as well as partisan rancor, he overwhelmed Peter Cartwright,
a picturesque and truculent Methodist circuit-rider whom the
Democrats had nominated as their candidate, by the unprecedented majority of fifteen hundred and eleven votes.

No one had given Lincoln more aid in this campaign than
faithful Billy Herndon. He had been exceedingly active in his
partner's behalf. A leader among the young voters of Sangamon
County, he had brought back into line those who had deserted
Lincoln in 1844. And now he was happy over his comrade's
success and proud that he was the only Whig congressman
elected in the State of Illinois.

But Lincoln, having reached the coveted goal, found no great satisfaction. He had struggled, schemed, and campaigned for the office, but now he wrote friend Joshua Speed, "Being elected to Congress, though I am very grateful to our friends for having done it, has not pleased me as much as I expected."

It would be sixteen months before he could take his seat in the House of Representatives. In the meanwhile there was a livelihood to earn and business to complete. So shoving politics to the background as best he could, he returned to the routine of writing pleadings, attending court, and riding the circuit.

VII. LAWYER LINCOLN
DEFENDS A SLAVE-OWNER

IMPATIENTLY awaiting the hour when he could take his seat in Congress, Representative-elect Lincoln became engaged in the Matson slave case, in which his position has been one of the greatest enigmas of his career. For the action found him fighting for a principle foreign to everything he had previously said or done in connection with the question of slavery.

The man who abhorred slavery with all his heart and soul for its iniquity and its danger to the Union, whose whole life was an all-embracing sympathy for the oppressed and downtrodden, and who within a few years was to become the Great Emancipator—now accepted a retainer from a slave-holder in an effort to send back into slavery a mother and her children, claiming to be free. Hero-worshiping biographers have seen fit to omit this incident from their writings, while a recent critic cites it as an example of the inconsistencies and confusion that existed in Lincoln's mind.[1] Before the facts of this case are related it will be well to chronicle Lincoln's experience with the burning question of slavery up to this point.

Only six years before the Matson litigation he had argued and

---

[1] Masters, *Lincoln the Man*, pp.90–91.

won the case of Bailey vs. Cromwell in the Supreme Court of Illinois.[2] Undoubtedly it involved his first comprehensive study of the slavery problem from a legal standpoint, although just four years earlier, as a member of the Illinois legislature, he had joined with another assemblyman, Dan Stone, in a protest against a resolution that voiced disapproval of the formation of abolition societies.

Lincoln's attitude toward slavery clearly defined itself in his famous case of Bailey vs. Cromwell. One Nathan Cromwell of Tazewell County, an owner of a so-called indentured servant, Nance, a negro girl, sold her to a neighbor, Bailey by name. The sale was conditioned on Cromwell's producing the necessary documentary proof that the girl was a slave and bound to servitude. As payment for Nance, Bailey gave Cromwell his promissory note. It appears that after the girl had been in Bailey's possession for about six months, she left his service, never to return, declaring that she was a free person. Cromwell never furnished the proof of her servitude and Bailey refused to pay the note. Cromwell's estate brought suit in Tazewell County and recovered judgment for the amount.

Lincoln, as counsel for Bailey, appealed to the Supreme Court. Judge Stephen T. Logan, soon to succeed Stuart as Lincoln's partner, and then at the zenith of his illustrious professional career, appeared for Cromwell.

Lincoln, the future Emancipator, argued that the girl was free by virtue of the Ordinance of 1787 as well as by the Constitution of Illinois forbidding slavery. The consideration of the note, he emphasized, was the sale of a human being, and therefore void. He argued that under the law of nations no person can be sold in a free State. He had given this grave question elaborate study and intensive investigation. The Supreme Court sustained Lincoln's position and reversed the circuit court, holding: "It is a presumption of law in the State of Illinois that every person is free, without regard to color. The sale of a free person is illegal."

Through Lincoln's able presentation of the case the slave girl was released from bondage. He was then only thirty-two years

[2] Scammon, Ill. Reports 71–73.

of age, and there can be no doubt that his study and investigation of the question of slavery occasioned by this case influenced his future convictions regarding the problem.

A number of years later, an old negro woman known as Polly came into the law office of Lincoln and Herndon and sobbed out a tale of woe that affected both lawyers intensely. She and her children had been born in slavery in Kentucky, she told them, but her owner, a man named Hinkle, had brought the family to Illinois. Later, unable to hold them in bondage in a free State, he had set them free. Shortly thereafter her son found work as a waiter and deckhand on a steamboat and sailed down the Mississipi. While the boat was docked at New Orleans, the young negro foolishly went ashore. That night he was seized by a policeman and thrown into jail for the violation of a law which prohibited any colored person from being at large after dark without a pass from his owner. By the time he was brought to trial and ordered to pay a fine, his boat had sailed and he was left stranded. Of course he was unable to pay his fine. Under the law there was but one fate in store for the negro—to be sold to the highest bidder in satisfaction of the sentence. It was then that the old negro mother learned of her son's plight. In her misfortune she came to Lincoln and his partner and begged for aid.

Lincoln was incensed over what he regarded as an outrage against the rights of a free person. He besought Herndon to visit Governor Bissell to urge him to use his official influence for obtaining the immediate release of the youth. Herndon returned from the State House with a report that the governor regretted that he had no legal or constitutional right to act in the premises, and therefore could do nothing at all.

"By the Almighty!" exclaimed Lincoln excitedly, when he heard what the governor had said, "I'll have the negro back here or I'll have a twenty years agitation in Illinois until the governor does have a legal and constitutional right to do something in the premises."

But in the meanwhile immediate action had to be taken to save the young negro from being sold. So while the "twenty years agitation" was still in the formative stage, Lincoln and

Herndon, after appealing in vain to the Governor of Louisiana, engaged Colonel A. P. Fields as their correspondent in New Orleans, and from their own meager purses and contributions from a few friends, sent him sufficient money to pay the fine and other expenses of the case. In due time the youth was returned to his home in Illinois, and the two lawyers were content with only the heartfelt gratitude of the old negro mother as their fee.[1]

Now returning to a date only six years after the Bailey vs. Cromwell case, we find the future Emancipator in a very strange and anomalous position. We see him as counsel for Robert Matson, a more or less disreputable slave-owner who was endeavoring to send back into bondage another negro mother and her children, claiming to be free.[2]

Early in 1843, about four years before the commencement of the litigation in question, Robert Matson, a Kentuckian, purchased a large tract of land in Coles County. He named it Black Grove and brought to it a number of slaves for household work and labor in the fields. After the harvest he returned the slaves to Kentucky, but speedily replaced them with another group of negroes, believing that if he permitted them to remain only a short time in Illinois they would not acquire the status of freemen. It was a common practice in such instances to explain to the officers of the law who cared to investigate that the slaves were *in transitu* and not residents.

However, he permitted one slave, Anthony Bryant, to remain from year to year, to act as overseer or foreman. Thus this negro acquired his freedom. He learned to read, and "by keeping his forefinger on the line to spell his way slowly through the Bible." He became a leader among his people and an exhorter or preacher at their religious gatherings. In the spring of 1847 Bryant's wife Jane, a mulatto, and her four children arrived at Black Grove from Kentucky as members of the new replacement con-

---

[1] Brooks, *Abraham Lincoln and the Downfall of American Slavery*, p. 125; Herndon and Weik, *Lincoln*, 11, 378–79.

[2] Duncan T. McIntyre, "Lincoln and the Matson Slave Case," *Illinois Law Review* (1906), 1, 386; Jesse W. Weik, in *Arena Magazine* (April, 1897), XVII, 752–58.

tingent of slaves. Before their scheduled return to Kentucky after the gathering of the crops, Jane aroused the displeasure of Matson's mistress and housekeeper, a white woman named Mary Corbin. She threatened immediately to break up the reunited Bryant family and order Jane and her brood returned to Kentucky, there to be sold for labor "way down South in the cotton fields." This was equivalent to a death sentence for a slave.

In terror Anthony hurried to the nearby village of Oakland, uncertain how to proceed in saving his wife and children from their doom. Here he knew nobody. By mere accident he stopped in front of Gideon M. Ashmore's hotel, where he told his woes to the innkeeper. At the recital of the facts Ashmore became thoroughly aroused. He hurriedly called into consultation a young physician, Hiram Rutherford, who too became deeply stirred by the threatened injustice.

Ashmore and Dr. Rutherford, rabid Abolitionists both, believed that Jane and her children, having been brought from Kentucky, a slave State, to the free State of Illinois, had become free. Resolutely they determined to defend the Bryant family and resist their return to Kentucky. But when Matson executed before William Gilman, a justice of the peace, an affidavit based upon the Fugitive Slave Law, alleging that his slaves refused to return to lawful service in Kentucky, the negroes were arrested and lodged in jail in Charleston.

Matson employed Usher F. Linder, an able attorney residing in Charleston, to protect his interests. Orlando B. Ficklin, another leader of the bar, was retained on behalf of the Bryant family. For two days testimony and arguments were offered in Squire Gilman's court. Mr. Ficklin had demanded a board of three magistrates to try the case, and a Mr. Shephard and a Captain Easton were named to collaborate with Squire Gilman. The justice of the peace and Captain Easton were known pro-slavery sympathizers, while Mr. Shephard was thought to favor the hapless negro defendants.

At the conclusion of the trial Gilman dismissed the large crowd assembled in the courtroom and proceeded with his associates to prepare the judgment.

For several days Squire Gilman, Captain Easton, and Mr. Shephard deliberated over their decision. Doubtless they realized that the whole community was aroused to fever heat. They had seen men about the courthouse with angry, resolute faces, awaiting the result of the trial. Pistols were everywhere in evidence. Loud talk was heard, excitement ran high, and bloodshed seemed imminent. Although two to one pro-slavery, the board of magistrates suddenly discovered that it had no jurisdiction as to the question of the freedom of Jane and her children. But as the negroes were without proper letters of freedom, in violation of the black law, Squire Gilman remanded them to the custody of the sheriff, to be advertised and disposed of according to law. Immediately Dr. Rutherford and Ashmore caused a writ of habeas corpus to be filed in the circuit court demanding their release.

For forty-eight days the negro family remained in jail, and the sheriff had to file a claim against Matson for $107.30 for "Keeping and Dieting five negroes forty-eight days at thirty-seven cents each per day."

Matson in the meantime had been arrested and convicted on a charge of having lived in improper relations with Mary Corbin. Angered by the attempts of Dr. Rutherford and Ashmore to free the Bryant family, he brought suit against both, demanding damages in the sum of twenty-five hundred dollars for the detention of his slaves. As soon as the summons was served on Dr. Rutherford he rode to Charleston to engage a lawyer, and at this point of the tangled litigation appears the man destiny was preparing to become the Great Emancipator of seventeen years later.

For Dr. Rutherford wanted Abraham Lincoln, attending circuit court in Charleston, to act as counsel for himself and to lead the defense of the Bryant slaves. He found the Springfield lawyer at the tavern sitting on the veranda, and he hastily told him of the facts leading up to the controversy with Matson. But Lincoln, with much reluctance, replied that he could not accept the retainer because he had already been consulted in behalf of Matson and was, therefore, under professional obligations to him. Grievously disappointed, Dr. Rutherford left Lincoln and engaged Charles H. Constable to conduct his defense.

When the circuit court finally convened Lincoln, associated with Linder, appeared as Matson's counsel. Judges Wilson and Treat of the Supreme Court had come to Charleston to hear the case. Attorney Ficklin, realizing that Matson had prepared to bid in the slaves when they were to be sold for the payment of the jail fees, went before the opening session of circuit court and procured an order stopping the sale until the adjudication of the habeas corpus proceedings.

Mr. Constable made the opening argument in favor of the motion and Mr. Linder, for Matson, eloquently argued that inasmuch as Matson had never intended to liberate his slaves by permitting them to sojourn in Illinois, their status never changed and they remained slaves. The Federal Constitution, he declared, recognized slavery, and wherever the Constitution held sway one's property rights in slaves as in any other chattels were protected.

In defense, Mr. Ficklin and Mr. Constable argued that the Ordinance of 1787 and the Constitution of Illinois prohibited slavery, and cited many English cases in support of their contention.

"I shall never forget," said Mr. Ficklin, "how Lincoln winced when Constable quoted from Curran's defense of Rowan: 'I speak in the spirit of the British law, which makes liberty commensurate with and inseparable from British soil; which proclaims even to the stranger and sojourner the moment he sets foot upon British earth, that the ground on which he treads is holy and consecrated by the genius of universal emancipation, no matter in what language his doom may have been pronounced; no matter what complexion incompatible with freedom an Indian or African sun may have burnt upon him, no matter in what disastrous battle his liberty may have been cloven down; no matter with what solemnities he may have been devoted upon the altar of slavery; the first moment he touches the sacred soil of Britain the altar and the god sink together in the dust; his soul walks abroad in her own majesty; his body swells beyond the measure of his chains that burst from round him and he stands regenerated and disenthralled by the irresistible genius of universal emancipation!' "[1]

Abraham Lincoln, with the Supreme Court decision in the Bailey vs. Cromwell case still fresh in his mind, then arose to make the closing argument. He was the cynosure of all eyes in the crowded courtroom. His anti-slavery sympathies were well known. What arguments would he offer to doom this mother and her children to lifelong slavery?

"But strange to say," relates Duncan T. McIntyre, a member of the Coles County bar, "he did not once touch upon the question of the right of Matson to take the negroes back to Kentucky. His main contention was that the question of the right of the negroes could only be determined by a regular habeas corpus proceeding, and not by a mere motion, as was then attempted. His argument was masterful in that he was carefully and adroitly shunning the vital question at issue in the case."[2]

Judge Wilson then wanted to know whether Lincoln's objection was simply to the form of the action by which the question should be tried, and the lawyer answered affirmatively.

"Now, if this case was being tried on issue joined in a habeas corpus, and it appeared there, as it does here, that this slaveowner had brought this mother and her children, voluntarily, from the State of Kentucky, and had settled them down on his farm in this State, do you think, as a matter of law, that they did not thereby become free?"

Honest Abe was being put to the supreme test.

"No, sir," he answered after a pause, "I am not prepared to deny that they did."

"The moment those words fell upon the ears of the large audience that was packed into the courtroom Mr. Lincoln stood before them a bigger, greater man than ever before," observes Mr. McIntyre.

But Mr. Lincoln had admitted away his case.

[1] *Speeches of John Philpot Curran*, p. 169.
[2] McIntyre, "Lincoln and the Matson Slave Case," *Illinois Law Review (1906), 1,386.*

"This then," he added rather weakly, "is the point on which this whole case turns: Were these negroes passing over and crossing the State, and thus, as the law contemplates, *in transitu,* or were they actually located by the consent of their master?

"If only crossing the State that act did not free them, but if located, even indefinitely, by the consent of their owner and master, their emancipation logically followed. It is, therefore, of the highest importance to ascertain the true purpose and intent of Matson in placing these negroes on the Black Grove Farm."[1]

An attempt was made to prove through Joe Dean, a worthless fellow, and by other ignorant farm-hands that the sojourn of the slaves at Black Grove was not permanent, that they were never domiciled there, and that they were only *in transitu*; but this testimony was easily discredited.

Lincoln was pitiably weak. His arguments in behalf of a cause his conscience detested were spiritless, half-hearted, and devoid of his usual wit, logic, and invective. He lost the case. Jane Bryant and her four children were released from imprisonment. "And they shall be and remain free and discharged from all servitude whatever to any person or persons, henceforth and forever," concluded the court's decree.

Matson, learning of the judgment, fled from the State, according to Dr. Rutherford, without paying Lincoln one penny of his fee.

The next morning the man who was to annihilate the hated institution of human slavery mounted his old gray mare and ruefully set out for the next county on the circuit. As he threw across the animal's back his saddle-bags filled with soiled linen and crumpled court papers and struck out across the measureless prairie, he gave no further sign, if he experienced it, of any regret, because as a lawyer he had upheld the cause of the strong against the weak.

Curiously enough, when Ashmore sought donations of money with which to defray the expense of sending the happy Bryant

---

[1] In 1867, in the case of Crandall vs. Nevada, 6 Wallace 35, the Supreme Court of the United States decided that citizens might travel across state lines without impediment and carry their property with them.

family to Liberia, one of the first and most willing donors was Lincoln's own partner, Billy Herndon.

This case has been pointed out as proof that Lincoln as a lawyer was not above reproach; that he was insincere and that he did not know his own mind on the burning question of negro slavery. But was that true? If during all his life he uttered a single word in extenuation of slavery it has not come to the light of history. On the contrary, he hated that odious institution with every beat of his heart. That hatred was in his blood and every fiber of his being. "I have always hated slavery. I consider it a great moral evil to hold one-sixth of the population in bondage," he was to state on a momentous occasion. To no Abolitionist was that inhuman system more abhorrent—not only for its inherent inequity but also for its potential danger to the Union.

How, then, account for his acceptance of the Matson case? William H. Seward or Salmon P. Chase would certainly have declined it. Wendell Phillips, that firebrand of the Abolitionist cause, who was later to call Lincoln "the slave hound of Illinois," abandoned a lucrative law career rather than abide by his oath to uphold the Constitution, which sanctioned court rulings that a fugitive slave had no right to trial by jury. He even refused to vote or otherwise participate in the affairs of a government that refused a man—merely because of his color—his inalienable rights as a human being. Garrison denounced the Constitution as a "covenant with death and agreement with hell."

But Lincoln was no fanatic on the question of slavery. He realized the sad and unfortunate fact that slavery, odious as it was to him, was still the law of the land. He never ceased to think that the methods of the Abolitionists were too dangerous and exceedingly disrupting. It was his opinion that slavery could be abolished only by some gradual, orderly plan. His morality was coupled with the profoundness of the politician and farsightedness of the statesman. Slavery must be restricted to places where it was lawful and eradicated only by means consistent with the Constitution and with the Union. He believed firmly in law-enforcement and the obedient acceptance of every law until in response to public opinion it was changed. He felt that so long as slavery was countenanced by the Constitution men opposed to that institution had no right to interfere with the property rights of slave-owners.

In one of the earliest of his public utterances, made even before his twenty-eighth birthday, in urging a strict observance of all the laws, he declared: "Let me not be understood as saying there are no bad laws, or that grievances may not arise for the redress of which no legal provisions have been made. I mean to say no such thing. But I do mean to say that *although bad laws, if they exist,* should be repealed as soon as possible, still, while *they continue* in force; for the sake of the example they should *be religiously observed.* So also in unprovided cases. If such arise, let proper legal provisions be made for them with the least possible delay, but till then let them, if not too intolerable, be borne with."

And so it appears that with all his heartfelt sympathy for the downtrodden and oppressed, he participated in few cases in behalf of runaway negroes because, as John W. Bunn observed, he was unwilling "to be a party to a violation of the fugitive slave law, arguing that the way to overcome the difficulty was a repeal of the law." Mr. Bunn recalled that "in one case at least he [Lincoln] advised that a few dollars be paid to those who were holding the negro."

So when A. J. Grover at Ottawa was explaining to him how he had aided a runaway slave and was now in danger of going to jail for violating a law that was "not only unconstitutional but inhuman," the future Great Emancipator replied, "Oh, it is ungodly! Oh, it is ungodly! No doubt it is ungodly. But it is the law of the land, and we must obey it as we find it!"

With this understanding of Lincoln's attitude toward slavery and runaway slaves, we can better appreciate the reason of his entering the Matson case. There was nothing inconsistent in this act, no lack of sincerity, nothing to justify a reproach of his conduct as a lawyer. His opposition to murder did not deter him from accepting retainers to defend murderers, and his hatred of slavery did not keep him from representing Matson in his attempt to enforce his rights then recognized by the law of the land.

And though this retainer must have failed to meet the approval of his conscience, it typified his obedient acceptance of law as he found it. It typified his whole attitude toward the all-consuming question of slavery—non-interference with the rights of the slave-owners except by some orderly, legal, constitutional plan such as emancipation by compensation. It typified his refusal to become excited and fanatical over the problem when others were losing their heads.

Upon such principles he built—slowly, calmly, and sanely. Sound enough were these principles to withstand the assault of the keenest minds and ablest constitutional lawyers. So that when the proper moment arrived, the man who deemed it proper to use his ability as a lawyer to help Matson in his endeavor to send Jane Bryant and her brood back into bondage was ready with his own hands to strike the fatal blow against slavery.

VIII. A LAWYER IN CONGRESS

WHEN finally on December 6, 1847, sixteen months after his election, Lincoln took the oath of a United States representative and assumed his seat in the Thirtieth Congress, he might have observed this significant fact: as in Springfield, so in Washington, nearly all the lawmakers were lawyers.

For the *Congressional Directory*, the Sangamon representative furnished the following information concerning himself:

"Born February 12, 1809, in Hardin County, Kentucky.

Education, defective.

Profession, a lawyer...."

With few exceptions, every prominent actor in the grim tragedy even then impending was like himself a practicing attorney. At once he felt at home with them. His experience here was to be but his Illinois legislative career on a national scale.

Upon Lincoln's arrival at Washington a letter awaited him from Robert Smith of Alton, who had requested him to collect a claim due him from Senator Douglas. Lincoln answered that he disliked dunning the Senator so soon, but that within a short time he would attend to the matter. When he did see Douglas on December 10, he also presented a claim of Richard Yates, the future war governor of Illinois. That evening he wrote to Yates that Douglas "says it is all right and that he will pay it in a few days."

Lincoln reminded himself that he had forgotten to file certain papers in the Illinois Supreme Court case of James Wilson, for which he had received an advance fee of twenty dollars, and he instructed Herndon how to attend to it. Also there were some outstanding fees, and he urged his junior partner to try to collect them. When Herndon replied that he succeeded in collecting one of the fees Lincoln wrote: "Dear William: Your letter, advising me of the receipt of our fee in the bank case, is just received, and I don't expect to hear another as good a piece of news from Springfield while I am away." He was in need of these funds for paying a debt at the bank and a number of outstanding small bills for dry goods and groceries, and immediately directed his partner to settle the accounts with his share of the fee.

Lincoln was eager to make an impression on the folks back home, and so he informed Billy, "As you are all so anxious for me to distinguish myself, I have concluded to do so before long."

A few days later he made his first speech, a committee report, and wrote: "By way of getting the hang of the House I made a little speech two or three days ago on a post-office question of no general interest. I find speaking here and elsewhere about the same thing. I was about as badly scared, and no more, as I am when I speak in the court."

The law partnership with Herndon, at least nominally, still remained in force and effect. But ever more important to Lincoln just then was Billy's assistance and advice as a sort of political partner. Herndon at home, in close contact with Lincoln's constituency, was a valuable asset. He was, therefore, delighted with the news in Herndon's letter that friends were already planning for his re-election.

But whatever hopes he harbored that his constituents might insist on returning him to Congress were blasted by his own coming course regarding the Mexican War.

The war had been raging nearly twenty months when Lincoln assumed his seat in Congress. Already twenty-seven million dollars had been spent and twenty-seven thousand American soldiers had lost their lives in the acquisition of an unbroken string of victories; and no State had been more loyal and courageous than Illinois in sending volunteers to the front.

Then came President Polk's message to the Thirtieth Congress. He declared in the course of his address that Mexico had begun hostilities by "striking the first blow, and shedding the first blood of our citizens on our own soil."

Lincoln listened, and felt resentment in his heart at what he regarded as the President's attempt to convert the American attack into a defensive operation. He regarded Polk's statement as a perversion of history and justice.

With the thousands of alarmed slavery opponents who opposed territorial expansion in general and the war in particular as "unholy, unrighteous, and damnable," he saw in the alleged desire to protect Texas nothing but a subterfuge to get another huge slave State into the Union. He had promised Herndon that he would soon distinguish himself. His opportunity was here. Making a comprehensive study of the events leading up to the conflict, he concluded that his party's opposition to the war was justified—that it had been unnecessarily and unconstitutionally commenced by the President at the behest of the slave power. He resolved to join the Whig attack on the Administration.

Like a lawyer preparing for a battle in court he made ready for the assault. Law was his rapier blade, and he wielded it with telling force. The President's declaration that the "soil was ours" on which the Americans were attacked by Mexico, grated harshly on his sense of justice and fair dealing. It sounded untrue. In court he would have questioned the sufficiency of the pleading or filed a "motion to make more definite and certain." Now he introduced his famous Spot Resolutions—eight queries, direct and unambiguous, demanding that the President answer authoritatively: Where was the "spot"? Historically? Geographically? Was the "spot" on which the blood of American citizens had been overtly shed actually American territory? Was it not true that the American citizens whose blood was shed were members of our armed forces sent into a Mexican settlement against the better judgment of their commanding general, who believed the step was unnecessary for the defense of American interests?[1]

Formidable questions in formidable array were they. But the President chose to ignore them altogether.

Following this outburst, Lincoln hastened to write his law partner concerning a note about which one of their clients, Louis Candler, was bothering him, "not the least of which annoyance is his unreadable and ungodly handwriting." But he took this occasion to inform Herndon about the speech he had made in Congress, "a copy of which I sent you by mail."

Three weeks later Lincoln resumed his attack against the President. Speaking in behalf of his resolutions he again demanded that the Administration answer fully, fairly, and candidly and point out "the spot" on American soil where the first blood was shed. Let him answer with facts and not with arguments, and if he refuses to answer, "then I shall be fully convinced of what I more than suspect already—that he is deeply conscious of being in the wrong; that he feels the blood of this was, like the blood of Abel, crying to Heaven against him."

Once again he is a lawyer arguing in court as he gives utterance to these words:

"Title—ownership to soil or anything else—is not a simple fact, but is a conclusion following on one or more simple facts; and [that] it was incumbent upon him [the President] to present the facts from which he concluded the soil was ours on which the first blood of the war was shed.

"Accordingly ... he enters upon that task; forming an issue and introducing testimony. ... Now, I propose to try to show that the whole of this—issue and evidence—is from beginning to end the sheerest deception."

Then, like a lawyer in court, he set about "to examine the President's evidence as applicable to such an issue."

[1] *Congressional Globe*, Thirtieth Congress, 1st Session, p. 64.

"My way of living," said Lincoln, "leads me to be about the courts of justice; and there I have sometimes seen a good lawyer struggling for his client's neck in a desperate case, employing every artifice to work round, befog, and cover up with many words some point arising in the case which he dared not admit and yet could not deny." It appeared to him that "just such and from just such necessity is the President's struggle in this case" in his failure either to admit or deny the declaration that he had sent "the army into the midst of a settlement of Mexican people who had never submitted by consent or by force to the authority of Texas or of the United States and that there and thereby the first blood of the war was shed."

In the course of his tirade he made a blunder—an error in pleading, so to speak—which was to be used against him time and time again when as President he resisted with all the force and power at his command the attempts of the Southern States to secede. Altogether unnecessary and redundant to his present case, in endeavoring to demonstrate that Texas in revolting against Mexico had acquired for herself only the territory wherein her revolution was successful "by obtaining the actual willing or unwilling submission of the people," he declared: "Any people anywhere being inclined and having the power have the right to rise up and shake off the existing government, and form a new one that suits them better. This is a most valuable, a most sacred right—a right which we hope and believe is to liberate the world."

To Usher F. Linder he wrote that in law "it is good policy never to plead what you need not, lest you oblige yourself to prove what you cannot."[1]

Having unnecessarily pleaded the foregoing justification of the right of Texas to revolt, he was to be challenged in 1860 to answer why the same "most valuable" and "most sacred right" was being denied to the eleven million citizens who had organized the Confederate States of America.

Although President Polk again ignored Lincoln's tirade, his constituents back home did not. They could not understand Lin-

---

[1] Lincoln to Linder, February 20, 1848, *Works*, 11, 3.

coln's attitude. It was a dangerous business to criticize a war when fellow countrymen were daily risking their lives on the fields of battle. True, Lincoln had voted for all supplies for soldiers, but on every bill intended to embarrass and censure the President he was aligned with the enemies of the Administration. Neighbor John J. Hardin and hundreds of others had given their lives for their country. Lincoln's stand was unpatriotic, damnable, and treacherous. "A second Benedict Arnold," the Illinois *State Register* was calling him.

Faithful Billy Herndon became greatly alarmed. He felt that Lincoln was digging his political grave. He disagreed with his partner's attitude.

"I will stake my life that if you had been in my place you would have voted just as I did," Lincoln wrote back. "Would you have voted what you felt and knew to be a lie? I know you would not. Would you have gone out of the House—skulked the vote? I expect not."

He was eager to have Herndon, of all people, understand him. If Billy did not understand him, then no one could. He justified his contention that the war was unconstitutionally begun by the President. Polk's act was an usurpation of the war-making powers inherent in Congress, he argued.

But Lincoln's failure to make a deep impression with his Spot Resolutions in no manner deterred him from taking an aggressive stand on other questions that interested him. He concerned himself especially with bills dealing with the administration of justice and the courts. So when a bill to increase the salary of a judge in western Virginia from eighteen hundred to twenty-five hundred dollars a year was being considered, Lincoln said he felt unwilling to be either unjust or ungenerous, but he wanted to understand the real case of this judicial officer. In Illinois but one district court had been held annually. There were now to be two. Could it be that the western district of Virginia furnished more business for a judge than the whole State of Illinois? Actually, the matter came to this, he argued: that the people in the western district of Virginia have eleven courts in one year for their own accommodation; and being thus better accommodated than their neighbors elsewhere, they wanted their judge to be a little better paid.

When the House resolved itself into a Committee of the Whole to consider the state of the Union, on the civil and diplomatic appropriation bill, Lincoln, the aggressive first-termer, arose to attack the Administration's stand on the general subject of internal improvements.

The adopted policy of the Democratic Party was that the "Constitution does not confer upon the general government the power to commence and carry on a general system of internal improvements," and that "internal improvements ought not to be made by the general government; first, because they would overwhelm the treasury; and second because, while their burdens would be general, their benefits would be local and partial, involving an obnoxious inequality."

Lincoln displayed his wide knowledge of constitutional law and history by taking issue with this attitude. He uncovered the fallacies of the President's arguments, and quoted as his authorities two of the most eminent lawyers of the age, Mr. Justice Story and Chancellor Kent.

To prove his contention that Congress has the authority to appropriate public moneys for internal improvements, Congressman Lincoln read at length from the law commentaries of these great jurists. Concerning Chancellor Kent's authoritativeness, Lincoln said: "He was one of the ablest and most learned lawyers of this age, or of any age. It is no disparagement to Mr. Polk, nor indeed to anyone who devotes much time to politics, to be placed far behind Chancellor Kent as a lawyer. Can the party opinion of a President on a law question, as this purely is, be at all compared or set in opposition to that of such a man, in such an attitude, as Chancellor Kent? This constitutional question will probably never be better settled than it is, until it shall pass under judicial consideration."

Lincoln's fidelity to the Constitution, which he was to display in the crucial days of the Civil War, was strikingly revealed when he discussed the possibility of amending the Constitution to enable the general government to undertake great objects of improvement thought expedient though unconstitutional. He declared: "I have already said that no one who is satisfied of the expediency of making improvements needs be much uneasy in his conscience about its constitutionality. I wish now to submit a few remarks on the general proposition of amending the Constitution. As a general rule, I think we would much better let it alone. No slight occasion should tempt us to touch it. Better not take the first step, which may lead to a habit of altering it. Better, rather, habituáte ourselves to think of it as unalterable. It can scarcely be made better than it is. New provisions would introduce new difficulties, and thus create and increase appetite for further change. No, sir; let it stand as it is. New hands have never touched it. The men who made it have done their work and have passed away. Who shall improve on what they did?"

During his sojourn at Washington, Lincoln attended some of the sessions at the Supreme Court and heard such giants of the bar as Rufus Choate, Reverdy Johnson, and Daniel Webster arguing, pleading, and building the fabric of American law. Three days after the termination of the Thirtieth Congress, he too was to be admitted to the practice of law before this high tribunal. A Mr. Lawrence signed the necessary motion for his admission. On the same day Lincoln argued his first United States Supreme Court case.[1]

Here he first met Chief Justice Roger B. Taney, with whom he was to clash so vigorously in the days to come. Often he went to the library in the Supreme Court building and borrowed books which he tied in his bandanna handkerchief. Then with his cane stuck through the knot he would throw the bundle over his shoulder and go forth to his boarding-house to read at his leisure.

He also made numerous trips to the Patent Office to make inquiries on behalf of clients or constituents. Thus Benjamin Kellogg, Jr., of Pekin[2] and Amos Williams of Danville requested

[1] Lewis vs. Lewis, 7 Howard 776, March 7, 1849.
[2] Letter to Benjamin Kellogg, Jr., April 21, 1848, in P. M. Angle, *New Letters and Papers of Lincoln* (hereafter cited as *Letters*), p.43.

him to obtain information about patents for their inventions. To Williams Congressman Lincoln wrote: "Send me a description of your 'invention' or 'improvement' together with $20 in money and I will file it for you."[1]

Two drafts totaling nearly fifteen hundred dollars were sent to Lincoln for collection from Joseph Gales and William Winston Seaton, Washington publishers of the *National Intelligencer*, a leading Whig organ. "Please let me hear from you on the subject," was the manner in which he dunned the publishers.[2]

Lincoln took a part in the successful campaign that made General Zachary Taylor the President of the United States, and later returned to Washington on the reassembling of the Thirtieth Congress for its second session. He then introduced resolutions to emancipate the slaves of the District of Columbia. The House was indifferent and his bill was denied even a hearing. It never came to a vote. Thus ended his career as a congressman.

Fortunately, two years before, he had announced he would not seek a second term. His unpopularity had not only made his reelection an impossibility but had also brought a disheartening defeat to his former law partner, Stephen T. Logan, whom the Whigs had nominated as his successor.

Lincoln had made no serious impression upon either the Nation or his party. Fellow congressmen knew him only as a droll, honest, amiable fellow who could have been crowned the champion story-teller of the Capitol.

All in all his career in Congress had been a failure—an unfruitful episode. Facing politically a blank wall, he sought as his reward for faithful services to his party the office of Commissioner of the General Land Office, but the Whig administration gave the post to Justin Butterfield, and offered Lincoln either the governorship or secretaryship of Oregon Territory. Apparently this was the full measure of his importance to his party at that time. Fortunately for himself and his country, at his wife's insis-

---

[1] Letter to Amos Williams, December 8, 1838, *ibid.*, p. 48.
[2] Letter to Gales and Seaton, January 22, 1849, *ibid*, p.51.

tence he declined to "throw himself away" on the distant territorial post.

He would rather remain in Springfield and resume the practice of law.[1]

---

[1] Lamon, *Life of Lincoln*, p. 334; Herndon and Weik, *Lincoln*, 11, p. 306; Nicolay and Hay, p. 297.

IX. LINCOLN'S RETURN TO LAW AND THE CIRCUIT

His political fortune at low ebb, his finances attenuated by its pursuit, disillusioned and deeply humiliated, Lincoln at the age of forty found himself back in Springfield, a politician repudiated by his own party, a lawyer without a practice. It was indeed a new and chastened man who now retreated from the world at large to seek solace by burying himself in the law.

Grant Goodrich, a prominent member of the Chicago bar with an extensive and lucrative law practice, urged Lincoln to become his partner, but Lincoln refused the offer. He voiced a fear of consumption. He could not stand confinement in a big city law office, he explained. Riding the circuit, though not so profitable, was much more to his liking. He preferred a return to his dingy office in Springfield and a new start.

The hoary adage that the law is a jealous mistress proved true in Lincoln's case. His mind, absorbed for so many months in the consideration of politics to the entire exclusion of legal questions, had ceased to think habitually in the terms of law. In fact, said Herndon, Lincoln seemed to have lost all interest in the law. Many clients, formerly accustomed to bringing their legal problems to Lincoln, during his absence had gone to lawyers more experienced than Herndon. The former congressman, therefore, returned to a law practice conspicuous by its absence.

Of course, the junior partner had retained all the business possible, and when Lincoln came back he offered to share with him the fees collected from these clients. The fee book kept by Herndon for the year 1847 contained more than fifty entries headed: "These cases attended to since Lincoln went to Congress." Lincoln, however, refused to accept any money, maintaining that he had no right to share in the earnings gained during his absence.

"I responded," related Herndon, "that as he had aided me and given me prominence when I was young and needed it, I could afford now to be grateful if not generous. I, therefore, recommended a continuation of the partnership and we went on as before."

The renewed partnership established an office on the second floor of a brick building on the public square, opposite the courthouse. A narrow flight of stairs led into a medium-sized room containing two windows which looked into a dingy back yard. The office was uncarpeted and plainly furnished with a long green baize-covered table in the center, forming a "T" with a shorter table at one end; an old-fashioned secretary with pigeon-holes and drawers for the legal papers; and a good-sized bookcase supplying ample shelving for the law books. An old rocking-chair was Lincoln's favorite seat.

Some five years later, when Whitney saw the office, the windows appeared to him "innocent of water and the scrubman since creation's dawn or the settlement of Springfield." John H. Littlefield, who studied in the Lincoln & Herndon office, found while endeavoring to clean up the room that a quantity of seed such as congressmen distribute to farmers had been left among a pile of old papers and accumulated rubbish and had taken root and sprouted in the dirt. "It did not seem as if the inspiration of a genius could haunt such a place," said Whitney, "and yet, in this uncouth office, the later creed of the Republican party was formulated."

Lincoln's life as a lawyer was thereafter divided into two periods, the one preceding and the one following his term in Congress. His real career and fame in the profession commenced after his return from Washington. Believing himself politically dead, he now turned to law with a devotion and singleness of purpose which never before marked his practice.

Political defeat, Herndon observed, wrought a marked effect on Lincoln. "It went below the skin and made a changed man of him." Lincoln, interested in politics ever since his arrival in Illinois, now determined to eschew politics and devote himself earnestly and entirely to law.

The junior partner could notice a difference in Lincoln's demeanor as a lawyer from this time forward. Lincoln himself began to sense "a certain lack of discipline—a want of mental training and method." He began to study his law problems with a renewed industry. He realized that the twelve years which passed since his admission to the bar had wrought great change in the law and lawyers of the State. The courts were becoming graver and more dignified. Lawyers were learning that a broad and profound knowledge of underlying legal principles and close reasoning were more important than the pyrotechnics of the courtroom and ear-splitting stump oratory.

Lincoln began to read, study, and think as never before, and the boisterous and ruder characteristics which marked his earlier actions gradually gave way to the more ethical and refined bent of his mind.

In the main he was a profound student. No man ever realized his own educational shortcomings more keenly. No man had a greater capacity to grow. To bring himself up to the general standard of culture of the men he had been meeting in the East now became his ambition.

Ever a natural logician and patient investigator, he now began a course of study embracing mathematics, poetry, and astronomy. Soon he could demonstrate with ease all the propositions in the six books of Euclid. In later years he was destined to make frequent practical use of this knowledge.

A well-worn copy of Shakespeare became his companion. And at times he would find delight and mental refreshment in the poems of Byron and Burns.

Law business was not sufficient in Springfield to keep all of Lincoln's time occupied. The Supreme Court convened for only a few days annually, while the circuit court held only two sessions a year, each lasting but a few weeks. Nor did the United States District Court sitting in Springfield consume much of his time. Unhampered by political activities he would have had an enforced idleness six months out of the year on his hands; and like Viola, he might have

. . . Pined in thought,
And with a green and yellow melancholy
. . . sat, like Patience on a monument,
                    Smiling at grief,

were it not for the fact that he now entered upon circuit riding to an extent hitherto unknown to his professional activities.

Lincoln had engaged in this arduous, itinerant practice almost from the outset of his legal career. He had become a familiar figure on the Eighth Judicial Circuit of Illinois ever since its formation in 1839. Previously, for a short time, he had practiced in the circuit court over which Judge Stephen T. Logan presided. But this future partner of Lincoln's resigned from the bench in 1837, because of the inadequate pay, and began building up one of the most successful law businesses in Illinois. The youthful Stephen A. Douglas was then the State's attorney for Logan's circuit. Lincoln, as a member of the legislature, supported David Davis for the office of State's attorney for the Eighth Judicial Circuit after Douglas became a member of the Assembly, but the Democratic majority overwhelmed the Whigs and elected David B. Campbell instead.

Two years later, in 1841, the legislature, under the adroit leadership of the ambitious and energetic Little Giant, swept the nine circuit judges of Illinois out of office, increased the number of Supreme Court judges from four to nine, divided the State into nine circuits, and assigned each judge to preside over a circuit in addition to his duties on the Supreme Court bench. Among the five new Supreme Court judges elected by the General As-

sembly was Douglas, only twenty-seven years old. Another ap-
pointee was Samuel H. Treat, who was assigned to the Eighth
Circuit. In his courts Lincoln practiced until his departure for
Washington.[1]

From county seat to county seat Judge Treat traveled in regular
rotation, holding court twice a year at the various counties at
fixed sessions of two days to a week in each. With the itinerant
judge went a cavalcade of lawyers, including Lincoln, Stuart,
Logan, David Davis, Edward D. Baker, John J. Hardin, and
James Shields. Over muddy roads and broken bridges, through
swollen, treacherous streams, through sleet and snow, in rain, in
fair weather and foul, amid hardships known only to the pioneer,
they rode on horseback or in rickety buggies to administer justice
to a folk uncouth, simple, and unrefined, yet a splendid, brave,
and independent race of pioneers, straightforward and possessing
a wealth of common sense.

Lincoln, Stuart, Logan, Davis, and Baker were known as the
"big five" of this early horseback circuit.[2]

According to Davis, Lincoln during this period "shows the
want of early education, but has great powers as a speaker."[3]

Profound legal learning was then unnecessary. "Good sound
common sense, the gift of speech, a mixture of natural shrewdness with politics, and a regular attendance upon the courts in
the circuit were the principles requisite for success."[4]

"There is some fun and a good deal of excitement in practicing law in this prairie state, but not much profit or personal
comfort," Davis wrote to a relative. "We have been deluged by
rain this spring. The windows of heaven are certainly open. Bad
roads, broken bridges, swimming of horses and constant wettings
are the main incidents in Western travel."[5]

---

[1] Thomas A. Ford, *History of Illinios*, pp. 212; James C. Conkling, *Bench
and Bar of Central Illinois*, Fergus Historical Series, p. 47.

[2] Stringer, *History of Logan County*, pp. 314–15, 318.

[3] Davis to William P. Walker, Decatur, Illinois, May 4, 1844, Davis MSS.

[4] John Dean Caton, *Early Bench and Bar of Illinois*, p. 225.

[5] Davis to Julius Rockewell, May 14, 1844, in Harry Edward Pratt, "David
Davis," *Transactions of the Illinois Historical Society* (1930), p. 163.

As Lincoln's circuit practice increased, his absences from home grew longer and longer. In 1842, his sojourns already stretched weeks at a time. "You speak of the great time that has elapsed since I wrote you." Lincoln said in a letter to his friend Speed, written during that year. "Let me explain that. Your letter reached here a day or two after I had started on the circuit. I was gone five or six weeks."[1]

After his return from Congress it was not uncommon for him to remain on the circuit for the full three months of the court sessions. For the Eighth Circuit had then grown to gigantic proportions, and distance made it inconvenient if not impossible for Lincoln to return home frequently.

During his term in Congress, a new constitution again reorganized the judicial systems of Illinois by creating a Supreme Court of only three judges and providing for the election of circuit judges by popular vote for a term of six years. Under this arrangement, Lincoln's friend David Davis was elected in September, 1848, to succeed Judge Treat and to preside over the Eighth Circuit. With this good-natured, corpulent jurist, Lincoln rode the circuit until the nation called him to his greatest case.

At different periods the Eighth Circuit varied in size and in the number of counties which comprised it. At its greatest extent it covered seventeen counties. But as the population increased the resultant growth of legal business caused the legislature, from time to time, to cut the district down to a convenient and practical size. During the major part of Lincoln's circuit-riding activity the Eighth Circuit included fourteen counties—McLean, Logan, Tazewell, De Witt, Vermillion, Champaign, Woodford, Sangamon, Christian, Macon, Moultrie, Shelby, Edgar, and Platt, covering an immense expanse of sparsely settled territory. Here was an empire in itself—approximately one hundred and ten by one hundred and forty miles, or more than fifteen thousand square miles in area, virtually one fifth of the entire area of Illinois.[2]

To visit the fourteen county seats entailed a journey of approx-

[1] *Works*, I, 217.
[2] For changes in the Eighth Circuit see *Illinois Session Laws*, 1847, p. 31; 1849, p. 60; 1853, p. 63; 1857, p. 12.

imately five hundred miles. To reach the next court on time the itinerant lawyers had to start out long before dawn and ride late into the night. Four to five miles an hour were all the plodding horses could cover if the weather was favorable; but if the roads were bad, the riders had to be satisfied with the wearisome rate of one to two miles an hour.

Most of the lawyers practiced in a few neighboring counties where they were best known; nor did Lincoln, while Logan's partner, venture far from home in search of cases on the circuit. During the first years of his association with Herndon, however, he extended his practice greatly.

The junior partner remained in charge of the Springfield office while Lincoln went out "beating the bushes for more business." But it was not until after his return from Congress that he began to travel the entire circuit with Judge Davis. And they were the only members of the entire bar who regularly made the rounds of all the fourteen county seats—the judge because his duties demanded it, and Lincoln because he loved the nomadic and arduous life. Half of each year he spent in this peregrinative occupation—three months at the spring sessions and three months at the fall term of the court. On "an indifferent, rawboned specimen" of a horse which he himself groomed, he would set out from home, his saddle-bags stuffed with documents and a few changes of lighter apparel, a huge weatherbeaten cotton umbrella to shelter him from the elements, and a law book or two, to be gone for weeks at a stretch.

For nearly five years following Lincoln's return from Washington, only the stage-coach provided the inland means of public conveyance. Early in 1850, when the quagmire roads were somewhat improved, Lincoln hitched his horse to a ramshackle buggy and rode in greater comfort.

The thickly matted prairie grass and densely entwined roots caused rains to pass off very slowly. As the roads generally ran through the middle of the prairies, the highways became almost impassable in rainy weather, and the wheels of Lincoln's rattling buggy would sink deep in the sloughs as his plodding horse floundered and struggled on valiantly.

Bridges in the unsettled portions of Illinois were scarce. Ability to wade and swim, therefore, became necessary attributes of a circuit-riding lawyer, as he had to give almost as much thought to fording streams as to trying his cases.

Lincoln's extremely long legs caused his circuit-riding companions to appoint him as scout in testing the depth of the streams. By taking off his boots and stockings and rolling up his trousers he could easily find the shallow crossing-places and lead his cronies through the current. On one occasion after a severe rainstorm, a party of itinerant lawyers, including Judge Davis, stripped naked and with their clothes thrown in bundles over their shoulders, mounted their horses, and led by the gigantic, rawboned Lincoln, crossed the flood.

Frequently the riders would go on for stretches of fifteen miles or more without passing a single farm or meeting a human being.

Few were the villages Lincoln passed as he rode his lonely way over the dim trails or rough dirt roads of the expansive Illinois prairies. County seats, practically the sole centers of population, were mere hamlets of a few hundred inhabitants. Shelter for the night he found in rude farmhouses or wretched country taverns. Often he slept on the floor of these wayside hostelries. When not traveling with the judge, and provided he found a choice of taverns, he would select that at which the cost would be the least, since by necessity he was compelled to be prudent in his expenditures. At the inns the lawyers usually slept two in a bed except in the case of Judge Davis. He tipped the scales at three hundred pounds, and a bedfellow lean enough could not be found.

Poor lodging, wretched food, impassable roads, and swollen streams were the common experiences of the riders of the circuit, and not a few succumbed to the perils of the journey and constant exposure to all sorts of weather.

Yet generally it was a jovial and carefree company that rode along, judge and lawyers, forgetful for the time being of their legal difficulties, and regaling each other with jokes and oftentimes the coarsest of humor. It was this relaxation and unrestraint that caused to pass pleasantly what otherwise would have been monotonously long hours.

On reaching the county seat where the court was scheduled to hold session for from two days to a week, bench and bar, jurors and witnesses, litigants and hangers-on, and even persons accused of crime but free on bail would stop at the same inn, have their meals together, and join in the same recreation during the evenings.

Although judge and prisoners, lawyers and jurors, witnesses and travelers ate at the same table, the choice seats were reserved for the court and the bar. One time Lincoln sat in the wrong place, and when the innkeeper called his attention to the fact that he might sit at the head of the table, the lawyer asked: "Have you anything better to eat up there? If not, I'll stay here."

He could accommodate himself to any surroundings and circumstances, and make himself as comfortable in a rude, unhewed log cabin as in the Pike House in Bloomington, one of the finest hostelries on the entire circuit.

Unfastidious as he was about his food and lodgings, he was even more careless about his clothes and general appearance. He was six feet, four inches in height, his legs disproportionately long and feet and hands unusually large, and his thin chest and stooped shoulders gave him the appearance of a consumptive as he walked along with clumsy, awkward gait.

In one hand he usually carried his large faded green umbrella with the inscription "A. Lincoln" sewed in white thread inside. The knob was missing, and when the umbrella was closed a piece of cord had to be tied around the middle to keep it from flying open. In the other hand he carried a carpet-bag containing his court papers, a few books, and some changes of underclothing.

When Lincoln, in his rude buggy drawn by the rawboned nag, arrived in a county seat, he might well have been mistaken for a rough, intelligent farmer. He wore a faded brown hat, a short cloak, and usually a shawl thrown around the collar. His loose hanging coat and vest and trousers, which were too short to reach his shoe-tops, only served to emphasize the gauntness of his ungainly form.

His features were coarse and his skin dark and sallow. His

bushy, black hair stood out all over his head and had the appearance of being always in need of combing.

Although of an exterior unimpressive, to say the least, he did not lack dignity. In manner he was friendly, cordial, and frank. Something about his kind and amiable expression and sad, quizzical eyes gave everyone the impression that here was a man of truthfulness and integrity who could be trusted implicitly.

Nearly all Lincoln's associates of the bar remember his "wonderful wit and humor." But they also recall his melancholy, moodiness, and depression as a chief characteristic of this period.

On numerous occasions Herndon and Whitney saw Lincoln gloomy and dejected, staring absent-mindedly at the walls. "Melancholy dripped from him as he walked," the junior partner observed, but he could never understand the cause of this sadness. In fact, despite the many years of almost brotherly intimacy he never really knew and certainly did not understand his eccentric senior associate.

What if he were peculiar! His lovable traits made folks forget his idiosyncrasies. Acquaintances admired him for what he was and acclaimed him the most popular lawyer on the circuit.

Court day was a holiday in the average county seat. From the entire countryside came men, women, and children on horseback, in wagons, and afoot to assemble in indiscriminate confusion in and around the courthouse. There were properties to be transferred, taxes to be paid, old debts to be settled, and new ones to be made. There was confusing and uncertain land titles to be determined and numberless grievances to be redressed. The amount of litigation was enormous, and it seemed that men went to law on the slightest provocation. But most of the assembled court crowd came to hear the lawyers plead—to be entertained as if attending a theatrical performance. In addition to the formal legal arguments, they were certain also to hear an eloquent and vociferous political speech or two. For before the introduction of railroads, telegraphs, telephones, and daily newspapers the itinerant lawyers were the chief instructors of the people regarding the political issues of the day.[1]

[1] John M. Palmer, *Bench and Bar of Illinois*, 1, 15.

On the first day of the term after court adjourned, some prominent member of the bar would "make a speech" defending his own party. The following noon or night, a lawyer of the opposite party would reply, and so the lawyer-orators would alternate to the end of the term of court. Three to four hours was the usual length of one of these addresses.[1]

The courthouses in which Lincoln practiced varied in appearance and construction in the different counties. Sometimes the courthouse was a well-built log house, sometimes a room in a building also occupied as business or living quarters, but more often it was an attractive wood or brick structure whose graceful white tower or cupola overlooked a spacious square. Wide verandas with huge Doric or Ionic pillars often adorned the front. The interior was always plain and severe, with unpainted woodwork, knotty pine floors, and wooden benches. A raised platform of pine wood, with a white board on which to write his notes, served as the judge's dais. On one side stood a small table for the clerk, and on the other a larger table, sometimes covered with green baize, for the lawyers.

The court would be officially opened by the sheriff's announcing in a resonant voice, "Oyez! Oyez! The circuit court is now open for the despatch of business." The clerk would then summon the grand jury. The court would charge that august body, and send it to its special room. Then all was in readiness for calling the cases on the docket.

The courtrooms were always crowded. An almost steady flow of wit, humor, and repartee made the proceedings exceedingly informal.

The circuit lawyers having no offices would be in the courtroom listening to the cases even if they were not engaged in them. It was customary for the unoccupied barristers to help those who were engaged, with advice and suggestions. Such constant attendance at the court sessions furnished a fine schooling for the lawyers.

Lincoln habitually attended the sessions even when he had no

[1] Harry Edward Pratt, "David Davis," in *Transactions of the Illinois Historical Society* (1930), p. 163.

scheduled cases of his own on the docket. He was known to whisper comments on the proceedings or tell humorous stories to his neighbor, much to the annoyance of Judge Davis.

When not engaged in the trial of cases or in delivering political addresses, the judge and lawyers usually assembled about the fireplace in the inn or in the barroom of the tavern and spent their leisure in social conversation, playing cards, telling stories, and singing songs. Ward H. Lamon, Lincoln's partner at Danville, had a good voice and would mount a table and sing the popular songs of the day. Well might he have sung with his English brethren of the bar:

"All round the Circuit I goes without a guinea,
All round the Circuit for two months and a day,
And if anybody axes me the reason why I goes it,
    It's because I don't know how to earn it any other way."

William May, a former member of Congress, carried his violin with him and entertained with musical selections. But whenever Lincoln was present he became the center of attraction. He was the "life and light of the court," said his admiring friend Lamon. Abounding in an inexhaustible supply of humorous stories, his art of mimicry, the quizzical expression of his homely features and his good nature kept the group in a continuous roar of laughter. The judge who heard their cases cast aside his judicial dignity and joined in the merrymaking.

Though the circuit had its hardships and privations, it also had its compensations. Judges and lawyers met as friends on a common level. The long rides together and the continued close and friendly intercourse amid jest and song and unchecked vivacity erased all enmity occasioned by contests at the trial table and forum, and created a spirit of fellowship and fraternity unknown under present-day conditions.

Often, too, for the entertainment of the folks of the countryside and of the itinerant lawyers, Judge Davis would call into session an "Orgamathorical Court," a mock tribunal which held night sessions at the courthouse. Here various members of the bar, to the great delight of the spectators, amid much pretended severity and seriousness, would be tried for sundry "high crimes and misdemeanors." It was at one of these sessions that Lincoln was haled before Judge Davis and charged with the "offense" of impoverishing the bar by rendering legal services for unreasonably low fees.

Money was a rather scarce commodity, and circuit lawyers often received their fees in the form of produce, horses, and livestock.

Not having any office of his own in the various county seats, Lincoln would make use of his local associate's headquarters and there consult with his circuit clients. In cases where he acted alone he would confer with his clients in some obscure corner in the court clerk's office or in his bedroom or under a tree on the courthouse lawn—anywhere at all that lawyer and client could discuss their case.

Unless the case were intricate he took no notes and made no memoranda, but with an unusual talent embraced "the whole scope and plan and all essential details of a case within the area of his mind in an orderly and systematic manner." If a case were complicated, there being no time for research, he would confer with the client and associate counsel to ascertain all the facts, then see if the statutes could throw any light on the disputed issues. Then he would seclude himself and formulate in his own mind the plan of trial and the legal principles to be argued.

Practice on the circuit was admirably suited for the unique genius of Lincoln. Employed usually after reaching the county seat, and entrusted with the legal affairs of persons whom he probably never had seen or heard of before, he was obliged to try their cases with little or no preparation. Pleadings like answers, demurrers, motions, and the like had to be drafted at once and made ready for the opening of court within a few hours. He would enter upon the defense of persons confined to the log jail and charged with a misdemeanor or a crime, with just enough time before trial to enable him to learn the facts of the case.

With few law books available and both time and facilities lacking for the drafting of briefs of analogous cases, he was compelled to argue the instant case on broad principles of original reasoning and natural justice rather than on legal precedent. In this respect Lincoln encountered few superiors. Fortunately, few of these lawsuits involved complications. Though the interests involved were usually trivial from a monetary standpoint, they concerned the same principles of right and justice as those connected with the most important cases. Especially when the case hinged upon some human or moral issue did his knowledge and understanding of human beings and his forcefulness and sincerity make him the peer of any advocate at the bar; this despite the fact that Lincoln was ordinarily a slow thinker, and at his best only in cases where he had the opportunity for careful preparation.

The impromptu nature of his circuit practice is also reflected in the professional correspondence carried on by him from the various county seats. Owing to the lack of either stationery or writing facilities it was not uncommon for him to pen his replies to letters on the back of those very letters, and clients were often surprised to receive the return of their own correspondence with Lincoln's answer scrawled on the reverse page.

The perambulating court usually began its spring tour in February and took about three months to traverse the circuit. The fall trip commenced in September and lasted until Christmas.

Before the advent of railroads in Illinois, Lincoln, while traveling the circuit, found it practically impossible to return home until the full terms of court were completed. Absences from home lasting from nine to twelve weeks at a stretch were therefore not uncommon for him.

However, during the last years of his practice Lincoln traveled mostly on the primitive railroads of the day which linked together the various county seats. Thus he found it possible on frequent occasions to return to Springfield over the week-end and be back in circuit court the following Monday morning.

As early as 1853, Lincoln could mount a train of the Chicago and Mississippi Railroad at Springfield and ride to Bloomington and Lincoln. He writes of his leaving his home town on a Tuesday morning in 1854, arriving in Clinton in the afternoon for a three-day court session, and returning home on Friday night.[1] Three years later, when Lincoln's circuit was reduced to five counties, he could travel to every county seat by rail.[2]

The itinerant lawyers welcomed the adjournment of court over the week-end and hurried to their homes to spend Sunday with their families. But according to Judge Davis, Lincoln seldom went home until the full three months term of court was completed. "He was proverbially slow and would linger behind, pleading an accumulation of unfinished business or something equally commonplace and improbable as an excuse for not going. The next Monday, when the other lawyers returned, they would invariably find Lincoln still there anxiously awaiting their reappearance." An uncongenial home life was responsible for this reluctance to return to his family when the opportunity presented itself, although one never would have dreamed this from the care and devotion Lincoln lavished upon his children. He loved them with an affection that verged almost upon folly.

It was the tumultuous nature and unrestrained temper of his wife that made the gypsy-like wandering on the circuit from county seat to county seat so much more congenial than his own fireside. He loved the freedom of the open country, the informality in the mingling with the masses, the undisturbed moments to dream and brood, and the very solitude of it all. The usually moody and melancholy lawyer "was happy, as happy as he could be, when on the circuit, and happy in no other place," Judge Davis declared. "This was his place of enjoyment." And later when as leader of the Nation he was weighed down with the staggering responsibility of a great civil war, he found comfort and delight in stealing away from his crushing cares and for a few moments living over again, in reminiscence with his old friends Whitney and Swett, the bygone exhilarating and carefree days on the circuit. But now he welcomed the opportunity it

---

[1] Letter to Orville H. Browning, November 12, 1854, in Tracy, *Uncollected Letters*, p. 53; Angle, "Abraham Lincoln: Circuit Lawyer," in *Lincoln Centennial Association Papers* (1928), pp. 28–29.

[2] Benjamin P. Thomas, "Lincoln and the Courts," in *Abraham Lincoln Association Papers* (1933), pp. 60–61.

gave him to escape for six months of the year the scolding and incessant outbursts of wrath of his wife. It freed his mind from the hundreds of petty and uneventful trivialities of domesticity, and thrust him into a turbulent sea of politics and public life. His more or less unhappy union, therefore, turned out to be an accidental piece of good luck.

The roving, unsettled life of the circuit in which he had hoped to find escape from his bitter disillusion of politics only shoved him deeper into the turbulent sea of political controversy. Believing himself forever done with politics, he found himself discussing political questions of the day wherever he went.

Traveling up and down this vast circuit for so many years, he came to know personally more men, women, and children than any other citizen of the State. Six months out of each year he spent away from the comforts of his own home, passing his time among strangers, meeting lawyers and politicians and citizens of every walk of life. With them he talked and exchanged views on every conceivable question of the day. With the common people especially he loved to mingle. He shared in their intimacies and was constantly learning from them. "Billy, don't you shoot too high—aim lower and the common people will understand you," he told Herndon one day. "They are the ones you want to reach—at least they are the ones you ought to reach. The educated and refined people will understand you anyway. If you aim too high your ideas will go over the head of the masses, and only hit those who need no hitting."

With the farmers he discussed crops and farm stock; with the business men he talked of the necessity of more railroads and transportation facilities. He would reason upon the tariff, land values, and general industrial, agricultural, and political conditions to the great edification of the scores of listeners, who would be sure to throng around him at every store and tavern he visited. His wit and humor made him a universal favorite and an ever-welcome guest in every county seat. Here the common people learned to know and love him and he in turn to understand and love them. Their problems became his problems. Their aspirations became his aspirations. How important this was to become in his political struggles of the near future! Here he found schooling in the art of human understanding. Here amid a crude society and a gypsy-like life his mind became disciplined and his soul tempered for the great trials of the days to come. Here he built the foundation of a popularity destined to lead him to the White House.

X. CIRCUIT ASSOCIATES AND POLITICAL ALLIES

WHEN Lincoln and the other circuit lawyers arrived in a county seat, they had no definite advance employment, as a rule, but like traveling salesmen found it necessary to hustle out and see what cases they could pick up. All too often the yield of such business was discouraging, not even paying the expenses of the trip. When Henry C. Whitney once complained, while attending court at Danville that he had but two or three cases, Lincoln replied: "You have as much business here as I used to have; I listened to a French street peddler's antics here half a day once, simply because I had not one particle of business."[1]

Frequently Lincoln would have but one case during an entire session. Thus at one term in 1850 at Danville, the records show, he tried but one action, Murphenheim vs. Scott; after the jury

[1] Whitney, *Life on the Circuit with Lincoln*, p. 192.

disagreed, a compromise verdict for seven dollars and fifty cents was entered, each party to pay half the costs. What a fee he must have received after having traveled almost a hundred miles on horseback! At the fall term of 1852, at Danville, three cases involving trivial amounts comprised his entire business, yet the following week at Paris, at a term of five days, he was engaged in nineteen different cases.[1]

As one of the most popular and best beloved circuit riders, Lincoln managed generally to be one of the busiest. Frequently he would scarcely alight from his horse when he would be surrounded by two or three clients requiring his services.

In almost every county seat of the judicial district Lincoln could count upon some resident lawyer to furnish him with business—especially litigation for the Illinois Supreme Court or the United States District Court at Springfield. The local associate or correspondent was often a younger man who found it advantageous to advertise himself a "partner" of the more experienced Springfield lawyer. Actually, the so-called partnership pertained only to the particular case or two then on hand, and it was not uncommon for Lincoln to oppose his "partner" in other litigation at the same term of court.

Pleadings have been found signed Harlan & Lincoln (October 10, 1845), Lincoln & Lamon (May, 1855), Goodrich & Lincoln (October 9, 1855), Ficklin & Lincoln, and others—all during the time when the partnership of Lincoln & Herndon was in full force and effect.

Lincoln tried only about one third of his cases on the circuit alone. In the remainder he was associated with one or more attorneys. "Count me in," was Lincoln's characteristic way of accepting a fellow barrister's invitation to join him in a case.

These connections were to prove far more important in the molding of Lincoln's future than the mere additional revenue they brought to his nearly always empty pockets. For these circuit associates became in time bulwarks of strength during his politi-

---

[1] Charles W. Moores, "Abraham Lincoln, Lawyer," *American Law Review* (January–February, 1911) vol. 45, p. 81.

cal struggles. They became his loyal, devoted district leaders, upon whom he could rely at all times to promote his local interests among the voters of their respective regions.

As there were no law libraries in the average town where the circuit court sessions were held, and only a few elementary books available, there was neither the time nor the facilities to gather authorities and prepare briefs for the citation of parallel cases. Actions had to be argued on original principles rather than on precedent. This, of course, no lawyer could do skillfully unless, by diligent study or experience, he had mastered the rules and principles of law and the reasoning by which they are supported. Youthful and inexperienced local lawyers were naturally at a disadvantage in contested litigation, and therefore customarily retained a visiting leader of the bar as an associate in the trial of the cases.[1]

Lincoln's helpfulness and willingness to co-operate made him a great favorite with the young attorneys. They admired him especially for his unassuming ways. He was always kind, patient, and courteous while advising them regarding their knotty legal problems. He possessed the happy faculty of being able to set his young associates at their ease, encourage them, and instill them with self-confidence.[2]

"The result was, he became the much beloved senior at the bar," is the testimony of a lawyer who made the rounds with him. "No young lawyer ever practiced in the courts with Mr. Lincoln who did not in all his after life have a regard for him akin to personal affection."

When James Haines, then a beginner in the law practice in Tazewell County, retained Lincoln to become associated with him in the defense of a man indicted for obstructing a public road, the Springfield lawyer told him: "I want you to open the

---

[1] John Dean Caton, *Early Bench and Bar of Illinois*, p. 51; F. B. Stringer, *History of Logan County, Illinois*, p. 317; Whitney, *Life on the Circuit with Lincoln*, p. 42.

[2] Lawrence Weldon, in Allen Thorndike Rice, *Reminiscences of Abraham Lincoln*, p. 200; Whitney, *Life on the Circuit*, pp. 31, 111–12.

case, and when you are doing it talk to the jury as though your client's fate depends on every word you utter. Forget that you have any one to fall back upon, and you will do justice to yourself and your client."

The youthful barristers would usually prepare the necessary pleadings under Lincoln's directions. Relieved of the details of preparation and search for legal precedents, Lincoln could give free reign to his powers of logic, lucidity in statement, eloquence, strategy, and humor so necessary in the trial of cases on the circuit.

The young lawyers derived great prestige and much experience by associating thus with Lincoln. But these local "partnerships" were equally beneficial to the Springfield advocate. Not only did they give him a permanent assistant to handle the detail matters at every court, and the use of a local lawyer's office as his headquarters in the various county seats, but they also eliminated the necessity of taking Herndon along with him whenever he made the tour of the circuit. They reduced the firm's traveling expenses and enabled Herndon to remain to attend to the Springfield business.

The majority of these circuit associations were limited to an instant case in hand. At least one, however, assumed an aspect of permanency. This was the partnership with Ward H. Lamon of Danville. "Hill," as Lincoln always called him, became one of the closest and most confidential friends of the future President. This relationship continued uninterrupted to Lincoln's death. One of his first acts as President was the appointment of this Danville lawyer to the office of United States marshal of the District of Columbia.[1]

Lamon was about nineteen years younger than Lincoln, tall, handsome, aristocratic in appearance, a fastidious dresser, and renowned among his acquaintances for the amount of whiskey he could drink without losing his sobriety. He and Lincoln had few qualities in common, and the strange bond of loyalty and close friendship of these two men were objects of wonder to the

---

[1] Lamon, *Recollections of Abraham Lincoln*, pp. 14–15.

other lawyers of the circuit. But it can easily be understood why the frequently melancholy Lincoln longed for the companionship and gayety supplied by this dashing, boisterous, jolly good fellow.

This Danville attorney never rose to great heights at the bar. Fellow practitioners held him in rather low esteem as a lawyer, and gave him a still lower rating as a scholar. Lincoln, however, closed his eyes to all of Lamon's imperfections and clung tenaciously to their companionship.

Lamon advertised himself extensively as Lincoln's law partner. Under date of November 10, 1852, a newspaper advertisement announced:

"Lincoln and Lamon, Attorneys-at-law, having formed a co-partnership will practice in the courts of the Eighth Judicial Circuit and the Superior Court, and all business entrusted to them will be attended to with promptness and fidelity. Office on the second floor of the 'Barnum Building' over Whitcomb's Store."[1]

Whenever Judge Davis and the circuit riders reached Danville, Lamon felt it his duty to act as host to the travelers. After the completion of court business, when the cavalcade had assembled in Lincoln's or in the judge's hotel room, the Danville lawyer would bring in a pitcher of whiskey and bid his guests make merry. Lincoln never drank intoxicants but otherwise joined in the jollification. When the whiskey had made Lamon "mellow" enough, he would strike up some nonsensical tune on his banjo, sing ballads, and be the life of the party.

For about six years, until Lamon's election as State's Attorney, this partnership remained in effect. Through this association, Lincoln built up an extensive business in Vermillion County.

When W. W. R. Woodbury and William Fithian of Danville wrote to Lincoln for an opinion on a legal question concerning the title to certain lands in which the widow of a deceased friend was interested, the Springfield lawyer sent them his opinion. But

[1] From the *Iroquois Journal* of July 6, 1853, published at Middleport, Iroquois County, Illinois.

as it appeared that some court proceedings would be necessary in the administration of the estate, Lincoln warned them, "Better mention this to W. H. Lamon, lest he should, unawares, commit me to the other side."

Among the pleadings still preserved and signed by the firm of Lincoln & Lamon is the bill of complaint filed in the chancery case of Eleanor Smith in connection with the will of her late husband, in the Circuit Court of Vermillion County.

In Champaign County, Lincoln was frequently associated in the trial of cases with Leonard Swett and Henry C. Whitney. Pleadings are found signed. "Lincoln, Swett, Orme & Whitney," and also "Davis, Swett, Lincoln & Whitney." Lincoln had Swett as his trial associate more often than any other lawyer except Herndon. Whitney almost equalled Swett's record.

Leonard Swett, a native of Maine, had settled at Bloomington in 1849, in his twenty-fourth year, and immediately opened an office for the practice of law. At Mount Pulaski, Swett met Lincoln driving his horse, "Old Tom." These two with Judge Davis, driving two horses to his buggy, and David B. Campbell, the State's attorney, also in a buggy, formed a foursome in traveling the circuit. The young Bloomington lawyer soon gained a wide reputation for extraordinary success as a trial lawyer. Popular with all his circuit-riding companions, he became next to Lincoln, Judge Davis's favorite crony. In fact, so close did the three become that lawyers of the Eighth Circuit began to call Lincoln, Davis, and Swett "the great triumvirate."[1]

In 1858, when Lincoln was waging his historic campaign for the United States Senate against Douglas, Swett, who had never before held public office, acceded to Lincoln's request that he seek election as a member of the state legislature, so as to assure his friend of another vote. Swett was elected by an unprecedented majority for his district, and became a leader in the legislature in Lincoln's behalf. In 1860, he was to become a great aid to Judge Davis in procuring the presidential nomination for their circuit companion.

[1] Whitney, *Life on the Circuit*, pp. 67–70.

Swett and Lincoln collaborated as special partners in the defense of Father Chiniquy of Kankakee County. The priest was sued for slander by Peter Spink, one of his parishioners. This case was tried in Champaign County, and attracted wide attention. It was undoubtedly the most exciting slander suit in which Lincoln ever participated. Spink charged that the French Catholic priest had falsely accused him of perjury. Father Chiniquy would not deny that he had called Spink a perjurer, but plead justification. He would prove the truth of his accusation, he insisted, and urged his lawyer to "fight to the finish." Bitter feeling was aroused among the followers of the two principals and a change of venue was deemed advisable. When the case came up for trial in Urbana, Champaign County, hundreds of witnesses, onlookers, and parishioners crowded the courthouse, monopolized the hotels, or camped out in the surrounding woods during the four tedious days of trial. But the jury could not agree on a verdict. The case would have to be retried. The bitter feeling would have to be intensified, the slander repeated, the old hurts reopened. Lincoln abhorred this type of litigation. He urged the litigants to drop their charges and to make peace with each other. He was successful, and shortly afterwards a journal entry in Lincoln's handwriting appeared on the records of the court dismissing the suit.[1]

In the list of Lincoln's most intimate friends and confidants, the name of Henry C. Whitney holds high rank. To him more than any one man, with the exception of Herndon, the world is indebted for its knowledge and intimate glimpse of Lincoln in Illinois during the eventful years from 1854 to 1860. Although twenty-four years Lincoln's junior, the two became warmly attached to each other almost from the moment that Whitney, at the age of twenty-one, launched his law career at Urbana in 1854. "I did not feel the slightest delicacy in approaching him for assistance," Whitney later said in relating how he applied to Lincoln for advice in his law cases, "for it seemed as if he invited me to familiarity if not close intimacy at once; and

[1] Weik, *The Real Lincoln*, pp. 160–61; Whitney, *Life on the Circuit*, pp. 53–55, 136–37.

this from no selfish motive at all—nothing but pure philan-
thropy and goodness of heart to a young lawyer just beginning
his career.''

On the circuit the two often occupied the same bed. Whitney
developed an extensive practice, and in a large number of his
cases took in the Springfield lawyer as a co-counsel.

''As attorney for the Illinois Central Railroad I had authority
to employ additional counsel whenever I chose to do so,'' said
Whitney, ''and in Judge Davis' circuit I frequently applied to
Lincoln where I needed aid. I never found him unwilling to
appear in behalf of a great 'soulless corporation.' In such cases
he always stood by me, and I always, of course, tried to win.''
They appeared together in a number of very important railroad
cases.

Another of the coterie of young lawyers who became associated with Lincoln in the fifties was Lawrence Weldon, who upon
his arrival from Ohio in 1854 immediately opened an office for
the practice of law in De Witt County. Lincoln was already a
leader of the Illinois bar and was held high in the esteem and
confidence of the people of the State. Stephen A. Douglas was
making a campaign in defense of the Kansas–Nebraska Bill at
Bloomington in September, 1854, when Lincoln, in attendance
at the circuit court, greeted him. Weldon, standing near by, was
introduced to Lincoln by the Little Giant. Although much
younger than the Springfield lawyer, Weldon, within a very short
time, became the future President's trusted friend. From then on
they frequently rode the circuit together and were associated in
a number of cases.

Weldon almost worshiped Lincoln. ''He was particularly kind
to young lawyers,'' Weldon later said, ''and I remember with
what confidence I always went to him, because I was certain he
knew all about the matter, and would most cheerfully tell me. I
can see him now through the decaying memories of thirty years,
standing in the corner of the old courtroom, and as I approached
him with a paper I did not understand, he said: 'Wait until I fix
this plug for my ''gallis,'' and I will pitch into that like a dog
at a root.' While speaking, he was busily engaged in trying to

connect his suspender with his pants by making a 'plug' perform the function of a button."

In McLean and De Witt Counties, Lincoln and Weldon as co-counsel tried a number of cases.

Weldon traveled the circuit with Lincoln until his nomination for the Presidency. The young De Witt County lawyer took an active part in the campaigns of 1858 and 1860, and was one of the presidential electors on the Republican ticket. In such high esteem did Lincoln regard his young friend that shortly after assuming the office of President he placed Weldon, scarcely more than thirty years of age, in charge of the business of the United States in the southern district of Illinois during the turbulent war era, by naming him federal district attorney for that section.

Another faithful and devoted law associate who never lost an opportunity to champion the political fortunes of Lincoln was Joseph Gillespie. A trusted colleague in the legislature and a companion on the circuit, this able lawyer was one of Lincoln's few intimates.

During his first attempt for a United States senatorship, Lincoln wrote Gillespie, who also had his eye on the toga: "I have really got it into my head to try to be United States senator, and, if I could have your support, my chances would be reasonably good. But I know, and acknowledge, that you have as just claims to the place as I have; and therefore I cannot ask you to yield to me, if you are thinking of becoming a candidate yourself. If, however, you are not, then I should like to be remembered affectionately by you. . . . Let this be confidential."

Gillespie did yield to his friend, and Lincoln came within three votes of winning the office on the early balloting in the legislature.

"Bring Joe Gillespie here immediately; don't fail," Lincoln hurriedly telegraphed a friend in Alton on another occasion.

Together they tried a number of cases in the United States District Court at Springfield. Early in 1858, the two were associated in a case involving political questions. Concerning this matter, Lincoln wrote Gillespie: "This morning Col. McClernand showed me a petition for a mandamus against the Secretary of State to compel him to certify the apportionment act of last session; and he says it will be presented to the court tomorrow morning. We shall be allowed three or four days to get up a return; and I, for one, want the benefit of consultation with you. Please come right up."

Usher F. Linder, with whom Lincoln served in the Illinois legislature, was another able and well-educated lawyer who was frequently associated with him in the trial of cases. Born in the same county of Kentucky and in the same year as Lincoln, he also resembled him in stature, awkwardness, and general picturesqueness. In Edgar and Coles Counties they tried cases together under the firm name of Lincoln & Linder or Lincoln, Linder & Dill.

In the Supreme Court they were associates in the case of Laughlin vs. Marshall.[1] They collaborated in the slander suit of Bagley vs. Vanmeter at the Coles County Circuit Court in the fall of 1843. Their client, Bagley, must have engaged them on a contingent fee basis, as the agreement regarding their compensation reads: "I assign twenty dollars to Usher F. Linder and thirty dollars to Logan & Lincoln if said judgment shall amount to so much." The case yielded eighty dollars.

As already related, Lincoln and Linder were also associated as counsel for Robert Matson in his suit to recover the Bryant slaves. These two lawyers apparently were on such intimate terms that Lincoln did not regard it as presumptuous on his own part to make the unusual request contained in the following letter, written at Springfield:

"The change of circuits prevents my attending the Edgar court this Spring, and perhaps generally thereafter. There is a little Ejectment case from Bloomfield in which the name of Davidson figures . . . and for defending which I have been paid a little fee. Now I dislike to keep the money without doing the service, and I also hate to disgorge; and I therefore request of you to defend

[1] 19 Ill. 391.

the case for me; and I will, in due time, do as much or more for you. Write me whether you can do it.''

In "due time" Linder's son Dan was arrested for shooting a young man named Benjamin Boyle. The elder Mr. Linder was then seriously ill and confined to his bed. He appealed to Lincoln to handle his son's case. The Springfield lawyer gave the matter his immediate attention and was instrumental in procuring Dan's release without a trial. When the happy father offered him a fee for his services, Lincoln naturally refused it and expressed his happiness at having been able to serve a friend.

Samuel C. Parks, who like Lincoln became a Republican and worked assiduously for the cause of that party, frequently was associated with the Springfield lawyer in the trial of cases in Logan County. As a reward for his tireless efforts in behalf of Lincoln's nomination at Chicago, the latter, after his election as President, appointed Parks as associate justice of the Supreme Court in Idaho.[1]

Another frequent law associate was Orville H. Browning of Quincy, a very capable lawyer who served in the Illinois Senate when Lincoln was a member of the Assembly. A stalwart Whig, he was to become one of the founders of the Republican Party, instrumental in Lincoln's success at the Chicago presidential convention, and after becoming a United States senator from Illinois was to be President Lincoln's spokesman in the upper house of Congress. Still later, Andrew Johnson was to name him his Secretary of the Interior, and for a time Attorney General. This eminently successful lawyer was frequently associated with Lincoln in the trial of cases and in appeals to the Supreme Court.

In his diary, Browning wrote on a Monday in July: "Attending court. Commenced trial of Williamson, formerly postmaster at Lacon, who is indicted for robbing the mail. I am assisting Lincoln at his request." Tuesday's entry was: "Argued case against Williamson. The evidence was very strong, almost conclusive. I was so discouraged that I wished to decline a speech, but at the

---

[1] Bulletin 35, Abraham Lincoln Association, June, 1934.

persuasion of Lincoln I addressed the jury for something over two hours.''

Orlando B. Ficklin of Coles County, who served with Lincoln in the state legislature, although frequently opposed to him in cases on the circuit also associated himself with the Springfield lawyer in a number of others. In the case of Benjamin Twiney vs. Archibald Craig in Coles County Circuit Court at the October term, 1842, the pleadings in behalf of the plaintiff are signed by ''Ficklin & Lincoln p. q.'' And in the important case of the Illinois Central Railroad Co. vs. Morrison,[1] which was first tried in Coles County Circuit Court, Ficklin was associated with Lincoln and Whitney in the appeal to the Supreme Court.

Richard S. Thomas of Virginia, Illinois, was both a loyal political ally and frequent business associate of Lincoln's. ''Friend Richard,'' Lincoln once wrote to him, ''Now if you should hear anyone say that Lincoln don't want to go to Congress, I wish you as a personal friend of mine, would tell him you have reason to believe he is mistaken. The truth is I would like to go very much.''

Concerning a law case in which they were jointly interested, Lincoln suggested that the suit should be settled and the fee of two dollars should be divided equally.

Correspondence between Lincoln and Sam Marshall, a lawyer of Shawneetown, reveals the extent of their joint cases. ''Dear Sam,'' Lincoln wrote on one occasion, ''In your last letter you incline and complain that in mine I did not notice what you had said about the case of Stickney vs. Capel, nor of cases against the Shawneetown Bank. The truth is when I received your letter I glanced it over, stuck it away, postponing consideration of the cases above mentioned and forgot them altogether.'' He then proceeded to give a detailed account of some of the cases in which they were jointly interested. ''Dorman vs. Lane stands as it did, and I will do the best I can do with it.'' In Gatewood vs. Wood and Wood, ''we would have failed utterly to get into court but for an agreement with Mr. Eddy, which saved us.'' In another

[1] 19 Ill. 136.

letter to Marshall, Lincoln wrote, "The Forbes & Hill case, of which you speak, has not been brought up as yet."

To attorney Henry A. Clark of Woodford County, Lincoln wrote: "The cases of Cochran & Hall against Camp and others, and against J. L. D. Morrison are already continued. I have never had any definite arrangements with anyone about a fee on these cases and the consequence is I am bothered with them every court without understanding anything about them. I blame no one for this, but it would be better all round for me to either get out of these cases or get in deep enough to understand and prepare them."

Asabel Gridley of Bloomington, Lincoln's colleague in the legislature, generously turned over much of his lucrative law practice to his Springfield friend when Gridley forsook his profession to engage in banking, real estate, and railroad construction enterprises.[1]

In Christian, Shelby, and Macon Counties, Anthony Thornton was often associated with the Springfield lawyer in the trial of cases. Pleadings are there found signed "Lincoln & Thornton."

T. Lyle Dickey of Ottawa was still another frequent law associate of Lincoln's. Always a Whig and ever conservative, he became a very dear friend of the future President. He went with him to the historic Bloomington convention, where Lincoln delivered his famous "Lost Speech." With him he joined the newly founded Republican Party, but forsook it when he believed it was "too closely allied to the Abolitionists," whom he detested. Upon learning of Dickey's act, Lincoln told Whitney that he "did not know of any of his friends he felt so badly about losing as Dickey." In the Supreme Court, Lincoln and Dickey were associate counsel in several important cases.

Jackson Grimshaw appeared with Lincoln in a number of trials, including the case of The People vs. Hatch, Secretary of State,[2] to resit a writ of mandamus to test the validity of an act which the governor inadvertently approved and later vetoed.

[1] Browne, *Abraham Lincoln and the Men of His Time*, p. 333.
[2] 19 Ill. 283.

Later Grimshaw was one of a group that included Norman B. Judd, Ebenezer Peck, and Herndon, among others, who met in the rooms of Hatch in the State House early in 1860, and planned the launching of Lincoln's campaign for the Republican nomination for President.

Another frequent law associate was Norman B. Judd of the Chicago bar, general counsel for the Rock Island Railroad Company, who called on Lincoln to act as co-counsel in the famous Rock Island Bridge case. As chairman of the Republican Central Committee of Illinois he conducted the political campaigns of 1856–58 with consummate skill, and as one of the earliest advocates of the nomination of Lincoln was the chief organizer of the movement which resulted in his election to the Presidency.

O. L. Davis, a special partner in Vermillion County whom Lamon regarded as "the leading lawyer in that part of the State," did yeoman service for Lincoln in the campaign of 1858, and in 1860 became a delegate to the Chicago Convention. During the heat of the 1858 election Lincoln wrote to T. A. Marshall, of Charleston, Illinois: "I wish you, G. W. Rives of Edgar and O. L. Davis of Vermillion to co-operate in getting a Senatorial candidate on the track, in your district. Davis is here and agrees to do his part. The adversary has his eye upon that district, and will beat us, unless we also are wide awake. Under the circumstances a District Convention may or may not be the best way—you three to be the judge of that." Under the style of Lincoln & Davis or Lincoln, Lamon & Davis, the Vermillion lawyer frequently collaborated with Lincoln in the trial of cases in that county.

Another circuit associate was Henry E. Dummer of Beardstown, Cass County, whom Lincoln had succeeded as Stuart's partner in 1837. The many letters Lincoln wrote to him reveal that the Springfield lawyer regarded him not only as a trusted law associate but as a most intimate political confidant as well. "Friend Dummer," he wrote during a political campaign, "if it be consistent with your feelings set a few stakes for me in Beardstown." They looked after each other's interests and were always mutually helpful.

When Lincoln had a fee of fifty dollars due him from a Dr. Sprague of Beardstown, he wrote Dummer that he was in need of cash and urged: "Please get the money and send it to me. And while you have pen in hand, tell me what you may know about politics down your way."

When in Champaign County William D. Somers, a local lawyer, invited Lincoln to associate with him in the defense of an indicted horse thief. Lincoln and Somers went to the jail to interview the defendant, who paid the lawyers ten dollars for their fee. Lincoln then observed that the prisoner's wife, present as a visitor, was about to become a mother. "How about your wife? Won't she need this?" he asked the defendant. "She'll get along somehow," was the hesitant reply. But Lincoln understood. After whispering to Somers, he handed the woman five dollars, explaining that the remaining five dollars would be a sufficient fee for himself and co-counsel to divide.

Gustave Koerner, who was to play an important rôle in procuring the presidential nomination for Lincoln, in his *Memoirs* writes of "being engaged [with Lincoln] in an important case in 1854, for the City of St. Louis against the Ohio and Mississippi Railroad Company, or rather against the directors of that company."

Koerner's home was in St. Clair County, and he frequently sought Lincoln's assistance in the handling of litigation in the Supreme Court.

Grant Goodrich, who urged Lincoln to join him as a partner in Chicago, after the latter's return from Congress; Archibald Williams of Adams County, whom Lincoln described as the "strongest-minded and clearest-headed man" he ever knew, a colleague in the legislature and constant friend; Ninian W. Edwards, Lincoln's brother-in-law, Norman H. Purple, David Allen Smith of Jacksonville, William Martin of Alton, Benjamin S. Edwards, one of Springfield's ablest barristers, O. T. Reeves of Bloomington, Caleb B. Smith of Indiana, William N. Coler of Urbana, John M. Scott of Bloomington, W. B. Parker and Samuel W. Fuller of Pekin, Shelby M. Cullom and John A. McClernand are a few more attorneys who should be included in the long list of Lincoln's special law associates. And the list is not yet complete.

In various degrees, practically everyone of this numerous contingent contributed something to the makeup of the Lincoln who became the Republic's sixteenth President. Without their assistance and counsel, he might never have reached his exalted station.

XI. THE TRIAL LAWYER AND
JURY PLEADER

THE poor crippled widow of a Revolutionary soldier hobbled one day into the law office of Lincoln & Herndon and tearfully told the senior partner how a pension agent named Wright had defrauded her. Wright had induced the Government to grant her a pension of four hundred dollars, she said, but for his commission he had pocketed half of the award. Her bitter protests over this exorbitant fee had availed her nothing. And now she appealed to Lincoln for advice and aid.

The lawyer's wrath knew no bounds as he listened to the details of the transaction. As soon as the sobbing old woman departed, Lincoln walked over to the pension agent's office and demanded the return of the money. When Wright turned a deaf ear to the request, Lincoln indignantly reminded him that courts of justice still existed to deal with greedy rascals. Without further delay the lawyer brought suit.

The day before the trial, Lincoln asked Herndon to obtain for him a history of the Revolutionary War. That night he read it carefully.

"I am going to skin Wright and get that money back!" Lincoln resolutely told his junior associate as they walked to court the following day.

He had but one witness—the crippled old lady. But through her tears she told a most touching story.

Never was Lincoln so wrought up. "When in a lawsuit he believed his client was oppressed, he was hurtful in denunciation," his friend Judge Davis observed. "When he attacked meanness, fraud, or vice, he was powerful and merciless in his castigation."

Here was a situation ideal for the advocate—the crowded courthouse, the magnetic sympathy of the audience, the impassive attention of the jury, the little old widow softly weeping to herself. A dramatic suspense of the moment—and Lincoln arose to plead her cause.

He towered above every person in the audience. His slouchy appearance and ill-fitting clothes were forgotten. His sallow features marked by high cheekbones, large deep-set eyes of grayish brown shaded by heavy eyebrows, betrayed neither excitement nor anxiety as he calmly passed his fingers through his long coarse hair and wiped the perspiration from his face with a red silk handkerchief. But when he peered straight into the eyes of the jury they observed the look of grim determination on his face. In a voice clear, distinct, and well modulated he reviewed briefly the facts of the case. Then, straightening himself up and taking a few steps backward, he began to picture eloquently and minutely the scene at Valley Forge. Vividly he described the barefooted patriots creeping with bleeding feet over the ice.

"As he reached that point in his speech wherein he narrated the hardened action of the defendant in fleecing the old woman of her pension," says Herndon who was present in the courtroom, "his eyes flashed, and throwing aside his handkerchief, which he held in his right hand, he fairly launched into him."

Well might Lincoln have been likened to Mirabeau, "fierce as ten furies and terrible as hell," as he shook his bony fingers at

the pension agent with an effect that was indescribable and proceeded to "skin" the rascal.

Then he recalled how the plaintiff's husband had kissed her
and their baby and had departed for the war.

"Time rolls by; the heroes of 'seventy-six' have passed
away and are encamped on the other shore," he continued
pathetically in a low, sad voice. "The soldier has gone to rest;
and now, crippled, blinded, and broken, his widow comes to
you and to me, gentlemen of the jury, to right her wrongs.
She was not always thus. She was once a beautiful woman.
Her step was as elastic, her face as fair, and her voice as
sweet, as any that rang in the mountains of Virginia. But now
she is poor and defenseless. Out here on the prairies of Illinois,
many hundreds of miles away from the scenes of her child-
hood, she appeals to us who enjoy the privileges achieved for
us by the patriots of the Revolution, for our sympathetic aid
and manly protection."

Then, stretching out his long arms toward the jury, he concluded dramatically: "All I ask is, shall we befriend her?"

"The speech made the desired impression on the jury," Herndon recalls. "Half of them were in tears, while the defendant sat
in the courtroom, drawn up and writhing under the fire of Lincoln's invective. The jury returned a verdict in our favor for
every cent we demanded. Lincoln was so much interested in the
old lady that he became her surety for costs, paid her way home,
and her hotel bill while she was in Springfield. When the judgment was paid we remitted the proceeds to her and made no
charge for our services."

The notes from which Lincoln spoke outline his plan of attack
against the unfortunate defendant. It is a unique law brief, and
reads as follows:

"No   contract—not   professional   services—unreasonable
charge—money retained by Defendant not given by Plaintiff—
Revolutionary War—Describe Valley Forge privations—Ice—
Soldier's bleeding feet—Plaintiff's husband, soldier leaving
home for army—Skin defendant! Close!"[1]

---

[1] Herndon and Weik, *Lincoln*, II, 340–42; Holland, *The Life of Abraham
Lincoln*, p. 127.

His defense of "Peachy" Harrison was another case that revealed Lawyer Lincoln's fighting qualities.

Young Quinn Harrison, better known as "Peachy," was a grandson of Dr. Peter Cartwright, the Methodist circuit rider, who had bitterly assailed Lincoln when they opposed each other for a seat in the thirtieth Congress. But when that youth stood accused of murdering Greek Crafton, a student in Lincoln's own law office, the lawyer forgot all political differences to associate with Herndon, Logan, and Shelby M. Cullom, to defend "Peachy." The prisoner and the victim had been lifelong friends and their families were related by marriage. An argument had taken place, followed by blows. In the scuffle Crafton was stabbed. Three days later he died from his wound. The prominence of the families of both young men made the case of great public interest. John M. Palmer and John A. McClernand were retained to assist Amzi McWilliams, the regular prosecutor.

In this battle of legal giants the usually complacent and easygoing Lincoln displayed his absolute fearlessness. Aroused by righteous indignation, he forgot his humility and fought back for all he was worth when greatly angered by the many seemingly spiteful adverse rulings of the presiding judge, E. J. Rice. "Finally," relates Herndon, "a very material question, in fact one around which the entire case seemed to revolve, came up, and again the court ruled adversely. The prosecution was jubilant, and Lincoln, seeing defeat certain unless he recovered his ground, grew very despondent."

He felt a grave injustice was being perpetrated upon him and his client. "I have determined to crowd the court to the wall and regain my position before night," he told his partner at dinner.

When court reconvened, Lincoln arose, "wrought up to the point of madness." Having made a thorough study of the points involved, he now plied the court with "broad facts and pointed inquiries in marked and rapid succession." He was furious. He was eloquent. He was sarcastic. He pointed out that the court's rulings were contrary to law, unjust, and absurd. He kept his remarks just within the bounds of contempt of court, and "figuratively speaking, he peeled the Court from head to foot." The prosecutor objected strenuously, but Lincoln's "masterly arraignment of law and facts had so effectively badgered the judge that, strange as it may seem, he pretended to see error in his former position, and finally reversed his decision in Lincoln's favor. The latter saw his triumph, and surveyed a situation of which he was the master."[1]

But the trial reached its climax when the venerable crusader, the Reverend Mr. Cartwright, was called to the witness stand. Strangely enough, it fell to Lincoln to question the sorrow-stricken, white-haired grandfather.

"How long have you known the prisoner?" he asked tenderly. With a quavering voice that revealed his love for his unfortunate grandson, Cartwright replied, "I have known him since a babe. He laughed and cried on my knee."

Amidst his sobs he was led on by Lincoln's pertinent questions until he described how he had visited the dying Crafton youth, and said that just before his death young Crafton said to him: "I am dying; I will soon part with all I love on earth, and I want you to say to my slayer that I forgive him. I want to leave this earth with a forgiveness of all who have in any way injured me."

The testimony of the sorrowing preacher made a profound impression on the jury. Lincoln realized that only by playing upon the jurors' sympathies was there any hope for "Peachy's" acquittal. With all the eloquence and tenderness at his command he pleaded for them to show the same spirit of forgiveness as the unfortunate young victim had practiced toward his assailant. Peachy's speedy acquittal was the result.

While waiting for one of his cases to be called for trial in the courthouse at DeWitt County, in Clinton, May 19, 1854, Lincoln listened to the proceedings of the case of The People vs. Eliza-

---

[1] Herndon and Weik, *Lincoln,* I, 328–29; Captain Thomas W. S. Kidd, official crier, in Rochester *Herald*, January 17, 1904; also Ida M. Tarbell, *Life of Abraham Lincoln*, I, 251–52.

beth Shirtleff, Emily Lewis, *et al.* It appears that a Mr. Tanner had opened a saloon in the village of Marion and was enjoying a rather successful business. A group of female temperance advocates called on him and urged him to close up his place. Upon his refusal, like Carrie Nation of a later day, they took the law into their own hands by knocking in the heads of the barrels and pouring the liquor over the ground. Tanner caused fifteen of these crusaders to be indicted for trespass. Lincoln was not retained in this case, but when one of the defendants saw him sitting in the courtroom she urged him to join the defense. With the consent of the other counsel the Springfield lawyer took up the defense of the overzealous women. Addressing the jury, Lincoln declared:

"In this case I would change the order of indictment and have it read: The State vs. Mr. Whiskey, instead of The State vs. The Ladies; and touching these are three laws: The law of self-protection; the law of the land, or statute law; and the moral law, or law of God. First, the law of self-protection is a law of necessity, as evinced by our forefathers in casting the tea overboard and asserting their right to the pursuit of life, liberty, and happiness. In this case it is the only defense the ladies have, for Tanner neither feared God nor regarded man. Second, the law of the land, or statute law, and Tanner is recreant to both. Third, the moral law, or the law of God, and this is probably a law for the violation of which the jury can fix no punishment."

He then launched into an attack on the liquor traffic, its evil and ruinous effects upon society, and demanded its early suppression.

The jury found the ladies of Marion guilty, but the court fined them only two dollars and permitted them to go home without bond or paying the fine.[1]

The most notable of all of Lincoln's jury trials was the famous Duff Armstrong murder case.

William Armstrong, popularly known as "Duff," was the

---

[1] Herndon and Weik, *Lincoln,* II, pp. 343–44; Decatur *Gazelle,* clipped in *Illinois State Register,* May 27, 1854.

twenty-four-year-old son of Jack and Hannah Armstrong, who had befriended Lincoln during his youthful struggles at New Salem. They had treated Lincoln as one of the family. He had often played with Duff as a baby and had even rocked him to sleep. Jack Armstrong had been one of the leaders of the Clary Grove Boys and village champion wrestler, who had tussled with Lincoln on the lawn near Offutt's store, in the days gone by. Duff's arrest on the charge of murdering a man named James Preston Metzker in a drunken brawl was a severe shock to Jack Armstrong, and he died of a broken heart about the time that his son was to stand trial for his life. It was then that Lincoln heard of "Aunt" Hannah's double misfortune.

September 18, 1847, he wrote to her:

"*Dear Mrs. Armstrong:* I have just heard of your deep affliction, and the arrest of your son for murder. I can hardly believe that he can be capable of the crime alleged against him. It does not seem possible. I am anxious that he should be given a fair trial at any rate; and my gratitude for your long continued kindness to me in adverse circumstances prompts me to offer my humble service gratuitously in his behalf.

"It will afford me an opportunity to requite in a small degree, the favors I received at your hand, and that of your late lamented husband, when your roof afforded me a grateful shelter, without money and without price."[1]

Shoving aside all other business, Lincoln made ready for the trial. He communicated with William Walker, the lawyer already retained in Duff's behalf, and offered his co-operation. Walker gladly permitted him to take charge of the case. Incidentally, at this session of the court Lincoln also participated in the trial of the divorce case of Ruth Gill vs. Jonathan Gill in association with Attorney J. Henry Shaw of Beardstown, who, curiously enough, had been retained by the family of Metzker to assist Hugh Fullerton, the State's attorney for the district, in the prosecution of Armstrong.

The case of The People of the State of Illinois vs. William Armstrong was set for trial at the May term of the Cass County

[1] Tracy, *Uncollected Letters*, p. 27.

Circuit Court in 1858. In the Gill divorce case, the court had put over the question of alimony until the May term. So when Lincoln arrived in Beardstown on May 7, Shaw believed he had come to argue the motion for alimony. The following morning, however, when the court convened for the trial of Duff Armstrong, Shaw was amazed to see Lincoln as chief defense counsel.

Lincoln was anxious that the jury be composed of young men, believing that youthful hot blood would be more sympathetic to the plight of his young client. He was successful in selecting a venire whose members averaged less than thirty years of age. The jury impaneled, the trial began with Judge James Harriot presiding. There were about twenty-five witnesses, some of whom were examined by Walker and the others by Lincoln.

The State's star witness was Charles Allen. He had already testified at the trial of James H. Norris, also accused of participating in the murder. Norris was found guilty of manslaughter largely through Allen's testimony that under the bright moonlight he had seen Norris hit Metzker on the back of the head with a club-like object and Armstrong strike him in the right eye with a sling-shot. Now Allen repeated the same story, and the prosecution's case was seemingly clinched.

"Lincoln sat with his head thrown back, his steady gaze apparently fixed upon one spot of the blank ceiling, entirely oblivious to what was happening about him, and without a single variation of feature or noticeable movement of any muscle of his face," is the recollection of Judge Abram Bergen, then a young lawyer present in the courtroom.[1]

Lincoln took over the witness for cross-examination. With apparent unconcern he questioned Allen regarding unimportant details. Then as to the fatal blows themselves; tell about them again.

Did you actually see the fight? Yes. Well, where were you standing at the time? About one hundred fifty feet away from the combatants. Describe this weapon again. The sling-shot was

[1] Bergen, in *North American Review* (February, 1898). vol. 166, pp. 186–95.

pictured in detail. And what time did you say all this occurred? Eleven o'clock at night. How could you see from a distance of one hundred and fifty feet, at eleven o'clock at night? The moon was shining real bright. A full moon? Yes, a full moon, and as high in the heavens as the sun would be at ten o'clock in the morning. He was positive about that.

Then with dramatic suddenness Lincoln requested the sheriff to bring him an almanac for the year 1857. Turning to the date of August 29, the night of the murder, he pointed a long forefinger to the page and bade Allen to read. Did not the almanac specifically say that the moon on that night was barely past the first quarter instead of being full? And wasn't it a fact that the almanac also revealed that instead of the moon being high in the heavens in the position of the morning sun, it had actually disappeared by eleven o'clock? And wasn't it a further fact that it was actually so dark at the time that it was impossible to see distinctly from a distance of fifty feet, let alone one hundred and fifty feet?

These revelations caused a tremendous sensation. Of course, the court took judicial notice of the almanac, but Lincoln desired to have it introduced in evidence. He submitted it to the inspection of the prosecutors and the judge and then it was handed to the jury. The jury smiled and nodded approvingly. Allen as a witness was destroyed. But the case was not yet over. The prosecution strove valiantly to make up for the lost ground, but there were no other eye-witnesses.

The defense then called a number of witnesses—persons to testify as to Duff's good reputation; witnesses who had seen Metzker fall from his horse; a Dr. Charles E. Parker, who declared that just such a fall or the blow struck by Norris could very likely have caused the fatal injury. But extremely damaging to the State's case was the testimony of one Watkins, who swore that the sling-shot in evidence belonged not to Duff but to him; that it was continuously in his own possession on the night of the fight, but that he had thrown it away the following day, at the very spot where it had been found.

Then followed the arguments of counsel to the jury. The prosecutors reviewed all the sordid details of the "atrocious crime"; denounced the young ruffians who had been terrorizing the countryside; urged that the jury make an example of Duff, and demanded that they inflict upon him the penalty of death.

After Walker's argument, Lincoln arose. The silence of the room was broken only by the heartbreaking sobs of Duff's grief-stricken mother. Tall, gaunt, and homely, Lincoln had risen to great heights both at the bar and in the political arena in Illinois. And now he was about to begin the greatest jury speech of his career. The crowd in the courtroom had been attracted not so much by the case itself as by the prominence of Lincoln. It was a sultry hot day and the audience was sweltering. Unconcernedly Lincoln took off his coat and vest and removed the stock that clung uncomfortably to his large Adam's apple.

"Slowly and carefully," relates Walker, "he reviewed the whole testimony and picked it all to pieces." Allen's story should be given no credence, Lawyer Lincoln urged the members of the jury. Having been mistaken about the light of the moon, he was undoubtedly mistaken as to other points of his testimony, he declared. Soon one of his suspenders fell from a shoulder, but paying no attention to it, he allowed it to hang during the rest of the speech. When he spoke "his eyes brightened perceptibly, and every facial movement seemed to emphasize his feeling and add expression to his thoughts," is the testimony of Judge Abram Bergen. "Then vanished all consciousness of his uncouth appearance, his awkward manner, or even his high-keyed unpleasant voice, and it required an extraordinary effort of the will to divert attention to the man, so concentrated was every mind upon what he was saying."

Lincoln had mastered some technical questions in anatomy and explained his theory that it was more than likely that Metzker had died, not from any wound inflicted by Duff, but rather from the blow of Norris's club or from repeated falls from his horse. And he especially emphasized Watkins's testimony that he, and not the defendant, was the owner of the sling-shot. Lincoln cut open the weapon and demonstrated to the jury that it was made exactly as Watkins had sworn he had made it.

After completely analyzing the evidence for nearly an hour, Lincoln devoted another ten minutes to an appeal that melted the hearts of the jury and brought joy to the sorrowing mother and freedom to her erring son. He was not arguing this case for a fee, he declared. In fact, he was indebted to Duff Armstrong's mother and deceased father in a manner he could never repay. When he was a stranger in New Salem, penniless, homeless, and alone, Jack and Hannah Armstrong, struggling pioneers though they were, had opened wide the doors of their humble cabin and had given him shelter and food. He had rocked this very defendant, as an infant, to sleep in his rough-hewn cradle. Their home had been his home. He had virtually been one of the family. Deep in his heart he felt that the son of such kindly, lovable parents could be no base murderer. And now that big-hearted Jack Armstrong was in his grave, the grief-stricken widow, alone in her plight, should be saved from further sorrow. He drew a touching picture of the hopelessness, suffering, and desolation in store for the poor old mother, if the jury saw fit to deprive her of her boy. As a pleader for her son's life, God willed he should repay his debt to his old benefactors. He prayed that he would not be unworthy of the task.

Real tears trickled down his homely face. "But they were genuine," insists Mr. Shaw, the special prosecutor. "His terrible sincerity could not help but rouse the same passion in the jury. I have said it a hundred times that it was Lincoln's speech that saved that criminal from the gallows." For when Lincoln sat down some of the jurors were seen to wipe misty eyes with their rough toil-worn hands. The prosecutor concluded the State's case, and Lincoln handed Judge Harriott two carefully written requests for special instructions to the jury. Neither one referred to the moon incident, but dealt with the question of reasonable doubt and the endeavor of the defense to shift the guilt to Norris, already found guilty of the murder.

With the instructions completed, Duff's fate was soon in the hands of the jury.

"They'll clear him before dark, Hannah," Lincoln was heard to encourage the heartbroken mother as with his arm around her shoulder, he tenderly escorted her from the courtroom. He was right. By their first ballot the jurors acquitted the defendant.

"It is not yet sundown and Duff is free," Lincoln joyfully told Mrs. Armstrong when she returned. For answer she fell to her knees in a prayer of thanksgiving. She blessed Lincoln and offered him pay. "Why, Hannah, I shall not charge you a cent— never," he told her. "Anything I can do for you I will do for you willingly and freely, without charge."

Thus ended this remarkable case.[1]

The cases handled by Lincoln during his twenty-three years of practice at the bar comprised every kind, both civil and criminal. He participated in the pettiest and most trivial litigation in the justice of the peace courts, running the gamut to the most important in the Supreme Court of Illinois and three in the United States Supreme Court. These cases often involved the lives of accused murderers or vast property rights, and frequently established new principles of law destined to serve as guides and precedents for generations to come.

Specialization in law was then unknown, and the ability of a lawyer to adapt himself to all types of litigation, problems, and courts was the measure of his success. In this respect Lincoln had few superiors. His popularity as a lawyer is indicated by the large number of cases entrusted to him. Humble individuals and great corporations placed their affairs in his hands. When it is realized that only a very small proportion of the average lawyer's cases reach the highest appellate tribunals, one obtains an idea of the vast number of cases Lincoln must have tried in the lower courts from the fact that he appeared in one hundred seventy-eight cases in the Supreme Court of Illinois. In addition, he tried hundreds of actions in the circuit and district courts of the United States. This is a record equaled by few lawyers.

[1] For additional accounts of this famous case see: Lamon, *Life of Abraham Lincoln*, pp. 327–31; Arnold, *Life of Abraham Lincoln*, p. 87; Onstot, *Pioneers of Menard and Mason Counties*, p. 98; Herndon and Weik, *Lincoln*, II, pp. 358–59; Barrett, *Life of Abraham Lincoln*, pp. 63–66; Holland, 128–29; McClure, 97–99; Whipple, *The Story Life of Lincoln*, p. 261; Curtis, *The True Abraham Lincoln*, p. 75. Bergen, *North American Review* (February, 1898), vol. 166, p. 186.

His early cases were of a class common in a new and sparsely settled country—litigation arising from disputed land lines, neighborhood quarrels, trespasses by wandering cattle, and the like. Life in Illinois during the first half of the nineteenth century was crude and simple and so was the administration of justice. Knowledge of the fundamental elements of the common law and of principles of natural justice were chiefly relied upon to dispose of the simple litigation that arose. But as the country developed and population increased, the business of the region became more complicated, interests more diversified, and the legal problems arising therefrom naturally more complex. Technical knowledge became necessary. New legal principles had to be evolved to solve new problems. It was a period in American legal history when new precedents were being established. The early practitioners, aroused to devise new policies, new tactics, and fresh expedients, acquired the requisite technical knowledge to meet the new conditions and grew and kept pace with the changing order.

Typical of the bar of this shifting period was Lincoln. He was of the frontier, grew up with it, and now marched on with its progress. Competing with a coterie of lawyers who as a group have seldom been excelled for general training, logic, force of character, tenacity of purpose, ready wit, power of speech, and results obtained, he never lagged behind but developed his unique talents, kept ever forging to the front until he stood the acknowledged peer of the leaders of the profession.

His growth as a lawyer—from the days when trivial cases brought retainers of two and three dollars to the time when he could demand a five-thousand-dollar fee—marks the growth of the man in ability, confidence, learning, and power.

In the trial of hundreds of cases in all the courts his ideas and arguments helped build the fabric of jurisprudence and the great principles of government of his State. In many opinions of the Supreme Court of Illinois, in some instances still the established law of today, are reflected the labors of the unassuming Springfield lawyer who argued his cases before that tribunal, not infrequently on original principles.

All the lawyers on the circuit feared Lincoln—the trial lawyer's matchless power of overwhelming an adversary by the apt use of an anecdote or a bit of appropriate ridicule. Many were the cases that he laughed out of court. Especially trifling suits and those involving small amounts of money, he disposed of with a telling sally of wit or sarcasm if circumstances permitted. He used his unique sense of humor as a tool of his trade, and many a case that otherwise might have been hopelessly lost, he turned into a decisive victory with the aid of this effective expedient.

Judge Abram Bergen, who as a law student in Illinois frequently saw Lawyer Lincoln in action during the trial of his cases, has left a vivid recollection of one of the cases Lincoln laughed out of court. It was in a suit for ten thousand dollars damages brought by Paul Selby, a newspaper editor, against Colonel Dunlap, "a wealthy, aristocratic Democrat."

At the trial in the old Morgan County courthouse in Jacksonville, Selby and a number of witnesses testified that Colonel Dunlap had violently assaulted him because of a newspaper article he had written and which Dunlap considered offensive. Lincoln as counsel for the colonel realized that he could present no legal defense for his client, and hoped merely to keep the damages down to a minimum.

When he arose to address the jury, he slowly picked up Selby's petition, which was lying on the trial table, and scrutinized it closely. Suddenly he "indulged in a long loud laugh accompanied by his most wonderfully grotesque facial expression." Its effect was magnetic and "the usually solemn and dignified Judge Woodson, members of the jury, and the whole audience joined in the merriment; and all this before Lincoln had spoken a single word."

At length he became serious and apologized to the court for his "seemingly rude behavior." He then explained that he had just observed in the plaintiff's petition that the amount of damages claimed by Selby was at first written as one thousand dollars, but later changed to ten thousand dollars. He supposed that the editor "had taken a second look at the Colonel's pile and concluded that the wounds to his honor were worth an additional nine thousand dollars.''

The result was that the jury forgot the "tears, pathos, towering indignation and high-wrought eloquence'' of plaintiff's counsel. They forgot his plea for punitive damages; and to the complete satisfaction of Lincoln's client, brought in a verdict for a few hundred dollars.[1]

On another occasion Lawyer Lincoln was defending a man accused of passing counterfeit money. J. Parker Green was the State's important witness, and gave testimony that was very damaging against the defendant. At length the prosecutor turned the witness over to the defense counsel for cross-examination. Lincoln glared at J. Parker Green for a few seconds and then nonchalantly asked him to state his name.

"J. Parker Green," was the matter-of-course reply.

"J. Parker Green," Lincoln mused aloud. "J. Parker Green, J. Parker Green," he repeated as if pondering over some weighty matter. "What a peculiar name. What does the 'J' stand for?"

"John."

"Well, why don't you call yourself John—John P. Green— instead of J. Parker Green?

"Well——"

"Most ordinary folks would call themselves John P. Green instead of J. Parker Green, wouldn't they?"

"Well——"

And so for several minutes Lincoln pursued this line of questioning—to J. Parker Green's great discomfiture. It was all a huge joke in so far as the lawyer was concerned. But the witness became confused and embarrassed, and soon began to squirm uneasily in the witness chair.

The jury observed Green's demeanor and wondered why the

---

[1] James L. King, "Lincoln's Skill as a Lawyer," *North American Review* (February, 1898), vol. 166, pp. 186–95.

Paul Selby, in a letter in the *North American Review* (February, 1898), vol. 166, pp. 507–09, relates his version of the case. It differs from Bergen's in several respects.

simple matter of a name caused him so much trouble. Subconsciously they attributed his uneasiness to something that was not altogether right—perhaps some matter of suspicion he was endeavoring to conceal. The effectiveness of Green's previous damaging testimony was destroyed, and the defendant was promptly acquitted.

Lincoln's ridicule had simply laughed the case out of court.

Lawyer Lincoln's anecdotes were not intended merely to wring a laugh from the jury. They proved far more effective in illustrating his points than any abstract arguments he might have used.

Thus, while Lincoln was defending a man charged with assault and battery, the testimony revealed that the prosecuting witness had been the aggressor; that Lincoln's client in defending himself had turned upon his assailant and had given him a sound thrashing, for which reason the aggressor had caused the defendant to be arrested for assault and battery. In addressing the jury, Lincoln said:

"My client is in the fix of a man, who in going along the highway with a pitchfork on his shoulder, was attacked by a fierce dog that ran out at him from a farmer's door-yard. In parrying off the dog with the fork its prongs stuck into the brute and killed him.

" 'What made you kill my dog?' the farmer demanded.

" 'What made him try to bite me?'

" 'But why did you not go at him with the other end of the pitchfork?'

" 'Why did he not come after me with his other end?' insisted the dog's intended victim."

And Lincoln illustrated by whirling an imaginary dog in his long arms, and jabbing at the jury with the make-believe beast's extended tail.

The jury quickly got the point—that self-defense is a good plea of justification against one who commits the first assault even when extraordinary force is charged. And Lincoln's client won his freedom.

Lincoln's fondness for story-telling never caused him to obtrude upon the seriousness and dignity of his profession. "He felt the responsibility and gravity of his position and entered into all trials with the attention, dignity, and decorum demanded," Whitney observed. He never resorted to facetiousness to the detriment of his case.

This ability "to laugh cases out of court" was to prove as effective later in the White House as in the courts of Illinois. The stories that won him favor with the juries on the circuit were later to come to his rescue and bring relief to the extreme tension in the most trying of situations.

In the case where Lawyer Lincoln was defending a man accused of murder, it became important, he felt, that the jury should understand that though his client had struggled with the victim, the prisoner had been unable to withdraw from the fray. The accused was in the position, explained Lincoln, of the fellows who had gone with a party of men to hunt for wild boar. "But," said the lawyer, "the game came upon them unawares, and scampering away they all climbed the trees, save one who, seizing the animal by the ears, undertook to hold him; but despairing of success cried out to his companions in the trees, 'For God's sake, boys, come down and help me let go.' "[1]

Some years later, at one of the most tragic moments in our Nation's history, this homely tale, somewhat modified, was again related—this time to hide the ache in President Lincoln's heart and to suppress the tears that were forcing themselves to his eyes.

Governor Curtin, the great war governor of Pennsylvania, had come to the White House fresh from the field of Fredericksburg, where a disastrous battle had taken place. President Lincoln asked many questions about the encounter and especially about the wounded.

"Mr. President, it was not a battle, it was a butchery," the governor replied, as he proceeded to give a graphic account of his investigations. The recital overwhelmed Lincoln with sorrow. A deep-seated sadness overshadowed his uncomely face and it appeared that he would be moved to tears.

[1] Herndon and Weik, *Lincoln*, II, 329.

"Mr. President, I am deeply touched by your sorrow, and at the distress I have caused you," Governor Curtin sympathized, as he took Lincoln tenderly by the hand. "I have only answered your questions. No doubt my impressions have been colored by the sufferings I have seen. I trust matters will look brighter when the official reports come in. I would give all I possess to know how to rescue you from this terrible war."

A whimsical smile then dispelled the gloom on the President's face and gladdened his visitor's heart, as in characteristic fashion Lincoln drawled:

"This reminds me, Governor, of an old farmer in Illinois that I used to know. He took it into his head to go into hog raising. He sent out to Europe and imported the finest breed of hogs he could buy. The prize hog was put in a pen, and the farmer's two mischievous boys—James and John—were told to be sure not to let him out. But James, the worse of the two, let the brute out the next day. The hog went straight for the boys, and drove John up a tree. Then the hog went for the seat of James's trousers, and the only way the boy could save himself was by holding on the hog's tail. The hog would not give up his hunt nor the boy his hold. After they had made a good many circles around the tree, the boy's courage began to give out, and he shouted to his brother, 'I say, John, come down, quick, and help me let *this hog go!*'

"Now Governor, that is exactly my case. I wish someone would come and help me let this hog go."[1]

---

[1] Allen Thorndike Rice, *Reminiscences of Abraham Lincoln*, pp. xxv-xxiv.

XII. BUILDING THE LAW OF
THE LAND

ABRAHAM LINCOLN, the future preserver of a nation and the emancipator of four million slaves, arose one day in the chambers of the Supreme Court of Illinois to argue a case involving the alleged conversion of "a scrub male hog" of the value of three dollars.[1] Lincoln represented Andrew J. Stout, owner of the animal, who had recovered a judgment for three dollars in the Bond County circuit court when he had proved that his neighbor Patrick Byrne had castrated his hog. Despite Lincoln's able arguments before the Supreme Court which heard Byrne's appeal, that august tribunal decided that "castrating a scrub male hog running among one's stock is not such proof of a change of property as to be evidence of conversion."

One hundred seventy-eight cases[2] all told, ranging from this

[1] Byrne vs. Stout (15 Ill. 180), Lincoln for defendant-in-error.

[2] In Wren vs. Moss, Lincoln appeared twice, first in a motion for a writ of error involving the right of a divorcee to sue out a writ of error against the heirs and executors of the estate of the deceased husband (6 Ill. 560). The motion by Lincoln to do so was allowed. Wren vs. Moss *et al.* (7 Ill. 72) was a motion by Lincoln to require the defendants-in-error to join in

typical pioneer three-dollar-hog litigation to a controversy involving almost a third of a million dollars of taxes, constitute Lincoln's record of appeals before the Supreme Court of Illinois. It is a record probably unequaled by any other lawyer of his State; this despite the fact that Lincoln handled no cases at all during the two years he spent in Congress and during practically the whole of 1858, which he devoted to his campaign against Douglas.

A large portion of Lincoln's Supreme Court retainers came from other attorneys, many of whom took pride in advertising the Springfield lawyer as an associate or partner.

Lincoln practiced law at a time when Illinois courts had few precedents to direct them in their decisions. Legal principles

error, that is, to admit or deny that error had been committed by the trial court. This motion was also granted.

McCall vs. Lesher (7 Ill.46 and 7 Ill. 47) appears as two cases, the first being a hearing on a motion, and the second an appeal from the circuit court.

Ross vs. Irving and Pryor vs. Irving (14 Ill. 171) were consolidated at the hearing and one opinion covers both cases. The same is true as to the two cases of Myers vs. Turner (17 Ill. 179), Moore vs. Vail and Moore vs. Dodd (17 Ill. 185), and Miller vs. Whitaker and Young vs. Miller (23 Ill. 453), and also Columbus Machine Manufacturing Company vs. Ulrich (25 Ill. 169) and Columbus Machine Manufacturing Co. vs. Dorwin, 25 Ill. 169.

In Cunningham vs. Fithian (6 Ill. 269) his name was omitted by the official reporters, but in Cunningham vs. Fithian (7 Ill. 650) reference is made to the omission in the former case.

Lincoln's name does not appear in Walker vs. Hedrick (18 Ill. 570), a suit involving the validity of certain land grants; but in a brochure published by the Illinois Central Railroad Company it is explained that this action was brought under Lincoln's direction, and the case was argued upon the theory advanced by him and won by reason of the written opinion he prepared for the railroad.

He appears to have had some interest in the case of Atwood vs. Caldwell (12 Ill.96), although the printed report of the suit does not mention his name as one of the attorneys in the case. This case involved the liquidation of the Bank of Illinois. February 20, 1851, he wrote David A. Smith, a lawyer of Jacksonville: "I learn that Caldwell has executed his bond and qualified under the decree. I am now anxious to know whether the arrangement has been made to your satisfaction; and I do not like to ask Caldwell. Will you write me by return mail" (Angle, *Letters*, pp. 78–79).

remained to be established to guide and regulate men and women in their daily activities of life in a rapidly advancing civilization.

Many of Lincoln's early Supreme Court cases originated in the justice of peace courts. They involved trivial sums of money and were seemingly unimportant. But they concerned legal principles of importance hitherto undetermined. Often the contests resulting in petty verdicts created rules of action which settled the larger subsequent litigations incident to a more developed civilization. Lincoln and other able lawyers fought for principles regardless of the smallness of the amounts involved. They were making law and establishing legal precedents to guide the coming generations. They were laying the foundation of that system of jurisprudence which is the common law of Illinois today.

Between his first Supreme Court case, which he argued at the December term, 1840, and lost on a technical point of procedure,[1] and his one hundred and seventy-eighth case, which involved the vitally important question of the proper method of taxing railroad property,[2] arose almost every conceivable type of litigation. Out of the clash of opposing contentions of Lincoln and his adversaries were evolved new and important principles of jurisprudence. Questions of law hitherto undecided in Illinois received their first Supreme Court consideration and ended the various and conflicting decisions on the points involved. Some became landmarks in Illinois jurisprudence and have served as a guide to this very day.

Thus Lincoln helped settle a leading principle of the law of contracts in a case involving only $26.75 claimed as wages by a farmhand.[3] And in an unsuccessful attempt to replevin two mules for a client named Brundage, he became instrumental in establishing one of the most important precedents in the law

[1]Scammon vs. Cline (2 Scammon 456). He won his second case, Cannon vs. Kinney (4 Ill.9), although opposed by the formidable Logan. It involved the conversion of a horse.

[2] State of Illinois vs. Illinois Central Railroad, 27 Ill. 64.

[3] Eldridge vs. Rowe (7 Ill. 91), Lincoln for appellee.

of sales of that period. The decision that resulted from the conflict of arguments of Lincoln and his opponents, Logan and Hay, gave stability to a class of sales commonly known as conditional sales, and the courts have closely adhered to the rule ever since.[1] An action to set aside a conveyance of real estate on the ground of fraud, in which Lincoln and Logan represented the defendants in error, became one of the landmarks of Illinois law, and has been cited or followed in at least eighty-five other high courts.[2]

In a case involving only thirty-three dollars and fifty cents, Lincoln helped determine a very important principle of law concerning the affirmance of judgments of justice of the peace courts by circuit courts.[3] In three other cases at the same term of the Supreme Court his arguments contributed to the science of jurisprudence by fixing the law in reference to creditor's bills,[4] the laws of liability of sureties on a sheriff's bond,[5] and the rule of procedure concerning the maintenance of an action of debt on a judgment.[6]

"Justice has acquitted herself," Lincoln wrote in a brief in a false imprisonment action in which he won a verdict of three hundred and thirty three dollars for his client. The case became particularly instructive as to the rule governing new trials when newly discovered evidence is urged as a ground therefore.[7] Another one of his cases put an end to the various and contradictory decisions regarding the question of conflicting liens between a sheriff's execution and a landlord's distraint warrant, and fixed a firm rule to govern future court sales by judicial officers;[8] another determined several important questions of commercial

---

[1] Brundage vs. Camp (21 Ill. 330), Lincoln and Herndon for plaintiff-in-error.

[2] Bryant vs. Washington (7 Ill. 557), Lincoln for defendants-in-error.

[3] Benedict vs. Dillehunt (4 Ill. 287), Lincoln for appellee.

[4] Ballantine vs. Beall (4 Ill. 203), Lincoln for appellee.

[5] Elkin vs. The People (4 Ill. 207), Lincoln for appellee.

[6] Greathouse vs. Smith (4 Ill. 541), Lincoln for appellee.

[7] Schlenker vs. Risby (4 Ill. 483), Lincoln for appellee.

[8] Rogers vs. Dickey (6 Ill. 636), Lincoln for defendant-in-error.

law;[1] while still another involving only fifty dollars fixed the jurisdiction of justices of the peace in suits against executors and administrators.[2]

In a case in which Lincoln appeared as the successful counsel, the Supreme Court decided the important rule of property that the equity of redemption in foreclosure sales was liable to execution;[3] and shortly afterwards, in another case involving the purchase of a horse at a judicial sale, the general rule of *caveat emptor* was first applied to such sales.[4]

An overzealous constable seized a farmer's steer and oxen in the execution of process. From the resulting litigation, in which Lincoln represented the appellant, arose an important rule of procedure and liability of court officers which still stands as the law of Illinois and as a shield for honest inferior officers.[5]

One of the best-known precedents in Illinois jurisprudence, repeatedly cited and commented upon by high courts, which Lincoln helped establish, is a rule of property defining the status of a "creditor" within the meaning of the recording acts of the State.[6]

Lincoln represented a man in a seduction case and a verdict of six hundred and fifty-six dollars was returned against his client. But until this action the Supreme Court of Illinois had never before discussed the doctrine on which modern decisions on the subject were based, to the effect that it is no longer necessary for the parent to prove a loss of services of the debauched daughter in order to maintain the action.[7] At the same term of the Supreme Court he became instrumental in settling still another new question for Illinois jurisprudence, namely, that an unliquidated claim for damages cannot be set off against a claim founded on an entirely separate contract.[8]

[1] Kelly vs. Garrett (6 Ill. 648), Lincoln for plaintiff-in-error.
[2] Williams vs. Blankenship (12 Ill. 122), Lincoln for plaintiffs-in-error.
[3] Fitch vs. Pinckard (5 Ill. 69).
[4] England vs. Clark (5 Ill. 486).
[5] Parker vs. Smith (6 Ill. 411).
[6] Martin vs. Dreyden (6 Ill. 187), Lincoln for appellants.
[7] Anderson vs. Ryan (8 Ill. 187), Lincoln for appellants.
[8] Hawks vs. Lands (8 Ill. 227).

A saloon license is not transferable, Lincoln argued before the Supreme Court and that tribunal affirmed this contention and made it a rule of law.[1]

Then, clashing with his former partners Stuart and Logan, he succeeded in settling the question of resulting trusts in real estate, and the rights to property embracing large amounts became firmly fixed. Forty-seven high courts have followed or cited this precedent as an authority.[2]

The law governing bills of review underwent a serious consideration and adjudication for the first time in Illinois in a case in which Lincoln appeared for the successful appellant. This case has been cited or followed as an authority fifty-one times—even up to recent years.[3] Two of his cases involving the constitutionality of what was commonly known as the "occupying claimants" law determined that compensation shall be allowed to an adverse possessor of land for lasting improvements made prior to his receipt of notice of superior title. These cases have been cited or followed thirty-three times.[4]

Early in his career, Lincoln was retained by the appellees in the case of Manning Beams and Hiram Archer vs. George Denham and Nathaniel Buckmaster, an appeal from the Madison County Circuit Court.[5] In the court below an action had been commenced on a replevin bond. Shortly before the trial one of the complainants, who was also the principal in the bond, became too ill to attend court. His agent called upon the attorney for the opposition, who informed him that in view of the circumstances the case would be continued. Notwithstanding this agreement, either through a mistake or forgetfulness, the suit was permitted to go to trial and a default judgment for the entire penalty of the bond taken. The complainants appealed to the Supreme Court on

---

[1] Munsel vs. Temple (8 Ill. 93), Lincoln for plaintiff-in-error.
[2] Perry vs. McHenry (13 Ill. 227), Lincoln & Herndon for appellee.
[3] Griggs vs. Gear (8 Ill. 2).
[4] Ross vs. Irving and Pryor vs. Irving (14 Ill. 171), Lincoln for appellants. Cases argued jointly as both involved the same question.
[5] 3 Ill. 58. This is the first time this case is included in the list of Lincoln's Supreme Court cases.

the plea that they were not justly or equitably bound to pay the judgment.

The appellees contended that courts of equity should not interfere to grant new trials except in extraordinary cases, of which this was not one. Besides, they claimed that such negligence was shown by the complainants as to deprive them of all right of interposition by a court of chancery.

The appellees retained Lincoln to insure the retention of their victory won in the circuit court.

But, according to Joseph Gillespie, one of the attorneys for the complainants, it was not in Lincoln's nature to assume or attempt to bolster up a false position. He would abandon his case first. His study of the facts convinced him that the default judgment ought to be vacated, and he so informed his clients. When they insisted on resisting the Supreme Court appeal, Lincoln withdrew from the case. Other lawyers, A. Cowles and J. M. Krum, "less fastidious," took his place. At the hearing the Supreme Court upheld Lincoln's contentions that the facts were sufficient to authorize a court of chancery to grant relief to the complainants.[1]

Although many of Lincoln's Supreme Court cases involved but trivial sums of money, a large number concerned much wealth and vast property rights.[2] Some dealt with the constitutionality, interpretation, and construction of statues and legisla-

[1] Collated from accounts in Scammon's *Illinois Reports*, vol. 3, p. 58, and Herndon and Weik, *Lincoln*, II, 13–14, and Ward H. Lamon, *Life of Lincoln*, p. 321–22.

[2] Lincoln's victory in Illinois Central Railway Company vs. County of McLean (17 Ill. 291) saved the company many thousands of dollars in taxes and settled the constitutional question of railroad taxation.

Webster vs. French (II Ill. 254), Lincoln & Herndon and Logan for plaintiff-in-error, concerns the advertising of bids in the sale of public lands of the value of twenty-two thousand dollars.

Parlow vs. Williams (19 Ill. 132), in which Lincoln & Herndon for plaintiff-in-error won a sixty-five hundred dollar judgment, reflects the unsettled money situation of the period and resulted in the fixing of a rule of law pertaining to it.

tion,[1] others with the question of slavery and the inalienable rights of human beings,[2] and still others were of great political significance.[3] One of his cases caused a public sensation when it demanded that the Supreme Court mandamus Governor Bissell to issue to Lincoln's client certain bonds authorized by the legislature. But the court decided that it "does not possess the right to exercise coercive powers over the Executive."[4]

Lincoln was a pioneer in railroad litigation in Illinois, and a number of early railroad decisions are the result of his efforts.[5] Numerous important questions of commercial law, principles of procedure, and vital rules of property were first declared and made certain in cases in which Lincoln participated.

When Lincoln appeared in the Supreme Court to argue his first appeal, one of the justices of that tribunal was Stephen A. Douglas, then only twenty-seven years old. Until his resignation from the bench to assume a seat in Congress, he presided over a number of Lincoln's cases. In one he delivered the opinion of the Supreme Court affirming the circuit court's judgment against Lincoln's client for $364.50 on a promissory note.[6] The Little Giant thus received many opportunities to observe his future po-

[1] People vs. Blackford (16 Ill. 166), Lincoln for appellees. The case concerned the interpretation of a statute regarding the liability of sureties on the bond of a county tax-collector.

Kinsey vs. Nisely (23 Ill. 505), Lincoln & Herndon for plaintiff-in-error. Involves construction of Illinois laws concerning usury.

Sullivan vs. The People (16 Ill. 233), Lincoln for plaintiff-in-error. Involves construction of the laws of Illinois governing the sale of intoxicating liquors.

The people vs. Marshall (12 Ill. 391); Lincoln for relator persuaded the Supreme Court to declare an act of the legislature unconstitutional because it sought to merge two counties.

[2] Bailey vs. Cromwell (4 Ill. 71); Lincoln for appellate succeeded in securing the freedom of Nance, a slave girl.

[3] People ex rel. Lanphier, & Walker vs. Hatch (19 Ill. 283), involves a reapportionment act passed in 1857. Governor Bissell inadvertently signed the bill and then withdrew his approval. The Democrats tried to compel the Secretary of State to certify the act.

[4] The People ex rel. vs. Bissell, Governor (19 Ill. 229).

[5] See Chapter XV, "Railroad and Big Business Lawyer."

[6] Averill vs. Field (4 Ill. 390), Lincoln and Logan for appellants.

litical rival's skill in argument and debate. But little did he then dream that the carelessly dressed lawyer to whom he listened from the high judicial bench would some day throw down the gauntlet, and on the rostrum of public opinion contend with him over the vital issues of the day with such skill and adroitness as to win the admiration of the entire Nation.

In addition to his large Supreme Court practice, Lincoln also enjoyed one of the most extensive federal court businesses in Illinois.

On the third day of December, 1839, Lincoln was one of a group of six lawyers admitted to the practice of law in the United States district and circuit courts at Springfield, presided over by Judge Nathaniel Pope, the first United States judge in Illinois.

In this group were also Stephen A. Douglas, "always around," and Samuel H. Treat, who later became a federal judge before whom Lincoln was to argue many cases after the division of Illinois into two districts. But for the next sixteen years, following Lincoln's admission to federal practice, the State of Illinois had but one United States court. Springfield as the capital of Illinois was the seat of this vast judicial district; and Lincoln, as one of the best-known lawyers of that city, enjoyed an extensive federal court practice. From all over the State, lawyers and clients retained him in cases over which the United States court had jurisdiction. These concerned questions involving constitutional law, interstate commerce and admiralty, infringement of patents, bills in equity, common law actions, and violations of federal laws. They included some of his most famous cases.

In 1855, the Illinois district was divided into a northern and a southern division, with Springfield retaining the headquarters of the latter and Chicago becoming the seat of the new district court. Judge Drummond was assigned to the northern, and Judge Treat to the southern division. For some reason all the records were ordered transferred to the Chicago court. In the great fire of 1871, which practically wiped out that city, all these documents were destroyed. As a result there exist no official records of Lincoln's federal cases except those argued in the Springfield district after 1855.[1]

However, a recent discovery of some musty volumes stored away in the Federal Building in Springfield has brought to light a number of Lincoln's cases whereof the documents were burned.

[1] In the official printed reports of the United States courts are found eleven cases which Lincoln argued in the district court prior to the division of Illinois into two federal judicial districts. All the original records of these actions were destroyed in the Chicago fire. Six of these cases were heard by Judge Pope and the others by Judge Drummond, with Justice John McLean of the United States Supreme Court sitting as circuit judge.

Lincoln vs. Tower (2 McLean 473), action of debt brought on a judgment obtained in Massachusetts, June term, 1841, Lincoln for plaintiff.

January vs. Duncan (3 McLean 19), July term, 1842, action against guarantor of a note; Logan & Lincoln for plaintiff.

Sturtevant vs. City of Alton (3 McLean 393), Logan & Lincoln for defendant.

Lewis vs. Administrators of Broadwell (3 McLean 568), Logan & Lincoln for defendant.

Lafayette Bank vs. State Bank (4 McLean 208), Lincoln for plaintiff.

Voce vs. Lawrence (4 McLean 203), Lincoln and Grant Goodrich for plaintiff. Concerns the administration of oaths in connection with depositions taken in another State.

Moore vs. Brown (4 McLean 211), Logan & Lincoln for defendants. Action involves the question of the sale of land for taxes. The reports contain the notation that "on the suggestion of the counsel, the above question was certified to the Supreme Court as to the validity of the deed."

Kemper vs. Adams (5 McLean 507), July term, 1853; Lincoln for the defendants opposed Logan in an action of ejectment.

United States vs. Prentiss (6 McLean 65), October term, 1853; Logan & Lincoln for defendant, a United States marshal sued by the Government for recovery of money.

Columbus Insurance Co. vs. Curtenius (6 McLean 209), Lincoln for plaintiff.

Columbus Insurance Co. vs. Peoria Bridge Association (6 McLean 70), Lincoln for plaintiff, Logan for defendant.

United States vs. Bridge Co. (6 McLean 516) is another case in which Lincoln probably appeared. It involved questions similar to those in the Rock Island Bridge case. Lincoln's name does not appear in the printed report. But the case was decided during July, 1855, in the Chicago District Court, when Lincoln is known to have been present in Chicago.

It appears that in 1856 Congress enacted a law requiring the clerk of the Southern District Court to make transcripts from the records at Chicago of all cases involving title to real estate in his district and certain other prescribed types of cases originating in the southern district. Included in the records so copied by him are transcripts of twenty of Lincoln's hitherto unknown federal court cases. Their dates range from 1839 to 1852.[2]

[2] These dockets were discovered in 1933 by Benjamin P. Thomas, Executive Secretary of the Abraham Lincoln Association, Springfield, Illinois, while browsing through the records of the Federal Court in Springfield, Mr. Thomas has furnished the author with a list of Lincoln's cases found in these volumes, as follows.

John Hooper, George H. Martin, Newberry A. Smith vs. Benjamin Haines, surviving partner of B. Haines & Son. Stuart & Lincoln for plaintiff. Trespass on the case. December 5, 1839. Defendant defaulted. Damages accessed at $626.82.

Andrew W. Porter vs. William Brown for plaintiff. Logan & Lincoln for defendant. Foreclosure suit in chancery. June 8, 1840. Ordered that defendant pay $5,550.25, amount agreed on as due and costs. Also ordered that defendant be foreclosed on all lands and tenements in mortgage described and that they be sold to pay amount due complainant.

Benjamin Robinson vs. Abraham Martin. Robbins & Wells for complainant. Logan & Lincoln for defendant. Suit in chancery. Begun June 18, 1841. December 14, 1842, by agreement contract of sale rescinded and complainant ordered to reconvey land to defendant. Each party to pay own costs.

George W. Walker and John Hack vs. John A. McCoy. Logan & Lincoln for plaintiff. Purple for defendant. Action on a promissory note. June 4, 1845. Jury finds for plaintiff. Awards him the land in question and costs.

Joshua G. Moore vs. Horatio C. Nelson & John Ashworth. Logan & Lincoln for plaintiff. Baker & Bledsoe for defendant. Ejectment. June 12, 1844. Jury finds for plaintiff. Awards him the land in question and costs.

Thomas II. Larkin vs. Maurice Doyle. Logan & Lincoln for plaintiff. Action on promissory note. June 6, 1843. Defendant defaults. Clerk assesses damages at $1,152.26.

Joseph Vance vs. John Kilgore, Henry Jacoby, & Thomas Karr. Logan & Lincoln for plaintiff. Trespass on the case. December 6, 1843. Defendants default. Clerk assesses damages at $1,678.

James Fassett, Theodore L. Fassett & Alfred Fassett vs. Robert Blackwell. Logan & Lincoln for plaintiffs. Assumpsit. June 7, 1884. Defendant defaults. Damages assessed at $5,442.10.

James Fassett & Wallace Fassett vs. Robert Blackwell. Logan & Lincoln for plaintiffs. Assumpsit. June 7, 1844. Defendant defaults. Damages assessed at $1,340.41.

William D. Barrett vs. Gustavus Kilbourn. Logan & Lincoln for plaintiff. June 7, 1844. Defendant defaults. Ordered that plaintiff recover $500 amount of mortgage and damages of $117.66. Writ of *scire facias* issued against mortgaged property.

Moses Atwood, Wm. P. Jones & Aaron A. Hardy vs. Lewis W. Links. June 11, 1840. Stuart & Lincoln secured judgment of $1,643.76 and costs for plaintiff.

Wm. Brown *et al* vs. Thomas I. Little. December 16, 1841. Logan & Lincoln secured judgment of $2,187 and costs for plaintiff.

Thomas T. January for use of Joseph Stettimus & D. A. January vs. William B. Archer. Logan & Lincoln for plaintiff, who was granted $4.32 and costs. June 6, 1842.

James Woods, William T. Christy and James C. Christy vs. Benjamin L. Yates & Mary E. Yates. Logan & Lincoln for defendants. December 5, 1844. Defendants defaulted. Ordered that plaintiffs recover debt of $457.47 and damages of $158.81. Writ of *scire facias* issued against mortgaged premises.

John Moore for use of State Bank of Indiana vs. William January. Trespass on the case of premises. Logan & Lincoln for plaintiffs. Stuart & Edwards for defendants. July 21, 1852. Jury waived. Court finds for plaintiff in sum of $5,938.67 and costs.

Alexander Norton vs. George D. Gordon. Logan for plaintiff. Doughty & Lincoln for defendant. Action on note. January 5, 1853. Defendant withdraws plea and defaults. Plaintiff awarded $1,068.39 and $641.92 damages.

John Moore for use of State Bank of Indiana vs. Victor Buchanan & John Vandermark. Logan & Lincoln for plaintiff. Stuart & Edwards for defendant. Action on promissory note. July 31, 1852. Jury waived. Court finds for plaintiff and assesses damages at $5,418.16.

John Everhard vs. Osee Welch and Robert Dawson. Logan for plaintiff. Lincoln for defendant. July 21, 1852. Dawson defaulted. Jury waived. Court dismissed case against Welch. Dawson ordered to pay $529.20 and damages of $447.36.

John Everhard vs. Osee Welch & Robert Dawson. Logan for plaintiff. Lincoln for defendant. Dawson defaulted. Jury waived. Charge against Welch dismissed. Dawson ordered to pay $772.36 and damages of $641.40.

Bank of Missouri vs. A. G. Caldwell, Ebenezer Z. Ryan, D. A. Smith & George Dunlap, assignees of Bank of Shawneetown, Illinois. Browning, Bushnell, Williams & Lawrence for complainants. Scates for defendants. December 30, 1850. Complainant files bill in chancery accusing assignees of negligence and unfaithfulness and disregard of interests of creditors in liquidating affairs of bank. . . . Claimant is creditor to the extent of $109,000, payment of which

On March 7, 1849, three days after the expiration of the Thirtieth Congress, in which Lincoln served, the Springfield lawyer, on a motion of a Mr. Lawrence, was admitted to practice before the Supreme Court of the United States. During the same term of court Hannibal Hamlin of Maine, destined to become the Nation's Vice-President during Lincoln's first term as President, was also admitted to practice before this highest of tribunals.

In the chambers where so much American history was being written, Abraham Lincoln participated in three cases.[1]

has been refused.... The case went along until October 28, 1852, when Lincoln came into it on the side of the complainants. He, Logan, and Williams filed an amended bill alleging that in 1837 the bank loaned to the trustees of Shawneetown a sum of money to grade and pave the river bank along the town, owners of certain lands in the town executing mortgages to the bank as security, and that interest and principal remain unpaid to the amount of $38,311.29.

See also Bulletin of the Abraham Lincoln Association, Springfield, Illinois, March, 1933, p. 7.

[1] Lewis vs. Lewis (7 Howard 776) involved the construction and operation of the statute of limitations of the State of Illinois. Lincoln and Mr. Lawrence argued the case of the appellee and a Mr. Wright appeared for the appellant. The majority opinion of the court, delivered by Chief Justice Taney, opposed Lincoln's version of the issue, but Mr. Justice McLean in a dissenting opinion held in accordance with the Springfield lawyer's contentions.

At the same term of court, Lincoln's name was entered on the docket of the Supreme Court as a counsel for the City of Chicago in the case of the United States vs. Chicago (7 Howard 185). The published report of the case states, "The cause was argued by Mr. Toucey, attorney general, on behalf of the United States—no counsel appearing for the City of Chicago." Supreme Court records do not reveal whether or not Lincoln participated in the oral argument of the case. The litigation involved the right of the City of Chicago to open streets through property belonging to the United States and adjacent to the city. The court decided in favor of the Federal Government.

Lincoln's last Supreme Court case, Forsythe vs. Reynolds (15 Howard 3), was at the December term, 1853. He appeared on behalf of the appellant in association with two other lawyers. The published report states that the "cause was argued by Mr. Williams for the appellant. Briefs were also filed upon that side by Mr. Williams for the appellant. Briefs were also field upon that side by Mr. Lincoln and Mr. Gamble." Salmon P. Chase, later President

Though none determined any important principle of law, Lincoln's participation in them permanently placed his name on the roll of Supreme Court practitioners alongside the names of William Pinkney, Daniel Webster, Rufus Choate, Reverdy Johnson, Jeremiah Black, Salmon P. Chase, and other immortals of the American bar.

The completion of a rail connection between Springfield and Chicago in 1855 enabled Lincoln to make frequent trips to the newly created United States District and Circuit Court. Thus in the summer of that year, following a busy term on the circuit, Lincoln spent about two weeks in Chicago, where he tried a number of important federal cases. Returning home, he immediately became engaged in the United States District Court at Springfield. In September, 1857, he spent four weeks in Chicago trying cases in the district court. Most of this time was devoted to the Effie Afton case.[1]

His very last professional appearance in any court, which marked the close of his illustrious career as a lawyer, was the case of Dawson vs. Ennis, which he tried in the Springfield District Court on June 20, 1860, after he had been nominated for the Presidency of the United States. With two other lawyers he represented the plaintiff, who sought to recover damages in the amount of ten thousand dollars because the defendant had violated an agreement not to sell a certain patented plow. The verdict in favor of the defendant was not announced until five days after Lincoln had assumed his colossal responsibilities as head of his dissension-torn Nation.

It has frequently been asserted that Lincoln cited few authorities in the argument of his cases. This contention seems to be amply borne out by the available reports of his Supreme Court and federal cases. He did not rely to any great extent upon precedent.

Lincoln's Secretary of the Treasury and subsequently Chief Justice of the Supreme Court of the United States, argued the case for the appellee. The case involved the ownership of certain land in Peoria, Illinois, and the construction of United States statues governing land grants to settlers.

[1] For reference to numerous of Lincoln's federal court cases, see Angle, *Lincoln*, 1854–1861.

He was content for the most part with analyzing and rebutting the arguments and legal authorities presented by his adversaries and supporting his own contentions with fundamental principles of natural justice and clear reasoning. To him the law was perfection of common sense, logic, and reason. Without probing deeply into the mass of analogous decisions he marshaled the facts of the controversy confronting him and applied to them the test of reason. His own extraordinary power of reasoning, invincible logic, and strong common sense enabled him to determine what the law ought to be under the circumstances, and then with all the force of his keen mind he sought to carry conviction of the righteousness of his client's cause and to win the court over to his view of the law.

It is not to be inferred, however, that Lincoln never prepared comprehensive briefs in support of his arguments. The law library was located in the courtroom of the Supreme Court Building, just across the street from the office of Lincoln & Herndon. Here the lawyers from all over the State gathered to search for their authorities and prepare their briefs. Lincoln spent much time in the library. The recognized authorities of American and English law were at his disposal. Whenever he believed it necessary he studied special cases thoroughly, and carefully prepared his arguments.

In many of his legal battles before the Supreme Court he reinforced himself with all the precedents he could find in the available law books. Thus, doubly armed, with the fundamental principles of law in the forefront and the array of authorities in reserve, he was a match for the most formidable adversary in the legal arena. His briefs that have been preserved are interesting as characteristic specimens of his style of expression, as well as of his method of reasoning. Those that have been published in connection with reports of his Supreme Court cases are marked by the brevity, simplicity, and directness that later characterized his important state papers.

An interesting action in which a brief in Lincoln's handwriting is still preserved is the slander case of Patterson vs. Edwards.[1]

[1] 7 Ill. 720.

Lincoln's brief to the Supreme Court, praying for the rehearing of an adverse ruling, is a specimen of his habitual logic and clear statement of facts.

Another brief, contending that a wagering contract concerning the result of the presidential election of 1856 was against public policy and void, ended with an interesting preachment against gambling.[1]

Generally speaking, Lincoln's most successful work as a lawyer was done in the State Supreme Court.[2] His slow-working mind ordinarily required plenty of time for deliberation to function at its best. Supreme Court cases were never hurried affairs. Usually they allowed sufficient time for careful preparation. As a result, well-reasoned arguments and, where necessary, briefs strongly supported by authorities distinguished his efforts in these cases.

Lincoln was a pioneer in the profession, accepting whatever litigation came his way. With but few precedents to guide him, his own skill, logic, reasoning, and common sense aided the courts in settling the law for the coming generations. From out of his legal clashes with many of the great lawyers whose names are impressed upon the jurisprudence of Illinois were evolved some of the most important principles of the substantive law of that great commonwealth, defining the rights of her citizens and the procedure which the law gives to secure and enforce those rights.

Together with these associates of the circuit he helped build the law of the land. Standing before the courts, he pointed the course they should go, representing not only his immediate clients, but all those who should come after them.

---

[1] Smith vs. Smith, 21 Ill. 244.

[2] Of his one hundred and seventy-eight cases in the Supreme Court Lincoln won 96, lost 81, and withdrew from Beams vs. Denham (3 Ill. 58) before the hearing.

XIII. "JUDGE" LINCOLN

WHEN pressure of personal business or illness prevented Judge Davis from attending to his duties on the circuit bench, the judge usually arranged with his friend Lincoln to hold court in his stead. This procedure had no sanction in law and was altogether irregular, but lawyers and litigants seldom voiced any objection because such assignment of the judicial function avoided delays, enabled cases to be disposed of in the regular order, and worked for the conveniences of all concerned—lawyers, litigants, jurors, witnesses, and officers of the court.

The close friendship which enabled Judge Davis early to recognize Lincoln's ability, coupled with the fact that Lincoln was the only lawyer to make the rounds of the entire circuit, accounts for his frequent appointments to hold court for the Eighth Circuit jurist. On one occasion, Lincoln presided for a whole term of court as Judge Davis's substitute. But usually his judicial services were limited to one-, two-, or three-day sessions.

Whitney recalled that two cases over which "Judge" Lincoln presided were reversed by the Supreme Court because of this irregular assignment of the judicial function. Lincoln realized that the procedure was unsanctioned by law, and would not preside at a trial unless all parties consented.[1]

[1] Whitney, *Life on the Circuit*, I, 192.

Although Lincoln officiated as judge in a considerable number of cases—sometimes presiding for an hour or two, sometimes for a day, and sometimes for an entire term of ten days—the detailed reports of only a few of these actions are available.

One such case is Chadden vs. Beasley, tried in Urbana. The suit involved the collection of a promissory note that a number of prominent and well-to-do citizens of Champaign County had delivered to one Chase in consideration of his establishing a newspaper. He violated his agreement and fled the county, but not before he had negotiated the note to innocent holders for value who now sought to enforce its collection. The makers of the note, despite the fact that it had found its way into the hands of an innocent purchaser, felt that morally they were not bound to pay it, and retained legal counsel to resist the litigation. Lincoln, although greatly annoyed by the attempt of the lawyers to ward off a decision where no legal defense existed, listened patiently to their contentions.

"We had no legal, but a good moral defense," admitted one of the lawyers, "but what we wanted most of all was to shove it off till the next term of court by one expedient or another. We bothered the 'court' about it till late on Saturday, the day of adjournment. He adjourned for supper with nothing left but this case to dispose of. After supper he heard our twaddle for nearly an hour and then made this odd entry:

L. D. CHADDEN   CHAMPAIGN COUNTY COURT
vs.   April term, 1858
J. D. BEASLEY, ET AL.   ASSUMPSIT

Ordered by the Court:

Plea in abatement, by B. Z. Green, a defendant not served, filed Saturday at eleven o'clock A.M. April 24th 1856, stricken from the files by order of court. Demurrer to declaration, if there ever was one, overruled. Defendants who are served now, at 8 o'clock P.M., of the last day of the term, ask to plead to the merits, which is denied by the court on the ground that the offer comes too late, and therefore, as by *nil dicet*, judgment is rendered for Pl'ff.

Clerk assess damages.

A. LINCOLN, Judge pro tem.'

When one of the defense lawyers finally recovered from his amazement occasioned by this unique entry, he ventured to ask, "Well, Lincoln, how can we get this case up again?"

Lincoln eyed his inquirer scornfully and replied, "You have all been so mighty smart about this case you can find out how to take it up again yourselves."

Lincoln had come to Urbana at the request of Judge Davis, who was busy elsewhere, to wind up a three-day term of the Champaign County Court. The Springfield lawyer presided as judge *pro tem* from April 22 to April 24, 1858, and disposed of a large number of cases, most of which were uncontested.[1]

On another occasion when Lincoln was substituting for Judge Davis, an action came before him wherein a merchant was suing the father of a minor son for the sum of twenty-eight dollars for a suit of clothes furnished to the youth. The clothes had been sold to the son without the father's knowledge or consent, and to hold the parent liable for the minor's debt it became essential to prove that the clothes were a necessity and suitable to the son's station in life. The evidence was that the father was a prosperous farmer, and the merchant contended that he ought to pay the son's bill of twenty-eight dollars. But "Judge" Lincoln refused to accede to the plaintiff's plea of necessity and ruled against the merchant. "I have rarely in my life," he declared, "worn a suit of clothes costing twenty-eight dollars."[2]

In Tazewell County Lincoln presided over a case wherein a farmer named Hartsfeller sued his neighbor Trowbridge for damages resulting when the latter's cattle ate up the corn stored in Hartsfeller's crib. It appeared that Trowbridge had let a portion

---

[1] Herndon and Weik, *Lincoln*, II, 348–49; Angle, *Lincoln, 1854–1861*, p. 225. Herndon gives the year of the Chadden vs. Beasely case as 1856 instead of 1858. This is manifestly wrong, as April 24, 1856, fell on a Thursday and not on a Saturday, as Lincoln stated in his entry. April 24, 1858, fell on a Saturday.

[2] Herndon and Weik, *Lincoln*, II, 347–48.

of his land to the plaintiff, who raised a small crop of corn
thereon. Contrary to Trowbridge's orders, Hartsfeller cribbed the
corn on this same land. Trowbridge had enclosed his farm with
a fence and had turned his cattle loose to graze. One day the
animals entered the corn cribs and devoured the crop.

"And you say you went over and fenced the corn after you
asked him not to crib it on your land?" "Judge" Lincoln inquired of Trowbridge.

"Yes, sir."

"Trowbridge, you have won your case," was the terse
decision.

Whitney recalls that on one occasion when counsel were arguing their case to the jury, Lincoln, who had been sitting in the
place of Judge Davis, forgot the dignity of his office and left the
bench and went to a corner in the rear part of the courtroom,
where he told humorous stories to a group of lawyers gathered
around him.[1]

In an old judge's docket of the Sangamon County Circuit
Court for the year 1856 is found indisputable evidence of Lincoln's frequent substitution for Judge Davis on the bench. That
musty calf-bound volume, still well preserved, reveals that on
Monday, December 1, 1856, Lincoln presided over that court for
at least part of the day and made entries in twenty-two cases. It
appears that Judge Davis, leaving for his home in Bloomington
after the adjournment of court on Saturday, had made arrangements with Lincoln to officiate for him in case he should not
return on time to open court Monday morning. So before Davis's
arrival in the afternoon his substitute was able to dispose of
twenty-two uncontested cases. When the clerk called the case of
Barnard, Adams & Co. vs. Bristol, counsel apprised the court
that it had been agreed that judgment should be entered in favor
of the plaintiff but that execution should be withheld for three
months. So in "Judge" Lincoln's handwriting is found the entry:
"Judgt. for plaintiff by agreement for $182.98 and costs—execu-
tion stayed till March 1856." Eighteen default judgments were
rendered in five of these cases, juries of inquiry being summoned

[1] Whitney, *Life on the Circuit*, p. 263.

to fix the damages in amounts ranging from $14.63 to $335, while in five other cases the clerk assessed the damages in amounts from $153.75 to $313.87.

Another case was an uncontested divorce action wherein Lincoln granted a decree in favor of the petitioner.

Evidence of the universal trust and confidence folks had in Lincoln's sense of fairness and justice is manifested by the fact that among the attorney's whose cases came before Lincoln on this day were Lucius B. Adams and John A. McClernand. The former was the son of General James Adams, whom Lincoln so bitterly assailed back in 1837, when he accused the general of defrauding a widow of her land, and ruthlessly pursued him with a series of legal and newspaper attacks. McClernand, a fighting Democratic leader, was one of Lincolns most constant and bitter political opponents, ever ready to strike for partisan advantage.[1]

No characteristic in all of Lincoln's career appears more prominent than the judicial spirit—the passion for justice and the zeal to act as pacificator, arbitrator, referee, umpire, or judge. Even as a youth in Clary's Grove, he constantly was called on to judge cock-fights, horse-races, wrestling-matches, or fist-fights, or to reconcile the adversaries before the fisticuffs commenced. Frequently disputatious citizens had appealed to him to arbitrate some controversy, be it a difference over land boundaries, physical prowess, or disputed points of literature. His fine common sense, native tact, good-natured raillery and humor, and physical strength were invaluable to him in his rôle as judge, peacemaker, and arbitrator.

These attributes of youth were but symptomatic of the man, for when he became a lawyer his office at once assumed the appearance of a court of conciliation. The judicial spirit—the desire to act as peacemaker and leave the litigants friends—dominated whenever feasible.

The lawyer whom destiny was preparing for the rôle of leader and counselor of the American people in their hour of greatest trial found extensive opportunity in his dingy law office to practice the art of giving sane and cautious advice to others.

[1] Abraham Lincoln Association, Bulletin for December 1, 1929, p. 3.

The same experience that prepared him to counsel his litigious neighbors, when one by one they came to him with their petty quarrels and bickerings, enabled him in the momentous days to come to guide them collectively when their government and national life were threatened with destruction.

As a lawyer, Lincoln early learned that justice is the greatest interest of men on earth; that people nearly always prefer compromise to contests; and that in very heated controversy among men the truth lies somewhere between the two extremes. The law taught him that in bitter combats the nominal winner is often the real loser in the end. It fixed in his mind the high conception that right makes might.

Here is a bit of Lincoln philosophy which reveals the mind of the prudent counselor warning his clients against the pitfalls of litigation:

"Quarrel not at all. No man resolved to make the most of himself can spare time for personal contention. Still less can he afford to take on the consequences, including the vitiating of his temper and the loss of self-control. Yield larger things which you can show no more than equal right; and yield lesser ones, though clearly your own. Better give your path to a dog than be bitten by him in contesting for the right. Even killing the dog will not cure the bite."

Gifted with the power of expression, skilled in argument, and schooled in the substantive law, Lincoln found great enjoyment in trial work. But he did not encourage litigation. Whenever a settlement outside of court was possible he urged it upon the contending parties.

"Discourage litigation. Persuade your neighbors to compromise whenever you can." This was the philosophy he practiced and urged upon other lawyers. "Point out to them," he continued in lecture, "how the nominal winner is often a real loser—in fees, expenses, and waste of time. As a peacemaker the lawyer has a superior opportunity of being a good man. There will still be business enough."[1]

So when a client came to his office and wanted him to sue a

[1] *Works,* II, 142.

widow for six hundred dollars, Lincoln was heard to exclaim: "Yes, we can doubtless gain your case for you. We can set a whole neighborhood at loggerheads. We can distress a widowed mother and her six fatherless children, and thereby get for you six hundred dollars to which you seem to have legal claim, but which rightfully belongs, it appears to me, as much to the woman and her children as it does to you. You must remember that some things legally right are not morally right. We shall not take your case, but will give you a little advice for which we will charge you nothing. You seem to be a sprightly, energetic man; we would advise you to try your hand at making six hundred dollars in some other way."[1]

To Abraham Bale he wrote: "I understand Mr. Hickox will go or send to Petersburg tomorrow, for the purpose of meeting you to settle the difficulty about the wheat. I sincerely hope you will settle it. I think you can if you will, for I will charge nothing for what I have done, and thank you to boot. By settling, you will most likely get your money sooner and with much less trouble and expense."[2]

He sat as a court of equity in sifting out the cases he would or would not accept, trying them all first in his own "court of conscience." Litigation arising out of ill-feeling and vengeance he usually refused. Although retained in cases as a lawyer and not as an arbitrator, he could not divest himself of the judicial spirit. Thus, while searching the title of a parcel of real estate for a widow Lincoln discovered that by some mistake his client was holding title to three acres more than actually belonged to her. He traced this discrepancy and learned that Charles Matheney, a former owner now deceased, in making a conveyance had, by an error in the description, included more land in the grant than he intended. Lincoln called his client's attention to this mistake and persuaded her to make restitution to Matheney's heirs for the extra acreage.[3]

[1] James Judson Ford to William H. Herndon in Herndon and Weil, *Lincoln*, 11, 14–15.
[2] Angle, *letters*, p. 65.
[3] Herndon and Weik, *Lincoln*, II, 14.

"You have no case; better settle," John H. Littlefield, a student in the office of Lincoln & Herndon, heard the senior partner advise would-be clients time and time again. In the case of Harris and Jones vs. Buckles he wrote this characteristic note to S. C. Parks: "Tell Harris it's no use to waste money on me in that case; he'll get beat."[1]

On another occasion, when Lincoln was riding to Lewiston to try a case in the circuit court, a farmer whom the lawyer had known as Uncle Tom hailed him and sought to retain him to "git the law" on Jim Adams, a neighbor, concerning a land line dispute.

"Uncle Tommy, you haven't had any fight with Jim, have you?"

"No."

"He's a fair to middling neighbor, isn't he?"

"Only tollable, Abe."

"He's been a neighbor of yours for a long time, hasn't he?"

"Nigh onto fifteen years."

"Part of the time you get along all right, don't you?"

"I reckon we do, Abe."

"Well, now, Uncle Tommy, you see this horse of mine? [and he pointed to his plodding, weatherbeaten nag]. He isn't as good a horse as I could straddle and I sometimes get out of patience with him, but I know his faults. He does fairly well as horses go, and it might take me a long time to get used to some other horse's faults. You and Uncle Jimmy must put up with each other, as I and my horse do with one another."

And another lawsuit was averted and another friendship saved.

When a young man charged his guardian with converting part of the estate to his own use and requested Lincoln to file suit against him, the lawyer, upon learning that Enoch Kingsbury was the accused guardian, replied: "I know Mr. Kingsbury and he is not the man to have cheated you out of a cent. I can't take the case and advise you to drop the subject." And that was the end of the threatened litigation.[2]

---

[1] S. C. Parks in Lamon, *Recollections*, 324.
[2] McClure, pp. 359–60.

Quarreling neighbors came to him and were willing to submit their differences to his arbitration. When Samuel Wycoff and Dennis Forrest disputed concerning a small strip of land, each claiming it to be part of his tract, they selected Lincoln as arbitrator "to hear the evidence adduced by both parties, and thereupon decide which is the owner of the disputed land, and what line is hereafter to be the dividing line between us." So great was their confidence in his fairness that each bound himself in the penal sum of five hundred dollars as liquidated damages to abide by the decision he should make.

David Spear and Isaac P. Spear came to Lincoln's office and requested him to serve with Stephen T. Logan as an arbitrator in settling their differences over a valuable parcel of land. The two lawyers listened patiently to the conflicting contentions of the disputants, and finally decreed that to entitle Isaac P. Spear to a conveyance of the land, he should pay David Spear the sum of $6,557.78, less the hair allowance due Isaac for his half of a stock of goods transferred to David. The two arbitrators figured out to the penny the net amount due, and Isaac and David shook hands, perfectly satisfied.[1]

"There is something remarkable about these Lincoln settlements and arbitrations," observed Leonard Swett, his contemporary at the bar.

"The parties always submit. They seem to think they have to submit, which is very little short of the power he exercises over a jury, before which these arbitrated disputes would otherwise come. He is so positive and final with them as to make his judgment equivalent to a settlement of these cases. Only one man objected seriously and threatened to take his case into court. It happened he was one of Lincoln's clients; but when the man objected to Lincoln's arbitration, and said, 'I will take the case into court,' Lincoln gave him one of his deep searching looks, and said, 'Very well, Jim, I will take the case against you for nothing.' But that was unnecessary, for the penetrating look had settled Jim and his case."[2]

[1] Logan and Lincoln Arbitration Award, December 6, 1851, in Angle, *Letters* p. 80.

[2] Browne, *Abraham Lincoln and the Men of His Time*, FI, 339.

Not only among quarreling neighbors did his love of justice and fair play and ability to bring about amicable settlements receive recognition. Large railroad corporations, too, sought his services as arbitrator. On October 14, 1851, came a letter from J. F. Joy of Chicago. "Can you come immediately and act as arbitrator in the crossing case between the Illinois Central and Northern Indiana R. R. Companies, if you should be appointed?" it read. "Answer and say yes if possible."

Lincoln's brief and unofficial career as judge *pro tem* on the bench of the Eighth Judicial circuit and his recognized ability as an arbitrator naturally raise the question whether or not he possessed the qualities of a great judge. His friend Whitney doubts that he was endowed with the judicial temperament, and yet he is certain that if Lincoln "had been made a successor of John Marshall, he would by his moral and logical acquirements have achieved as great renown, in spite of his lack of judicial temperament."

To Whitney, Lincoln was by nature more of the advocate than the judge, and there is the old saying that a good lawyer rarely makes a good judge. And yet to a high degree every attribute of the ideal judge is found in Lincoln.

From the youthful days in Clary's Grove to the time that he held in his hands the destiny of a nation, Lincoln's career shows that he could sit as an impartial tribunal and fearlessly and honestly hear and determine the rights of men—their claims to property, to liberty, and to life itself. Endowed with strict uprightness, his personal character was ever above reproach, and his life and thoughts on so high a plane that the hand of corruption could never reach him. The most human and humble of men, he never could exalt property above human rights. Fearless and independent, he was not afraid of being unpopular, nor could he be coerced into any course of action by promises or threats. He was blessed with the rarest of all qualities of the great judge—the open mind—which, in the words of Sir Matthew Hale, is the ability not to be "prepossessed with any judgment at all till the whole business and both parties be heard."

He was a scholar whose capacity to grow and learn was limitless, whose knowledge reached beyond the leather covers of his musty law books to delve into the realm of common sense— into the hearts and souls of men—studying their strength and weaknesses, their motives and innermost thoughts.

By instinct a conservative, a study of his acts proves that he never yielded to the impulses of the moment, but, ever calm and self-restrained, moved slowly and acted carefully. Yet his was not the *stare decisis* habit of mind. Precedents never hampered him, nor was he a salve to fixed authorities. Original thought helped him rise above the wisdom of the past into new and higher spheres of progress. He dared to criticize the Supreme Court of the United States when his own good sense and investigations convinced him that its decision in the Dred Scott case was wrong.

There was nothing sacred to him about precedents and decided cases, except in so far as they contributed to the reason and justice of the case at hand. He often recounted the story of the justice of the peace who had been issuing marriage licenses without legal authority. When at last this right was questioned, he insisted that it was his prerogative and went to Lincoln for a legal opinion on the point. After hearing the facts, Lincoln said, "No, Uncle Billy, you have no right to issue marriage licenses." To which the irate functionary replied, "Abe, I thought you were a lawyer, but now I know you are not. I have been doing it right along."

As President he became the fountainhead of military justice and the court of last resort. His was the power of review over the decisions of all the military courts. He was the court of final appeal in cases of soldiers condemned for mutiny or desertion. Every death warrant had to be signed by him; and so to his office came a steady stream of parents, relatives, and friends of the doomed, imploring mercy.

Stern when the occasion demanded, yet his heart was as warm as that of a mother towards her babe. To a mother tearfully supplicating on bended knees for her son, the tall-powerful Civil War President was heard to say, "Please go, your son will live; only go, if you don't want to have me sob." To a father he said,

"If your son lives till I will order him to be shot he will live as long as Methuselah."

Somehow he saw to it that the severe and drastic rules of war were tempered with mercy. Extenuating circumstances were given weight; first offenders were given special consideration; ignorance of the law often was accepted as an excuse; freedom was offered in exchange for an oath of allegiance; the drastic laws for the confusion of the property of disloyal persons were enforced with discretion; and somehow deserters were allowed to escape the death penalty. To a commander who warned the merciful President that he was destroying discipline by refusing to carry out the stern decisions of war, he said: "General, there are too many weeping widows in the United States now. For God's sake, don't ask me to add to the number, for I tell you plainly I won't do it."

A man endowed with these attributes of kindness blended with statecraft, mercy with shrewdness, incorruptibility, coolness, humor, and knowledge of men would well have graced the bench of his State or Nation.

XIV. PROSECUTOR, BAR EXAMINER, AND ADVISOR TO PUBLIC OFFICIALS

LINCOLN'S outstanding ability as a lawyer brought him many professional honors in addition to the occasional appointments as temporary judge of the circuit court. Often he served by appointment as a special aid to local prosecutors confronted with difficult cases, or as a substitute for the State's attorneys during their absence or illness. Municipalities frequently called upon him to represent them as town solicitor when important litigation arose, or to furnish legal opinions to guide their officers. Then, too, for a number of years he served as an official examiner of applicants for the bar of Illinois.

The office of prosecutor in those early days was far from important. The pay was ridiculously meager, and as a result only young, inexperienced, or inferior lawyers would accept the position. In consequence only a small fraction of the grand jury indictments resulted in convictions. It was necessary for the State's attorney to be present at the impaneling of every jury and grand jury. If he were not there the presiding judge appointed a prosecutor *pro tem* who was paid out of the regular prosecutor's salary. But when an important case arose, it was usual for the

161

relatives of interested parties to employ an experienced member of the bar to assist or advise the young State's attorney. In this manner Lincoln received many a retainer.

In Menard County he was called upon to prosecute the two Denton brothers, indicted for the murder of their brother-in-law, named Brown. There had been a family quarrel. Axes had been used, and when the fray was over Brown lay dead. The prosecution could find no witnesses who had seen the fight, and Lincoln felt a conviction was next to impossible. He was acquainted with every member of the jury and knew they were not the kind to convict the brothers on mere circumstantial evidence. "I would like to throw the whole panel out, for I know every single one of them; but I can't object to a man among them," Lincoln declared to the associate prosecutor. He had no desire to try the case, so he merely acted as advisor while the prosecutor questioned the witnesses and argued to the jury. As Lincoln had predicted, the defendants were speedily acquitted.

Early in 1857, while attending circuit court at Bloomington, Lincoln was appointed to prosecute Isaac Wyant on the charge of murdering Anton Rusk. Leonard Swett, who had been retained as counsel for the defense, entered a plea of insanity on behalf of his client. Lincoln believed that the accused was only feigning the loss of his mentality and strenuously opposed the plea. He spoke for five hours to the jury in the concluding argument for the prosecution. Before the termination of this trial, both Lincoln and Swett received permission to go to Danville to attend to other business. Here Joseph E. McDonald, an attorney, overheard them and some others just returned from the adjoining county discussing various features of the case. McDonald was amazed to learn that the defendant was none other than his old friend Isaac Wyant, who had formerly resided in Indiana.

"I told them," relates McDonald, "that I had been Wyant's counsel frequently and had defended him from almost every charge in the calender of crimes; and that he was a weak brother and could be led into almost everything. At once Lincoln began to manifest great interest in Wyant's history, and had to be told all about him. The next day on the way to the courthouse he told me he had been greatly troubled over what I had related about Wyant; that his sleep had been disturbed by the fear that he had been too bitter and unrelenting in his prosecution of him. 'I acted,' he said, 'on the theory that he was "possuming" insanity, and now I fear I have been too severe and that the poor fellow may be insane after all. If he cannot realize the wrong of his crime, then I was wrong in aiding to punish him.' "[1]

The jury found Wyant not guilty.[2]

On another occasion Lincoln acted as prosecutor in a case where the defendant was charged with the theft of his neighbor's chickens. He secured a conviction. The following morning, as he rode along the highway bound for the next county seat, the foreman of the jury cantered by alongside to compliment him on the able and vigorous manner in which he had conducted the prosecution. "Why, when the country was young and I was stronger than I am now, I didn't mind backing off a sheep now and again," the juror remarked. "But stealing hens!"—words failed him in expressing his contempt for so petty a thief.

On March 28, 1860, less than two months before the Republican Party was to choose him to be its standard-bearer for the Presidency, we find Lincoln writing to Ward H. Lamon:

"Yours about motion to quash the indictment was received yesterday. I think I had no authority but the statute when I wrote the indictment—in fact I remember but little about it. I think yet there is no necessity for setting out the letter in *haec verba*. Our statute as I think releases the high degree of technical certainty formerly required.

"I am so busy with our case on trial here that I cannot examine authorities here as fully as you can do there. If after all the indictment shall be quashed it will prove that my forte is as a statesman rather than a prosecutor."[3]

During the fifties the State Supreme Court appointed Lincoln as a member of the board of examiners of applicants for admis-

[1] Herndon and Weik, *Lincoln*, II, 344.
[2] Angle, *Lincoln, 1854 1861*, p. 170.
[3] Tracy, *Letters*, p. 36.

sion to the Illinois bar. This office he held until the approximate date of his election to the Presidency.

It is to be remembered that Lincoln himself never was required to submit to any kind of examination when admitted to the practice of law. On March 1, 1841, the Supreme Court of Illinois adopted a rule requiring all applicants, excepting those who already had been admitted to the bar in some court of record in the United States, to appear in person in open court and undergo a test of their qualifications to practice law in the courts of Illinois. Although serving as one of the examiners, Lincoln never had much faith in the efficacy of the conventional question-and-answer type of test to determine a man's fitness for any position.

Later, as President, he wrote this characteristic letter to his Secretary of War: "I personally wish Jacob Freese, of New Jersey, to be appointed colonel for a colored regiment, and this regardless whether he can tell the exact shade of Julius Caesar's hair."

He was very lenient with applicants for the bar. On one occasion, he wrote to the presiding judge of a circuit: "Your honor, I think this young man knows as much about law as I did when I began to practice, and I recommend his admission to the bar."

Probably typical of the examination imposed upon students is the one described by Jonathan Birch, of Bloomington, who had arranged with Lincoln to examine him for admission to the bar. After adjournment of the circuit court at Bloomington, Birch went to Lincoln's hotel room.

"I knocked at the door of his room, and was admitted," he related, "but I was hardly prepared for the rather unusual sight that met my gaze. Instead of finding my examiner in the midst of books and papers, as I had anticipated, he was partly undressed, and, so far as the meager accommodations of the room permitted, leisurely taking a bath! I shall never forget the queer feeling that came over me as his lank, half-nude figure moved to and fro between me and the window on the opposite side of the room. Motioning me to be seated, he began his interrogatories at once, without looking at me a second time to be sure of the identity of his caller.

" 'How long have you been studying?' he asked. 'Almost two

years,' was my response. 'By this time, it seems to me,' he said laughingly, 'you ought to be able to determine whether you have in you the kind of stuff out of which a good lawyer can be made. What books have you read?' I told him, and he said it was more than he read before he was admitted to the bar.

"He then told me a story of something that befell him in a county in Southern Illinois where he once tried a case in which he was pitted against a college-bred lawyer. 'This lawyer was highly accomplished and the court and all the lawyers were greatly impressed by his erudition, but it was all lost on the jury and they were the fellows I was aiming at,' laughed Lincoln.

"Then he resumed the examination. He asked me in a desultory way the definition of a contract, and two or three fundamental questions, all of which I answered readily, and I thought, correctly. Beyond these meager inquiries, as I now recall the incident, he asked nothing more.

"As he continued his toilet, he entertained me with recollections—many of them characteristically vivid and racy—of his early practice and the various incidents and adventures that attended his start in the profession. The whole proceeding was so unusual and queer, if not grotesque, that I was at a loss to determine whether I was really being examined at all or not. After he had dressed we went down-stairs and over to the clerk's office in the courthouse, where he wrote a few lines on a sheet of paper, and, inclosing it in an envelope, directed me to report with it to Judge Logan, another member of the examining committee, at Springfield. The next day I went to Springfield, where I delivered the letter as directed. On reading it, Judge Logan smiled, and, much to my surprise, gave me the required certificate without asking a question beyond my age and residence, and the correct way of spelling my name. The note from Lincoln read:

" 'My dear Judge:—The bearer of this is a young man who thinks he can be a lawyer. Examine him, if you want to. I have done so, and am satisfied. He's a good deal smarter than he looks to be.' "[1]

---

[1] Collated from accounts of Weik, *The Real Lincoln*, pp. 132–33; *Outlook Magazine*, vol. 97, pp. 311–14, "A Student's Recollection of Abraham Lincoln"; *Century Magazine*, XVII, 670, "Lincoln as an Advocate."

Hiram W. Beckwith, who studied law in the Danville office
of Lincoln and Lamon, presented himself for examination to a
committee consisting of the Springfield lawyer and Lawrence
Swett. Another student by the name of George W. Lawrence was
tested the same day. After examining them, Lincoln wrote out
but one recommendation of admission for the two applicants,
and after Swett signed it, handed it to the young men. It read:
"We have examined Hiram W. Beckwith and George W. Lawrence touching their qualifications to practice law; and find them
sufficiently qualified to commence the practice, and therefore
recommend that Licenses be allowed them."[1]

Only a few months before the Republican Party named him
as its candidate for the Presidency, Lincoln found time to serve
with L. W. Ross and O. H. Browning in examining Henry S.
Greene at Springfield. January 28, 1860, they questioned the
young man as to his knowledge of the law and handed him a
note reading: "We, the undersigned, report that we have examined Henry S. Greene and find him well qualified to practice as
an attorney and counsellor at law. We, therefore, recommend that
he be licensed as such." Lincoln, being the head of the examining board, signed first.

Lincoln's ability and reputation as a lawyer brought him retainers from municipalities, counties, and public officials when they
were involved in serious litigation or in need of legal opinions
or interpretation of controversial points of law concerning their
affairs. Thus, when the officials of the city of Springfield were
in doubt as to the legality of accepting its own script from a
citizen as payment of his fine for violation of an ordinance, they
engaged Lincoln to represent the municipality in the resulting
litigation in the State Supreme Court.[2]

Laws determining the functions of municipal corporations were
still unsettled, and when the question arose whether the City of
Alton could legally issue bonds for the grading and improvement
of its streets, town officials retained Logan & Lincoln to obtain
an adjudication. Lincoln argued the question in the United States

[1] Angle, *Lincoln, 1854–1861*, p. 129.
[2] City of Springfield vs. Hickox, 7 Ill. 241.

Circuit Court at Springfield, and helped settle the law which places this function within the powers of a municipal corporation.[1]

When Mary Macready was badly injured by a fall on an old defective cellar door in front of a grocery-store in Alton, she retained Lincoln to sue the town for her damages. Lincoln called on the mayor, Joseph Brown, to discuss the matter. Claiming that his client had been permanently lamed, Lincoln thought that she ought to be paid five thousand dollars for her injuries, but she said to the mayor, "I don't like to take this suit against your town; can't we compromise it in some way?" Mayor Brown replied that he did not think the city was liable for an injury resulting from bad cellar doors in front of private property.

A year before, Lincoln, as attorney for one Browning, had brought suit against the City of Springfield in the Sangamon Circuit Court to recover damages for injuries sustained by Browning when he fell on a faulty sidewalk. When the trial court ruled that the municipality was not liable the case was appealed to the Supreme Court. Herndon argued the appeal and the Supreme Court reversed the lower tribunal. Lincoln & Herndon's client eventually was awarded seven hundred dollars, and the decision became a leading authority on municipal law.[2] Now Lincoln tried to convince Mayor Brown that the city of Alton was responsible for the condition of its sidewalks and that Mrs. Macready would recover judgment.

"I think it is best to compromise if we can," the lawyer insisted. "How much will you give the lady? She is lamed for life with a stiff ankle."

After dickering for several minutes Lincoln offered to accept fifteen hundred dollars.

Jokingly the town official asked, "If we give the fifteen hundred dollars, are we to have the limb?"

To which Lincoln, never to be outdone in a match of wits, replied that if his client was satisfied, and "if you are an unmarried man you can have the entire woman!"

---

[1] Sturtevant vs. City of Alton, 3 McLean 568.
[2] Browning vs. City of Springfield, 17 Ill. 143.

Apparently Mayor Brown rejected both the compromise and the offer of marriage, as on April 17, 1858, the firms of Lincoln & Herndon and Browning & Bushnell filed suit for Mrs. Macready in the United States Circuit Court at Springfield, demanding five thousand dollars damages from the City of Alton. Two months later, after a trial lasting two days, a jury awarded her three hundred dollars.

In the autumn of 1854, when a controversy arose whether the City of Springfield or the County of Sangamon was to pay the expense of caring for paupers, these political divisions turned to Lincoln for a legal opinion to settle the question. His decision to the perplexed officials was that the city must bear the cost. On a later occasion he was retained by the same county to furnish a legal opinion pertaining to the sale of swamp lands.

He appeared in several cases involving the location of county seats, and helped establish new and important principles of law for that pioneer period.[1] The town of Petersburg retained him in the litigation that arose over the construction of its new charter.[2] And the organizers of the new town of Delevan sought his opinion concerning the validity of an election held in the town. At the end of his opinion Lincoln wrote, "Five dollars is a sufficient fee."

He was called upon to advise Mr. Powell, the State Superintendent of Public Instruction, concerning a contemplated contract for the introduction of district school libraries. Henry B. Blackwell, representing a firm of New York publishers who proposed to supply the books, related that he and Mr. Powell met Lincoln as he as coming out of the courthouse in Springfield "with his green bag in his hand. Greeting us cordially he took up our affair, giving us the advice we sought, but with characteristic unselfishness he declined to accept compensation for his legal services on a question of public interest."[3]

At different times Lincoln furnished legal opinions or appeared

---

[1] Adams vs. County of Logan, II Ill. 336; Harris vs. Shaw, 13 Ill. 456; Turley vs. Country of Logan, 17 Ill. 151.

[2] Town of Petersburg vs. Metzker, 21 Ill. 205.

[3] Boston *Advertiser*, February 12, 1909.

in court on behalf of Lyman Trumbull, Illinois Secretary of State from 1841 to 1843;[1] Jesse K. Dubois, Auditor of State; Dr. James H. Higgins, medical superintendent of the Illinois State Hospital; Z. A. Enos, a newly elected county surveyor in doubt as to his right to collect certain fees; Christian County;[2] Peoria County;[3] and the State of Illinois.[4]

At the request of Governor William H. Bissell and Secretary of State Ozias M. Hatch, Lincoln appeared in the Illinois Supreme Court to resist a writ of mandamus aimed against the Secretary of State, which sought to test the validity of an act of the legislature that the Governor had inadvertently endorsed "approved" but which he had actually intended to veto. It was an important political contest, and three of the most prominent Democratic lawyers, Goudy, McClernand, and Blackwell, opposed Lincoln and his associate counsel, Jackson Grimshaw of Quincy.[5]

Again, when the Governor and State Treasurer of Illinois were in doubt about a new law requiring them to issue bonds to pay the state debt, they requested Lincoln and his former law partner, Judge Logan, to furnish a legal opinion interpreting the law and their powers thereunder.

Such retainers were indeed important training for Lincoln. The problems they presented necessitated a thorough study of various phases of government functions, both local and state. Interpreting point of law for township, county, and state officials kept him in intimate touch with public questions to which he otherwise might have paid little attention. It was a schooling in public affairs that happily augmented the training he received as an assemblyman and as a member of Congress. It was a preparation for the rapidly approaching time when he was to make clear to the greatest of all his clients—the American Nation—the effect of the Dred Scott decision and the interpretation of the Constitution itself.

[1] Trumbull vs. Campbell, 8 Ill. 502.
[2] County of Christian vs. Overholt, 18 Ill. 223.
[3] Campher vs. The People, 12 Ill. 290.
[4] The People vs. Ridgely, 21 Ill. 65.
[5] The People vs. Hatch, Secretary of State, 19 Ill. 283.

XV. RAILROAD AND BIG BUSINESS LAWYER

THE years during which Lincoln practiced law were not only a formative era in Illinois jurisprudence, but to a marked degree a period of industrial development as well. Of course, for the greater part of the period between 1837 and 1860, that State remained chiefly an agricultural country. Great commercial and manufacturing interests were still unknown. But with the recovery of confidence and credit that followed the panic of 1837, the retirement of the State from all internal improvement schemes, the transfer of the Illinois and Michigan canal to the holders of the bonds which the State had sold in order to carry on that project, and the issuing of charters and generous land grants in favor of railroad building enterprises, there arose a new era with new developments and new problems.

Justice Caton, discussing the unprecedented growth of corporations, said in the course of an able opinion in one of Lincoln's most important cases:

"Indeed, their multiplication is astounding, if not alarming. It may be, and probably is, true that more private corporations were

170

created by our own legislature at its last session than existed in the whole civilized world at the commencement of the present century."[1]

About the time that Lincoln was returning to Springfield to busy himself in the law after his disheartening two years in Washington as a congressman, the first Illinois railroad, with the exception of one other feeble primitive attempt, was worming its way out of Chicago. Within ten years most of the trunk-lines of the present systems were well established. Farmers, storekeepers, and landowners speculated in the new internal development projects. Townships, municipalities, and counties vied with one another in making concessions to the infant roads and subscribing for the capital stock, until their credit was practically ruined. New and serious problems arose. The powers of the railroads and other corporations had to be defined: the rights of individual landowners whose property was being affected had to be determined. A flood of new litigation swamped the courts. For most of the questions no guiding cases or precedents could be found in the reported cases of other jurisdictions, and the solutions had to be evolved from the general principles of law.

The leading lawyers of the State were retained in litigation on behalf of and against the railroads. Stephen A. Douglas, who as a United States Senator had introduced a bill authorizing a grant of public lands to the State of Illinois to aid in the building of the Illinois Central, became one of the lawyers of the railroad. O. H. Browning handled cases for the Chicago, Burlington & Quincy, Norman B. Judd for the Rock Island, Joseph Gillespie for the Alton, and Judge Logan for the Illinois River Railroad Company.

Lincoln, forging to the front, became legal counsel for some of the largest interests doing business in Illinois. Never was he unwilling to appear on behalf of a "great soulless corporation," according to Whitney. When in a case that he and Lincoln were trying for a railroad, the opposing counsel sought to win the jury's favor by emphasizing that the plaintiff was a "flesh-and-blood man with a soul like the jurymen had," while their

---

[1] The St. Louis, Alton & Chicago Railroad Company vs. Dalby, 19 Ill. 353, in which Lincoln with great success appeared for Dalby.

client was a "soulless corporation," Lincoln in his argument declared:

"Counsel avers that his client has a soul. This is possible, but from the way he has testified under oath in this case, to gain, or hope to gain, a few paltry dollars, he would sell, nay, has already sold, his little soul very low. But our client is but a conventional name for thousands of widows and orphans whose husbands' and parents' hard earnings are represented by this defendant, and who possesses souls which they would not swear away as the plaintiff has done for ten million times as much as is at stake here."

In addition to railroad corporations, Lincoln numbered among his clients municipal corporations, banks, gas companies, insurance companies, and large manufacturing and commercial concerns. It is a glowing tribute to his ability and rising reputation as a lawyer that these interests, financially able to employ the finest legal talent, so often entrusted their important affairs to him.

Among Lincoln's affluent clients were Nichalos H. Ridgely, Springfield banker and capitalist interest in the Gas Light Works which were laying many miles of pipe in the Sangamon district; the Bank of Illinois interests; Tinkham & Company's Bank, the Bank of the Republic of McLeansboro, McLean County Bank, the Bank of Missouri, Morgan County Bank, Bank of Commerce, Lafayette Bank, Bank of Indiana, Delaware Mutual Safety Insurance Co., the North American Insurance Co., Columbus Machine Manufacturing Co., S. C. Davis & Co., St. Louis merchants, and Page & Bacon, bankers and financiers of St. Louis.

However, Lincoln could hardly have been designated as a "corporation lawyer" in the sense that we understand that term today, as with the possible exception of the Illinois Central Railroad his connections with those corporate interests were not continuous. One day he might be representing a corporation and the next day file an action against it on behalf of a private individual. There has been some question whether or not his arrangement with his largest and most remunerative corporation client, the Illinois Central, was a continuous one. Although present-day officials of that corporation maintain that Lincoln's employment by the railroad was permanent in the sense that all of its business in the Springfield vicinity regularly was referred to him, it is obvious from the writings of Whitney, who collaborated with Lincoln in a number of these cases, that the Springfield lawyer could best be designated as one of the road's local counsel with no definite and regular employment. Practicing in the state capital and the seat of the Supreme Court, the cases assigned to him were practically the most important of the company's litigation.

In addition to the Illinois Central, Lincoln also represented the Ohio & Mississippi, The Rock Island, the Chicago, Alton & St. Louis, the Tonica & Petersburg, and the Alton & Sangamon Railroads.

The first corporation litigation in which Lincoln engaged consisted of two cases in which he represented the Alton & Sangamon Railroad. The litigation involved the very important question of the right of a subscriber to the capital stock of a company to be released upon a modification of the corporation charter. In these cases the subscribers sought to evade liability on their stock agreements because the route of the railroad was changed so that instead of running past their land, as originally planned, it was located several miles away. The Supreme Court, holding with Lincoln, ruled the subscribers liable on the theory that a railroad company may adopt a change of route provided that the change does not make an improvement of a different character from the one originally planned. These cases set an important legal precedent that was followed often by other courts.[1]

Several months later, Lincoln again represented the Alton in two more very important Supreme Court cases. Through them he helped determine the law regarding the question of estimating the measure of damages suffered by an owner whose land is condemned for a railroad right of way.[2]

His success in the Alton & Sangamon unpaid subscription cases brought him similar retainers from other railroads that were

[1] Banet & Alton & Sangamon Railroad, 13 Ill. 504; Klein vs. Alton & Sangamon Railroad, 13 Ill. 514.

[2] Alton & Sangamon Railroad Co. vs. Carpenter, 14 Ill. 190; Alton & Sangamon Railroad Co. vs. Baugh, 14 Ill. 211.

endeavoring to enforce stock subscription agreements, while individuals who wanted to be released from their stock contracts also sought his services.[1]

In the first known case in which Lincoln appeared against a railroad, John B. Watson retained the firms of Lincoln & Herndon and Stuart & Edwards to institute suit against the Sangamon & Morgan Railroad for a balance of $93,450 due for railroad crossties sold and delivered.

Lincoln and Grant Goodrich appeared in the Supreme Court on behalf of Judge Isaac G. Wilson, against whom the Chicago, Burlington & Quincy Railroad filed an application for a mandamus because he refused to appoint commissioners to condemn lands for railroad shops, turnouts, and depots, and fix the compensation therefore.[2]

All these cases furnished pioneer decisions affecting railroad construction and became precedents for numerous future decisions.

On a number of occasions Lincoln appeared in the courts in connection with huge railroad finance controversies.

One day at the March term, 1856, of the United States Court for the Southern District of Illinois, he represented the Chicago, Alton & St. Louis Railroad in three suits alleging debts of over four hundred thousand dollars due from the railroad. These claims were allowed.[3]

The following day he appeared in the same court in connection with another railroad finance case. This time his client was the Ohio and Mississippi Railroad, against which a claim of nearly a third of a million dollars was filed. Lincoln for the railroad confessed judgment. It was a friendly suit intended for the purpose of correcting the title to some of the road's property.

On another occasion, in the federal court case of Allen & McGrady vs. Illinois River Railroad, he filed a declaration claim-

---

[1] Tonica & Petersburg Railroad Co. vs. Stein, 21 Ill. 96; Sprague vs. Illinois River Railroad Co., 19 Ill. 174; Terre Haute & Alton Railway Co. vs. Earp, 21 Ill. 291.

[2] Chicago, Burlington & Quincy Railroad vs. Wilson, 17 Ill. 123.

[3] Angle, *Lincoln, 1854–1861,* pp. 114, 116.

ing a debt and damages in the sum of eight hundred thousand dollars under a contract whereby the plaintiffs grubbed and cleared trees along the railroad's right of way and graded it, constructed embankments, ditches, bridges, culverts, and trestles, and supplied the crossties. The suit resulted from the railroad's failure to fulfill its part of the contract.[1]

As Springfield attorney for the Chicago & Mississippi Railroad, successor to the Alton & Sangamon, Lincoln had been furnished a pass that allowed him free transportation on its lines. When that privilege expired, on February 13, 1856, he wrote to an official of the road for a renewal in this characteristic manner:

"Says Tom to John, 'Here's your old rotten wheelbarrow. I've broken it, usin' on it. I wish you would mend it, case I shall want to borrow it this afternoon.'

"Acting on this as a precedent, I say, 'Here's your old "chalked hat." I wish you would take it, and send me a new one, case I shall want to sue it by the first of March.' "

The "chalked hat" referred to the custom of the railroad conductors of placing a white ticket in the headgear of passengers who had paid their fare.

Incidentally it was against this road, after changing its name to the St. Louis, Alton & Chicago Railroad Company, that Lincoln in 1857 filed what was probably the most far-reaching case he ever argued in the Illinois Supreme Court. Representing Joseph II, Dalby and his wife Sarah, Lincoln sued the railroad for damages because the conductor and brakeman had outrageously assaulted them and ejected them from a train because they refused to pay the regular cash fare. Conclusive evidence was introduced that the Dalbys had attempted to purchase tickets, but the station agent had none to the point of their destination. They offered to pay the price of the tickets, but the conductor would accept nothing but the extra cash fare. The question arose whether an action for assault and battery could be maintained against a corporation for the act of its agents while acting in the scope of their employment. A verdict for one thousand dollars was recovered by the Dalbys, but they remitted five hundred

[1] *Ibid.*, p. 287.

dollars of this amount. In affirming the decree of the trial court, the supreme tribunal, in a lengthy and well-considered opinion holding the railroad responsible for such acts of its duly authorized agents, established the rule of law that was to govern the numberless accident cases that later followed.[1]

Only a few months after he had defeated the St. Louis, Alton & Chicago Railroad in the Dalby case, Lincoln must have felt highly flattered to receive a call from that corporation requesting him to represent it in a certain court procedure. The man then in charge of the road operations was Joel F. Matteson, formerly Governor of Illinois, and an ardent Douglas Democrat. His employment of Lincoln was strange indeed, as only two years before, he, Lincoln, and Lyman Trumbull had been rivals for the United States senatorship, and when Lincoln's supporters in the General Assembly were beginning to desert him and go over to Governor Matteson, the Sangamon lawyer and his loyal followers threw their strength to Trumbull instead; as a result, Matteson was badly defeated.

On November 25, 1858, shortly after his contest with Douglas, Lincoln wrote to Matteson:

"Last summer, when a movement was made in court against your road, you engaged us to be on your side. It has so happened that so far we have performed no service in the case, but we lost a cash fee offered us on the other side. Now, being hard run, we propose a little compromise. We will claim nothing for the matter just mentioned if you will relieve us at once from the old matter at the Marine and Fire Insurance Company, and be greatly obliged to boot. Can you not do it?"[2]

Lincoln's most remunerative case is the now famous suit of the Illinois Central Railroad vs. the County of McLean.[3] Its prominence in the life story of Lincoln comes not so much from the important rule of law established as from an incident altogether collateral to the case itself. This was the fact that for his services

---

[1] The St. Louis, Alton & Chicago Railroad vs. Dalby, 19 Ill, 353; L. B. Stringer, *History of Logan County, Illinois,* pp. 322–23.

[2] Nicolay and Hay, *Works,* v. 96.

[3] 17 Ill. 291.

he received, after being forced to resort to litigation to collect it, a fee of five thousand dollars—by far the largest of his entire career. This unusual law fee is entitled to an important place in American history, as it enabled Lincoln to finance his historic political campaigns soon to follow.

As an inducement to the promoters of the Illinois Central Railroad Company to undertake and complete the vast project, the legislature of the State of Illinois had passed a law deeding to the railroad large tracts of public lands acquired from the Federal Government. It also embodied in the elaborate charter granted to the corporation a provision by which the Illinois Central would be exempted from taxation of all its property for a period of six years. In lieu thereof, the company was to pay the State 7 per cent of its gross income.

Under the arrangement, the promoters commenced the construction of the road in 1851. Two years later a section of the railroad between La Salle and Bloomington was completed, and shortly thereafter officials of McLean County demanded that the Illinois Central pay to that county a tax assessment on all its property within McLean County. These officers contended that the road's charter exempted it from state taxes but not from levies for county purposes. The very existence of the Illinois Central depended upon its ability to prove McLean County wrong, for if that county were successful in its attempt then every other county, township, and school district through which the road ran would also be entitled to make similar assessments for local taxation and the Illinois Central would likely be bankrupted while still in its infancy. The impending litigation was of vast importance for both the railroad corporation and the political divisions.

McLean County officials, sensing the importance of the matter, apparently in an unofficial manner consulted Lincoln regarding it. But when shortly afterward Lincoln received an offer to become counsel for the railroad, he hurriedly wrote to T. R. Webber, county clerk, that the county had the first right to his services; but in fairness to himself he should be informed at once whether or not the county would actually retain him.

"The question in its magnitude to the Co. on the one hand and the counties in which the Co. has land on the other," Lincoln wrote, "is the largest law question that can now be got up in the State, and therefore in justice to myself I can not afford, if I can help it, to miss a fee altogether. If you choose to release me, say so by return mail, and there an end. If you wish to retain me, you better get authority from your court, come directly over in the stage and make common cause with this county."

After waiting eighteen days without receiving an answer Lincoln wrote to Mason Brayman, the Chicago attorney for the railroad: "Neither the county of McLean nor any one on its behalf has yet made any engagement with me in relation to its suit with the Illinois Central Railroad on the subject of taxation. I am now free to make an engagement for the road, and if you think of it you may 'count me in.' Please write me on receipt of this. I shall be here at least ten days."

Within four days' time Brayman engaged Lincoln on behalf of the road and sent him a draft for two hundred dollars as a retainer. Thus Lincoln, associated with James F. Joy, general counsel of the road, and Brayman, found himself arrayed against John T. Stuart and Judge Logan, his two former partners, and Benjamin Edwards, retained by McLean County.

This was Lincoln's first big case for the Illinois Central, and he was very eager to make a good showing. It meant future business. In the circuit court he sought to enjoin McLean County from collecting the tax that had been assessed by the county assessor against the railroad. Meeting with an adverse ruling, he immediately appealed to the Supreme Court to reverse that finding. By agreement between counsel, it was stipulated that the only question for the Supreme Court to review was: Could McLean County tax the road despite its charter provisions specifically exempting it from taxation by the State; and further, was it constitutionally competent for the legislature to grant the exemption?

Lincoln prepared for the case with great thoroughness. Twice he argued it before the Supreme Court. The court's decision hinged on its construction of the constitutional provision for uniform taxation of all property. In a comprehensive opinion delivered by Justice Scates, the court finally ruled that it was within the constitutional powers of the legislature to make exceptions to that provision, and that the law exempting the railroad's property under the arrangement where in lieu of taxes ordinarily levied for county purposes, a gross sum to be ascertained by a fixed rule of compensation is ordered, is a proper exception to the rule of uniformity, and therefore constitutional.

The successful outcome of the case was a notable and important victory, and saved the company countless thousands of dollars it might otherwise have been compelled to pay in taxes to the twenty-six counties through which its lines ran or in which it owned property. Lincoln felt that considering the difficulty of the questions involved, the large pecuniary interests affected, and the success attained, his fee ought to be commensurate with the importance of the litigation.

Lincoln's own partner, Herndon, who shared in the fee, has written that after the completion of the litigation, "Mr. Lincoln soon went to Chicago and presented our bill for legal services. We only asked for $2000 more. The official to whom he was referred—supposed to have been the superintendent George B. McClellan, who afterwards became the eminent general—looking at the bill expressed great surprise. 'Why, sir,' he exclaimed, 'this is as much as Daniel Webster himself would have charged. We cannot allow such a claim.' Stung by the rebuff, Lincoln withdrew the bill, and started for home. On the way he stopped at Bloomington. There he met Grant Goodwich, Archibald Williams, Norman B. Judd, O. H. Browning, and other attorneys, who, on learning of his modest charge for such valuable services rendered the railroad, induced him to increase the demand to five thousand dollars, and to bring suit for that sum."[1]

The Illinois Central in its account of the affair makes no mention of the request for two thousand dollars, but insists that when "Mr. Lincoln presented a bill for his fee . . . for five thousand dollars, the general counsel of the road advised Mr. Lincoln that while he recognized the value of his services, the payment of so

[1] Herndon and Weik, *Lincoln*, II, 352.

large a fee to a western country lawyer without protest would embarrass the general counsel with the board of directors in New York, who would not understand, as would a lawyer, the importance of the case and the consequent value of Mr. Lincoln's services. It was intimated to Mr. Lincoln, however, that if he would bring suit for his bill in some court of competent jurisdiction and judgment were rendered in his favor, the judgment would be paid without appeal.''[1]

Lincoln commenced his suit in the Circuit Court of McLean County during the April term, 1857. On the morning of Thursday, June 18, 1857, the case came up for hearing before a jury in the Circuit Court, with Lincoln's friend, Judge Davis, presiding. Surprisingly, no one appeared on behalf of the Illinois Central. On the strength of his own testimony and the written opinion of the six lawyers who had certified the reasonableness of his charge, a default judgment was entered in Lincoln's behalf for the full amount of five thousand dollars. But it had not been the intention of the company to let the case go by default. Later in the day, too late to attend court, John M. Douglas arrived at Bloomington from Chicago. He explained that he had been unavoidably delayed and hoped Lincoln would not take advantage of the mishap. The Springfield lawyer quickly consented to vacating the entry of the default judgment, and the case was set for a rehearing five days later.

The trial was a mere formality and took but a few minutes. Lincoln briefly recited the history of the litigation and explained the services he had performed on behalf of the railroad. Then, with the consent of Attorney Douglas, he read to the jury the opinion of Lawyers Goodrich, Judd, Williams, Purple, Browning, and Blackwell that the services were reasonably worth five thousand dollars. Douglas reminded Lincoln of the retainer he had already received, the case was submitted without argument on either side, and a verdict was brought in for the balance of forty-eight hundred dollars.

The fee was promptly paid, and Lincoln deposited the funds

[1] John G. Drennan, *Abraham Lincoln as Attorney for the Illinois Central Railroad Company* (brochure).

with the Springfield Fire and Marine Insurance Company. Shortly afterwards the money was withdrawn so that Herndon could be paid his half.

When Lincoln came to the office with Herndon's share, he counted out the money and made a gesture of handing it to the junior partner. But before Herndon could reach for it, Lincoln said: "Hold on, Billy; how often have you stretched yourself out on that sofa and discoursed on how the corporations are strangling the life out of this nation? This is corporation money."[1]

Notwithstanding the corporation "taint" on the money, Herndon eagerly took it. "Much as we deprecated the avarice of great corporations, we both thanked the Lord for letting the Illinois Central Railroad fall into our hands," he explained.[2]

Lincoln invested his share in a real-estate mortgage yielding 10 per cent interest. Had he not received his fee when he did, it is doubtful whether he would have been financially able to neglect his profession the following year to make his extensive campaign against Douglas.

Shortly after the termination of his personal suit against the Illinois Central, Lincoln received a request from Attorneys James Steele and Charles Summers of Paris, Illinois, to represent their client in an error proceeding in the Supreme Court against the same road. Lincoln was then uncertain as to his future connection with the company, so he replied: "I have been in the regular retainer of the Co. for two or three years, but I expect they do not wish to retain me any longer. . . . I am going to Chicago if nothing prevents, on the 21st inst. and I will then ascertain whether they discharge me and if they do, as I expect, I will attend to your business and write you."

Despite his belief that the officials of the railroad would never forgive him for filing his personal suit, his employment was not terminated and he remained in the railroad's retainer until his election to the Presidency. Company records disclose that "he was consulted frequently and that his opinions were highly respected." So when the case that Steele and Summers invited him

---

[1] Newton, *Lincoln* and *Herndon*, p. 315.
[2] Herndon and Weik, *Lincoln*, II, 353.

to handle in their behalf reached the Supreme Court, Lincoln appeared in association with O.B. Ficklin and Henry C. Whitney as counsel for the Illinois Central and won a notable victory for the railroad. The question involved in this case[1] was of vast importance to both the business public and the railroad interests in general, in that it established the right of a railroad to restrict its liability to a shipper by express agreement. The decision has been cited many times in other courts, including the Supreme Court of the United States.

Shortly afterwards, in another damage suit against the Illinois Central for the death of some hogs caused by a delay in shipment, Lincoln again appeared on behalf of the railroad in association with Whitney. The evidence clearly showed that the company was to blame and the verdict of six hundred dollars against the railway was affirmed.[2]

The destruction of the steamboat *Effie Afton* on May 6, 1856, through its collision with a pier of the recently completed Rock Island railroad bridge which spanned the Mississippi, gave rise to the most notable of all of Lincoln's court cases. It was a test litigation, and attracted national attention. Not only did it involve a contest between the steamship and railroad interests competing for the transportation supremacy of the Nation, but it also reflected the bitter rivalry of river ports like Chicago for the commercial ascendance of the rapidly growing West.

The owners of the *Effie Afton* filed suit in the United States District Court at Chicago, demanding damages from the Railroad Bridge Company for the loss of their ship and cargo. The bridge, they insisted, was an obstruction to navigation. The company on its part maintained that the accident, so-called, was in fact an intentional and premeditated act. This accusation the ship-owners angrily denied. The impending litigation, officially docketed as Hurd vs. Railroad Bridge Company, promised to be the "battle of the century" for the competing transportation rivals.

Lincoln's friend, Norman B. Judd, was then general counsel and a leading director of the Rock Island Railroad. Meeting in

[1] Illinois Central Railroad vs. Morrison and Crabtree, 19 Ill. 136.
[2] Illinois Central Railroad Co. vs. Hays, 19 Ill. 166.

conference with the other directors, he urged the immediate retention of the Sangamon lawyer to take charge of the case. And
so the self-styled "mast-fed" lawyer became leading counsel for
the defense in a case that attracted the attention of the entire
country.

The questions involved were extremely complicated, embracing mechanical engineering, bridge construction, river currents
and their varying velocity, the size and navigation of vessels,
and other highly technical problems. But Lincoln was thoroughly prepared.[1]

For fourteen days witnesses testified—eye-witnesses, boat-
owners and builders, river-men, civil and government engi-
neers—all passing through the searching examination of the contending lawyers. The opponents of the bridge endeavored to
convince the jury that the river could not legally be obstructed
by a bridge, and that this particular one was so situated as to
constitute a constant peril to all boats navigating the river.

When at length both sides rested their case and began their
arguments to the jury, Lincoln in closing the arguments of the
defense arose to answer the contentions of the plaintiffs.

A river is like a street or highway, he explained. Just as every
person has the undeniable right to cross the highway or pass
along it, as he pleases, so "one man has as good a right to cross
a river as another has to sail up or down it." That being the
case, shall the mode of crossing the stream be forever limited?
"Must it always be by canoe or ferryboat? Must the products of
the boundless fertile country lying west of the river for all time

---

[1] Lincoln had previously argued two cases in the United States district court
involving the question of the obstruction of navigable rivers by the construction of bridges: Columbus Insurance Co. vs. Curtenius (6 McLean 209), and
Columbus Insurance Co. vs. The Peoria Bridge Association (6 McLean 70).
In the latter case Lincoln represented the insurers of a canal boat and cargo
that were destroyed when the boat struck the piers of a bridge erected by the
defendants over the Illinois River near Peoria. The plaintiff insurance company
paid the loss, and retained Lincoln to recover the amount from the builders
of the bridge.

The experience garnered in these cases proved most valuable in the later
Rock Island Bridge litigation.

be compelled to stop on its western bank, be unloaded from cars and loaded upon a boat, and after the transit across the river, be reloaded into cars on the other side, to continue their journey east?'' To continue this, he insisted, was to hinder the civilization of the great undeveloped West. The necessities of commerce and the progress of the country demanded the unhampered construction of bridges across the river.

Carefully he explained to the jury the currents of the river at the point where it was crossed by the bridge, and declared that the captain of the boat had failed to use reasonable care in piloting the *Effie Afton* past that point.

After an adjournment of court, Lincoln returned with a model of the *Effie Afton*; he discussed the mechanism of the vessel, and demonstrated that the failure of the starboard wheel to run properly was the primary cause of the crash. Another boat called the *Carson* had gone through the draw in perfect safety, he pointed out, but the *Effie Afton* had entered wrong, ''so far wrong that she never got right. Is the defense to blame for that?''

He gave the jury an opportunity to relax and smile when he said: ''For several days we were entertained with depositions about boats 'smelling a bar.' Why, then, did the *Afton*, after she had come up smelling so close to the long pier, sheer off so strangely? When she had got to the center of the very nose she was smelling, she seemed suddenly to have lost her sense of smell and to have slanked over the short pier.''[1]

Sarcastically he added: ''It is suggested as a way out of the difficulty that a tunnel be built under the river; but that is not practicable, for there is not a tunnel that is a successful project in this world. A suspension bridge cannot be built but that the chimneys of the boats will grow up till they cannot pass. The steamboat men will take pains to make them grow. The cars of a railroad cannot without immense expense rise high enough to get even with a suspension bridge or go low enough to get through a tunnel; such expense unreasonable.''

He talked long, but he knew when to stop. ''Gentlemen,'' he said to the jury in conclusion, ''I have not exhausted my stock

[1] Weik, *The Real Lincoln*, p. 186.

of information and there are more things I could suggest regarding this case, but as I have doubtless used up my time, I presume I had better close.''

Following a lengthy final argument for the plaintiff by Timothy D. Lincoln, Judge McLean charged the jury. After several hours of deliberation the jury divided nine to three in favor of the bridge and then reported they were unable to agree. Ascertaining that an agreement was impossible, the judge dismissed the jury. But the fight continued, and not until long after Lincoln had become President and was busied with the crushing burdens of the Civil War were the issues of this case finally determined by the Supreme Court of the United States.

Lincoln, the former assistant surveyor, displayed great interest in cases involving mathematical or mechanical problems. So we find him often in the federal district courts engaged in litigation over patent rights and infringements.

The most famous patent suit in which Lincoln participated was the case of McCormick vs. Manny.[1] This action was not only of vast importance to both the plaintiff and the defendant but also of great interest to the entire farm population of the country. Through this celebrated litigation Lincoln met a man who was to play an important rôle in his future career. He was Edwin M. Stanton, then a young and industrious lawyer of Pennsylvania and destined to become Lincoln's Secretary of War.

P. H. Warner, who had procured certain important reaping machine patents for John M. Manny & Company of Rockford, Illinois, visited Lincoln at his home in Springfield and explained that Cyrus H. McCormick had instituted in the United States Court for the Northern District of Illinois a suit against Manny for alleged infringement of patent rights. He requested Lincoln to join counsel for the defense. McCormick, who was endeavoring to restrain Manny from manufacturing reapers, also demanded damages in the sum of four hundred thousand dollars. Of course, Lincoln accepted the employment. He was paid an advance retainer of five hundred dollars, with an agreement for a substantial fee upon the completion of the litigation.

[1] 6 McLean 539, affirmed in 20 How. (61 U.S.) 402.

Like the *Effie Afton* case, this, too, was to be a test suit. Several of McCormick's competitors came to the financial assistance of Manny, and a large fund was placed at the disposal of the defense counsel to fight the issue to the limit. Each side employed an outstanding patent lawyer, McCormick retaining Edward M. Dickerson of New York, and the Manny interests, George Harding of Philadelphia. These leaders of the profession were to conduct the technical side of their respective cases. As associate counsel to argue the legal aspects of the controversy, the plaintiff retained that eminent lawyer, Reverdy Johnson, one of the giants of the American bar. For forensic counsel, Harding suggested that the defense employ his fellow Pennsylvanian, Stanton, then residing at Pittsburg.

Ralph Emerson of Rockwood, Illinois, a former law student who had abandoned the legal profession to become a member of the firm of Manny and Company, urged defense counsel to call in Lincoln as their associate because of his influence and standing in the Chicago courts. Emerson, by reason of frequent contacts with the Sangamon attorney, held the highest regard for his ability and judgment.

Thus Lincoln found himself associated with and arrayed against some of the ablest and most successful lawyers of the Nation. Watson gave Lincoln the impression that he was to deliver the closing argument for the defense, and Lincoln began to prepare accordingly.

July 23, 1855, Lincoln sent the following letter to Watson, who had gone to Washington:

"At our interview here in June, I understood you to say you would send me copies of the Bill and Answer in the case of McCormick vs. Manny & Co., and also of depositions, as fast as they could be taken and printed. I have had nothing from you since. However, I attended the U.S. Court at Chicago and while there, got copies of the Bill and Answer. I write this particularly to urge you to forward on to me the additional evidence as fast as you can. During August, and the remainder of this month, I can devote some time to the case, and of course I want all the material that can be had. During my stay at Chicago, I went out to Rockford, and spent half a day, examining and studying Manny's Machine.''

Anxious to be thoroughly prepared, he carefully studied the testimony that Watson sent him from time to time, and eagerly looked forward to the moment when he could match his forensic skill with the eminent Reverdy Johnson. But soon he met with a double disappointment. In the first place, by agreement of counsel, the case was removed from Chicago, where he was well known and had great influence in the District Court, and was set for trial in Cincinnati, where he would be a stranger. Secondly, his associates Harding, Stanton, and Watson, having no faith in the ability of the comparatively unknown Western lawyer to argue questions so highly technical as were involved in this action, reversed Watson's original suggestion that Lincoln close their case, and gave the assignment to Stanton instead.

Only when all the parties and lawyers met in Cincinnati was Lincoln first apprised of the decision that removed him from important participation in the case. His pride was hurt, and he was deeply disappointed; but he accepted the situation gracefully. Throughout his sojourn in the Ohio city, Lincoln was snubbed and ignored by Stanton; and in fact neither he nor Harding treated the Sangamon lawyer as though he had any further connection with the litigation. Immortality was awaiting the unpolished barrister from the prairies of Illinois, but how was Stanton to know it? Now this able lawyer of vehement impulses and ruthless indifferences to personal feelings felt only disdain for Lincoln's character and ability. Now he saw only the gaunt, awkward exterior and uncouth, rural clothes. He was yet to proclaim the man he was now snubbing and insulting as his master.

''His heart was as great as the world, but there was no room in it to hold the memory of a wrong,'' Emerson truly said of Lincoln; for not only was he to make Stanton his Secretary of War, but he was also to offer to Harding the important office of Commissioner of Patents.

Harding and Stanton won this famous case without Lincoln's assistance, but Watson sent the Springfield lawyer a two thousand dollar check for the balance of his fee. Refusing it at first because he had taken no part in the actual trial, he accepted it after Watson insisted that he was entitled to it for having prepared for the trial and for remaining in readiness. The entire incident was a most humiliating affair for Lincoln, and after Stanton concluded the case for the defense and court adjourned, Lincoln returned to Springfield crestfallen.

Only to Herndon did he confide what had occurred. "That man Stanton handled me pretty rough," he admitted. But never again did he allude to the subject.

Lincoln's last appearance before the State Supreme Court was on behalf of the Illinois Central. It was an action brought by the State of Illinois at the December term, 1859, against the railroad company to recover taxes assessed against the road by the State Auditor, inasmuch as the six-year period of exemption—the bone of contention in the McLean County case—had expired. State auditor Jesse K. Dubois, Lincoln's intimate friend, had assessed the property of the road at $19,711, 559 and fixed the tax at $132,067.41. Lincoln wrote to the auditor:

"Dear Dubois: M. M. Douglas of the I.C.R.R. Co. is here and will carry this letter. He says they have a large sum ($90,000) which they will pay into the treasury now, if they have an assurance that they shall not be sued before January 1859—otherwise not. I really wish you could consent to this. Douglas says they can not pay more and I believe him.

"I do not write this as a lawyer seeking an advantage for a client; but only as a friend, only urging you to do what I think I would do if I were in your situation. I mean this as private and confidential only, but I feel a good deal of anxiety about it."[1]

A test suit in the Supreme Court was deemed advisable to determine the basis of assessing the property; but not until the November term of 1861—nearly a half year after Lincoln had become the Nation's Chief Magistrate—did the Supreme Court finally decide the case.[2]

One of the most important cases that Lincoln argued in the federal courts was that of Johnston vs. Jones and Marsh. It is

[1] *Works*, II, 354.
[2] State vs. Illinois Central Railroad, 27 Ill. 64.

remembered as the famous sandbar litigation, and involved the title to extensive and valuable lake-front property created by accretion on the shores of Lake Michigan in or near Chicago.

The case first came to trial in 1855, and the district court's decision was reversed by the Supreme Court of the United States.[1]

At the second hearing the jury disagreed. When the third trial was called in 1860, Lincoln had risen to such eminence at the bar that the defendants, to enhance their chances for victory, invited the Springfield lawyer to join their staff of counsel.

Although nominally Lincoln appeared for the defendants William Jones and Sylvester Marsh, it was known that the real party in interest was one of the railroads operating in Illinois.

After a trial that lasted nearly two weeks during the end of March and beginning of April, 1860, a verdict was returned in favor of Lincoln's clients. His participation in the case had been the prevailing factor in the defense victory.[2]

One day during the trial, Isaac N. Arnold invited Judge Drummond and all the counsel on both sides to dine at his residence. Lincoln and Douglas were then active candidates for the presidential nomination of their respective parties. So when someone proposed the toast, "May Illinois furnish the next President," it was drunk with enthusiasm by the friends of both Lincoln and Douglas, related Mr. Arnold.[3]

A story exists that Lincoln's growing reputation as a corporation lawyer brought him the invitation to become the general counsel of the New York Central Railroad at an annual salary of ten thousand dollars. This offer is supposed to have been made by James B. Merwin, a cousin of and acting for Erastus Corning, a prominent financier and president of the powerful railway company. Mr. Corning became greatly impressed with Lincoln following his Cooper Institute address, and desired to engage his legal talents for the eastern corporation. But Lincoln refused the

---

[1] Jones vs. Johnston, 18 Howard 150.
[2] Whitney, *Life on the Circuit*, 254; Beveridge, *Abraham Lincoln, 1809–1858*, 1,597.
[3] Arnold, *Lincoln*, p.90.

tempting plum—if ever it was offered—to continue in the more alluring field of politics.[1]

Though this story may be apocryphal, it is indeed a glowing tribute to Lincoln's growth and his reputation as a lawyer.

The numerous retainers that came steadily from the corporations and important business interests speak volumes for the eminence he had attained in legal circles. These intimate relations with the powerful commercial and industrial interests of the period—ever factors of the greatest potency in the decisions of political bodies—contributed much to Lincoln's "availability" as the Republican Party's "man of the hour" at the historic presidential convention of 1860.

[1] "A Great and Fateful Decision," by Major J. B. Merwin, as told to Charles T. White, in the New York *Evening Sun*, February 12, 1917. John W. Starr, Jr., *Lincoln and the Railroads*, pp. 127–28.

XVI. HONEST, PRACTICAL, AND SHREWD

THE case of the People vs. Patterson was on trial in the Circuit Court of Champaign County. The large white-walled courtroom of unpainted woodwork and pine floors was crowded to capacity. Not a single seat was empty in the rows of crude wooden benches. Women in calico and sunbonnets sat with hard-faced frontier farmers and backwoodsmen in homespun jeans. All were listening intently. A murder trial was a rare treat for these pioneers and brought recreation, excitement, and intellectual stimulation into their drab and colorless lives.

Patterson, the accused murderer, pale as cellar-grown grass from long confinement in the county prison, huddled shrinkingly in his chair. His eyes gazed blankly upon the floor. Now and then he raised them and seeing the sheriff close by disconsolately let them fall again to the floor.

Orlando B. Ficklin and Ward H. Lamon, the State's attorneys, called witness after witness to the stand and adroitly wove a web of evidence that soon broke down the "presumption of innocence" which cloaked the prisoner.

On the defense side of the trial table sat Attorney Abraham Lincoln, Leonard Swett, and Henry C. Whitney. Lincoln, the senior counsel, appeared gloomy and dejected. Judge Davis, presiding, observed that the enthusiasm and buoyancy that marked his friend's countenance at the beginning of the trial was now gone.

Eyewitnesses recounted the sordid details of the crime. Others testified regarding circumstances that the prosecutors believed proved motive and intent. The tall sad-visaged defense lawyer from Springfield scrutinized the witnesses with his keen, penetrating, dreamy eyes and sought out the character of each.

For the most part his cross-examination of these witnesses was weak and spiritless. His lack of fighting spirit was a mystery to the courthouse crowd. They craved excitement, but the redoubtable Lincoln appeared submissive and destitute of enthusiasm or aggression.

At the end of the second day of the trial, Lincoln and Swett returned to their hotel room. They were discussing the case. The usually complacent Lincoln appeared greatly perturbed. He had accepted a fee to defend Patterson. He had believed in the accused's innocence and now he was firmly convinced the man was guilty. The discovery unnerved him.

What should he do? Abandon the case or go on with the defense? His conscience bothered him. It cried out that the cause he was advocating was contrary to justice. His duty, he felt, was loyalty to his client. But how far must this fidelity go? He had entered upon the case and had learned the innermost secrets of his client. Apparently Patterson had not told him all the facts. And yet the accused murderer's liberty, perhaps his life, depended upon the lawyer's faithfulness, his eloquence and skillfull advocacy. Was the lawyer honor-bound to stick by his client at all costs? Would it be right for him to forsake the accused man now?

The question was indeed perplexing.

Lincoln the lawyer knew that even the guilty are entitled equally with the innocent to a fair and legal trial. He knew that every accused person is entitled to counsel whose sacred duty it is to preserve for his client all rights and immunities secured by law, to object to the introduction of all improper testimony, to protest against erroneous instructions by the court, and to do all else within his power to prevent injustice from being perpetrated. Even if a number of witnesses swore the accused was guilty, how should the lawyer know positively that they told the truth? And even should the defendant himself admit his guilt, was there not to be taken into account the question of his sanity or criminal intent at the time of the offense?

Swett, Whitney, and other lawyers of their circuit could argue a bad case nearly as well as a good one. But not Lincoln. When his own conscience, acting as judge and jury, determined the client's guilt, or told him that he was on the wrong side of justice, he could not feign enthusiasm for the cause. He could not argue the case and convince the jury to do that which he himself felt was wrong.

"No man was stronger than he [Lincoln] when on the right side, and no man weaker when on the opposite," Whitney observed.

"You'll have to get some other fellow to win this case for you," Lincoln was heard to advise a prospective client who had "a pretty good cause in technical law, but a pretty bad one in equity and justice."

"I couldn't do it," he explained. "All the time while standing talking to that jury I'd be thinking, 'Lincoln, you're a liar,' and I believe I should forget myself and say it out loud."

Such was the compelling honesty of his nature.

He could not go on with the Patterson case. He felt he could not succeed in a case in which he did not believe. At length Lincoln turned to his associate.

"Swett," he said pleadingly, "the man is guilty. You defend him. I can't."

Swett demurred. He began to reason with his companion. But Lincoln added: "I am satisfied that our client is guilty and that the witnesses for the State have told the truth. It is my opinion that the best thing we can do for our client is to have him plead guilty to the lowest punishment."

Swett was not altogether surprised by this suggestion. But he refused to agree with it.

"Lincoln, you don't know what evidence I have in reserve to combat the witnesses of the State," he said.

"I don't care what evidence you've got, Swett," Lincoln replied. "The witnesses for the State have told the truth and the jury will believe them."

But Swett insisted that they go on with the trial. Lincoln returned to court but took no active part in the examination of the witnesses. He sat behind Swett and offered suggestions and advice. At length when it came time to argue the case to the jury, Swett, a very effective jury advocate, made a touching appeal for the acquittal of Patterson. Despite his protest, Lincoln was induced by his associates to make the closing argument.

"His logically honest mind chilled his efforts," Whitney believed. "While he made some good points, the honesty of his mental processes forced him into a line of argument and admission that was very damaging."

Lincoln's feeble, spiritless defense was useless. As he had predicted, the jury found Patterson guilty. Lincoln, Swett, and Whitney each received two hundred dollars as a fee.[1]

Contrary to popular belief, Lincoln did not abandon guilty clients in the midst of a case. Once in the case, he had no scruple against effort to acquit the client by all legal means. But as in the Patterson case, he preferred not to do it himself. He realized his weakness under such circumstances. He would have his associate argue the case while he served in an advisory capacity. He believed that in so doing he was more loyal to the best interests of the client than in making a spiritless and half-hearted fight.

"The framework of his mental and moral being was honesty, and a wrong cause was poorly defended by him," said Judge Davis. "The ability which some eminent lawyers possess of explaining away the bad points of a cause by ingenious sophistry, was denied him. In order to bring into full activity his great powers, it was necessary that he should be convinced of the matter which he advocated. When so convinced, whether the cause was great or small, he was usually successful.... Mr.

[1] Collated from accounts by Henry C. Whitney, *Life on the Circuit*, pp. 130–32, 136, 262, and Ward H. Lamon, Life of Abraham Lincoln, p. 322.

Lincoln thought his duty to his client extended to what was honorable and highminded, just and noble—nothing further."[1] "If you can say anything for the man, do it. I can't," Lincoln told S. C. Parks, with whom he was engaged in the defense of a man charged with larceny. During the course of the trial he had become convinced that the prisoner was guilty and ought to be convicted. But he did not abandon the case. He urged his co-counsel to conduct the argument, as he feared "the jury will see from my face the man is guilty and convict him."[2]

In another murder case, Swett pleaded with the jury to acquit the defendant because he was the father of several small children and his wife was about to give birth to another. Whitney says that Lincoln too adverted to the prisoner's family, "but only to disparage it as an argument, saying that the proper place for such appeals was to a legislature who framed laws, rather than to a jury who must decide upon evidence. In point of fact, our client was found guilty and sent to the penitentiary for three years; and Lincoln, whose merciless logic drove him into the belief that the culprit was guilty of murder, had his humanity so wrought upon that he induced the governor to pardon him after he had served one year."[3]

On one occasion Lincoln wrote to a client: "I do not think there is the least use of doing anything more with your lawsuit. I not only do not think you are sure to gain it, but I do think you are sure to lose it."

In a case where one of his own witnesses was evasive in his replies on cross-examination, Lincoln arose and, by permission of the trial judge, publicly and severely reprimanded the reluctant witness. "It was a dangerous experiment which might have brought discredit on our most important witness," said Anthony Thornton, who was Lincoln's associate in the case. "His object, however, was accomplished and the witness answered promptly all questions on cross-examination."[4]

[1] From Address of Judge David Davis, Indianapolis, May 19, 1865.
[2] Lamon, *Life of Abraham Lincoln*, p. 324.
[3] Whitney, *Life on the Circuit*, pp. 130-32; Weik, *The Real Lincoln*, pp. 193-94.
[4] Anthony Thornton in Chicago *Tribune*, February 12, 1900, p. 14.

As in his public career, so in the law, Lincoln "could look a long distance ahead and calculate the triumph of right."

"Such was the transparent candor and integrity of his nature that he could not well or strongly argue a side or a cause that he thought wrong," observed Judge Thomas Drummond. "Of course, he felt it his duty to say what could be said, and to leave the decision to others; but there could be seen in such cases the inward struggle of his own mind."[1]

To which should be added the additional observation of Whitney that "It was morally impossible for Lincoln to argue dishonestly. He could no more do it than he could steal. It was the same thing to him, in essence, to despoil a man of his property by larceny or by illogical, or flagitious reasoning; and even to defeat a suitor by technicalities, or by merely arbitrary law, savored strongly of dishonesty to him. He tolerated it sometimes, but always with a grimace."[2]

To Lincoln's indefatigable pursuit of the truth, his candor, and his fidelity to his convictions can be attributed much of his success at the bar. When a case engaged his moral sense, no matter if the law was clearly against him, his dynamic power of conviction and extraordinary sincerity often enabled him to overwhelm all the technicalities of the law, win over both judge and jury, and secure the verdict.

But the same inflexible and fastidious morality, oftentimes inconvenient, robbed him of much so-called success at the bar and also defined his limitations as a lawyer. His strict obedience to conscience weakened his usefulness to clients whenever their cause became incompatible with his sense of morals. Justice and truth were paramount with him, and he could not espouse an unjust cause. It was not in Lincoln's nature to bolster up a false position, nor could he simulate truth. Well-nigh irresistible when convinced his client was right, he was easily defeated when he became convinced he was wrong.

He believed that to be a real lawyer one had to be honest

---

[1] Nicolay and Hay, *Abraham Lincoln: A History*, I, 303–04; Barrett, *Life of Abraham Lincoln*, p. 818; Browne, *Abraham Lincoln*, pp. 235–36.

[2] Whitney, *Life on the Circuit*, p. 261.

intellectually as well as morally. He had no patience with the popular conception that no lawyer could be thoroughly honest.

"Let no young man, choosing the law for a calling, yield to that popular belief," he advised law students. "Resolve to be honest at all events. If in your judgment you cannot be an honest lawyer, resolve to be honest without being a lawyer. Choose some other occupation rather than one in the choosing of which you do in advance consent to be a knave."[1]

Once while attending circuit court at Bloomington, Lincoln was called upon by Judge Davis to express the censure and indignation of the profession to a youthful lawyer charged with unprofessional conduct. The young man regretfully admitted his indiscretion and with tears in his eyes beseeched Judge Davis to dismiss the disbarment proceedings and permit him to leave the bar and the county and start life anew in some other State. Inclined to grant the request, the judge was nevertheless determined that the lawyer who had disgraced his profession should not leave without first receiving a severe and open reproof for his offense.

Seeing Abraham Lincoln in the crowded courtroom and knowing well the lofty views he had developed concerning his chosen profession, Judge Davis called him to the bench and urged him to speak to the youth on behalf of the bar.

The Springfield lawyer had no desire to heap any more condemnation upon the head of the penitent youth. But he too felt that the offense was too grievous to be dismissed lightly. In a low voice that expressed the sorrow he felt, Lincoln addressed the recreant.

"Sir," he said, "you have polluted the ermine of this court of justice, that should be as pure and spotless as the driven snow or the light of the brightest stars in the firmament. Justice is not a fiction; and though it is often held to be a sentiment only, or a remote ideal, it is real, and it is founded and guarded on all sides by the strongest powers of Divine and human law. The court will not pronounce your disbarment; you have done that yourself. The people will trust no one, without sincere reforma-

---

[1] *Works*, II, 142.

tion, who has been wrong and reckless, as you admit, in one of the most confiding relations that ever exists between men.

"A client is in court by his lawyer so often and the custom so generally prevails that if he is not represented by honorable and trustworthy counsel, the right is of little value, and he is virtually denied the justice to which our laws entitle him. The Wisest has said that 'no man can serve two masters.' In your default you have used the information obtained in your preceptor's office while he was counsel for the plaintiff. You have done so when you were counsel for the defendant, his adversary in the action, using such information surreptitiously and without permission of the plaintiff, who fully confided in your preceptor as counsel and in you because of your relation of law student in his office. In this way you have been using the knowledge which you have gained from both parties in a way that no faithful and conscientious lawyer should do, and certainly very much to the detriment of one of them.

"A lawyer who becomes by his admission to the bar of any of our courts part of the judicial establishment of the land, should have integrity beyond question or reproach. Courts of law as of equity can sustain no other without themselves becoming venal and corrupt. A tarnished lawyer is a homeless man. Therefore, seek until you find a real reformation in honest work, and the court will approve."

When Abraham Lincoln finished these impromptu remarks the deep silence which prevailed in the courtroom was broken only by the soft sobbing of the contrite youth. The impressive words, so firm with reproof yet filled with genuine sympathy, had accomplished their purpose.

The older lawyer slowly walked over to the young man, took hold of his hand, and said, "We bid thee Godspeed in a work that will make you a better man." In sorrowful silence Lincoln then returned to his seat.[1]

Lincoln's extreme conscientiousness and intense veneration of the truth which prevented him from resorting to half-truths, subterfuges, sophistry, and appeals to prejudice in the trial of his

---

[1] Browne, *Abraham Lincoln and the Men of His Time*, p. 360.

causes have caused biographers to magnify his heart at the expense of his head.

Because he could not enthusiastically and wholeheartedly argue cases that clashed with his moral sense, nearly every writer who has given as much as a passing thought to Lincoln's career as a lawyer has endeavored to portray him as a heavenly agent of justice and a knight-errant of law and equity, who scorned the proffered fees of the rich and powerful in order to help the weak and distressed; who served them gratis or charged fees so ridiculously low as to gain the censure of contemporary lawyers for impoverishing the bar.

Lincoln's honesty is robbed of all human quality by eulogists who picture him as a lawyer perversely honest who refused all cases where there was the least doubt of his clients' innocence or question about their integrity; who admitted away many a case in order to concede the opposition its due. They endow him with god-like qualities while performing the dry-as-dust functions of his profession, and depict him as a lawyer who would never take advantage of the technicalities, expediencies, limitations, and fine protective points of the law.

This is far from being a true picture of Lincoln the lawyer.

He was a realist—shrewd, practical, and matter of fact.

Although he was eager to right a wrong whenever it was within his power to do so, it is not true that he went out of his way in search of cases of injustice to combat, nor that like Don Quixote he sought unduly to befriend the weak and oppressed from the ruthlessness of the powerful.

It is a great misconception that Lincoln was in the habit of foregoing his fee and withdrawing from every case in which there was a doubt of his success or question of his clients' honesty; nor is it to be inferred that he looked with suspicious scrutiny upon all cases that came into his office. Inherently honest himself, he suspected no guile in others. Like any other lawyer he welcomed the general run of business. Provided the case was not morally bad, he would accept it and endeavor to the best of his ability to win it.

"Mr. Lincoln would advise with perfect frankness about a

potential case," Whitney said, "but when it was *in esse*, then he wanted to win as badly as any lawyer; but unlike lawyers of a certain type he would not do anything mean, or which savored of sharp practice, or which required absolute sophistry or chicanery in order to succeed.

"As an attorney for the Illinois Central Railroad I had authority to employ additional counsel whenever I chose to do so, and in Judge Davis' circuit I frequently applied to Lincoln when I needed aid," Whitney adds. "I never found him unwilling to appear in behalf of a great 'soulless corporation.' In such cases he always stood by me, and I always of course, tried to win. There was nothing of the milksop about him, nor did he peer unnecessarily into a case to find some reason to act out of the usual line; but he had the same animus ordinarily as any other lawyer."[1]

Lincoln did not accept every case that came to him. "He is known to have been many times on the verge of quarreling with old and valued friends, because he could not see the justice of their claims, and, therefore, could not be induced to act as their counsel," Lamon recalls.[2]

On the circuit Lincoln frequently had to depend upon the local young lawyer with whom he was associated to prepare the case for trial. And when retained directly by the client, seldom had he sufficient time to probe deeply into the truth or falsity of the client's statements. More than once while in the midst of the trial of a case he discovered to his chagrin and dismay that his client had lied to him concerning the facts of the action. Then his conduct of the case would become heartless, spiritless, and devoid of courage and enthusiasm. Realizing his weakness when on the wrong side, he avoided such cases whenever consistent with the ethics of his profession. It was not unusual for him to convince a fair-minded client of the injustice of his cause and persuade him to drop it altogether.

While trying a case in behalf of a client to collect an account, the defendant produced a receipt acknowledging payment in full.

[1] Whitney, *Life on the Circuit*, pp. 262-63.
[2] Lamon, *Life of Lincoln*, p. 317.

Lincoln immediately gathered up his papers and left the court-room. Judge Treat sent a messenger to him with an order to return. He found Lincoln in his room at the hotel, but the lawyer refused to go back. "Tell the judge that I can't come—my hands are dirty, and I came over here to clean them," he replied. To him the maxim, "He who comes into equity must come with clean hands," was more than mere words.[1]

In another case, when Lincoln discovered that his client, a livestock breeder, being sued for damages, was in the wrong, he abandoned his previous effort to oppose the plaintiff's contentions and sought only to keep the damages to be assessed against his client down to a fair figure.

Lincoln, ever tender-hearted and generous, who could not refuse any honest request, would permit sentiment to interfere only so far with his duty to his clients. He wrote to Attorney L. M. Hays who had referred a case to him: "At our court just past, I could have got a judgment against Turley, if I had pressed to the utmost; but I am really sorry for him, poor and a cripple as he is. He begged time to try to find evidence to prove that the deceased, on his deathbed, ordered the note to be given up or destroyed. I do not suppose he will get any such evidence, but I allowed him until next court to try."

But after allowing the defendant plenty of time to collect his evidence, Lincoln proceeded to take judgment against Turley for $116.90.[2]

Lincoln was placed in an embarrassing position when Nancy Green, whom he had represented in procuring a divorce from her husband Aaron Green, requested him to bring suit against Mentor Graham. The impecunious schoolmaster who had befriended Lincoln in the early days at New Salem and taught him grammar and loaned him copies of Burns's poems and Shake-

---

[1] *Ibid.*, p. 324.

[2] Angle, in *Letters*, p. 110, spells the defendant's name as "Turley" while Tracy, in *Uncollected Letters*, p. 46 spells it "Tenley." Angle's version was deciphered by S. M. Bamberger, an autograph dealer of Newark, New Jersey, owner of the original letter of October 27, 1852, and is probably the correct one.

speare's dramas, was indebted to her on a note in the sum of two hundred dollars. Graham was unable to pay, and she insisted that court proceedings be instituted to enforce payment. Lincoln realized if he would not take the case some other lawyer would. So at the November term, 1845, of Menard Circuit Court he filed suit. In that court at Petersburg is still to be seen the declaration Lincoln filed against his old friend. Judgment was procured, but Lincoln did nothing to force payment. However, he did urge Graham to do his best to satisfy Mrs. Green's claim.

On another occasion the necessity of serving a client compelled him, as the attorney for John Warner, to recover a claim against John Calhoun, under whom he had served as a deputy surveyor. Having obtained a judgment he had to examine Calhoun concerning his holdings and recent transfers and assignments of properties.

However, when Robert F. Williams, a lawyer of Bloomington, asked Lincoln to participate in a case in which he was acquainted with both of the litigants, Lincoln replied: "As there is likely to be some feeling, and both parties are old friends of mine, I prefer, if I can, to keep out of the case."[1]

Undue effort has been made to point out how Lincoln's proverbial honesty often caused him to concede important points to the opposition or volunteer admissions that seemed nigh fatal to his client's case.

The many stories and anecdotes told in support of this view detract from rather than add to Lincoln's ability as a lawyer. To a casual observer he may have appeared to be giving away the case by understating his own side and admitting points of the opposition. But we have the word of an able barrister like Leonard Swett, who participated in many a hard-fought court battle with Lincoln, that he surrendered only the vulnerable positions and gave away only that which he could not hold. He admitted that only which his adversary was entitled to and was going to get anyhow. For Lincoln was a natural strategist who well understood the power of honesty and sincerity. He was a superb general in the courtroom who realized the worth of yielding several

[1] Angle, *Letters*, p. 168.

unimportant points to gain one strong one. Here was an early application of that tact and diplomacy that was to enable him years later, as President, to yield to Stanton and other cabinet members against his own conviction in order to avoid a rupture that would have brought disaster. Here was that extraordinary prudence that ever subordinated the minor issue to the greater; and which after all, is the first test of diplomacy and statesmanship.

"Where most lawyers would object he would say he 'reckoned' it would be fair to let this in or that," said Mr. Swett, "and sometimes, when his adversary could not quite prove what Lincoln knew to be the truth he 'reckoned' it would be fair to admit the truth to be so-and-so. When he did object to the court, and when he heard his objections answered, he would often say, 'Well, I reckon I must be wrong.' Now, about the time he had practiced this three-fourths through the case, if his adversary didn't understand him, he would wake up in a few minutes learning that he had feared the Greeks too late and find himself beaten. He was wise as a serpent in the trial of a cause, but I have had too many scars from his blows to certify he was harmless as a dove. When the whole thing was unraveled, the adversary would begin to see that what he was so blandly giving away was simply what he couldn't get and keep. By giving away six points and carrying the seventh he carried his case, and the whole case hanging on the seventh, he traded away everything which would give him the least aid in carrying that. Any man who took Lincoln for a simple-minded man would soon wake up with his back in a ditch."[1]

A story that taxes one's credulity involves Lincoln's first case before the Supreme Court of Illinois.[2]

It was during the course of arguing this case to the Supreme Court, according to a statement of Judge Samuel H. Treat to Herndon, that Lincoln declared:

---

[1] Herndon and Weik, *Lincoln*, II, 334; *ibid.*, II, 3; Whitney, *Life on the Circuit*, p. 251.

[2] Scammon vs. Cline, 3 Ill. 456. Richard V. Carpenter in *Journal* of the Illinois State Historical Society, October, 1911, pp. 317–23.

"This is the first case I have ever had in this court, and I have, therefore, examined it with great care. As the court will perceive by looking at the record, the only question in the case is one of authority. I have not been able to find any authority to sustain my side of the case, but I have found several cases directly in point on the other side. I will now give these authorities and submit the case."

It is a great tribute to Lincoln's extraordinary reputation for honesty that Herndon, Lamon, Schurz, Leland, Stoddard, and other biographers, writing shortly after his death, should accept this tale without even raising the question of its plausibility and reasonableness.

What a laughing-stock Lincoln would have made of himself before the Illinois bar, and how derelict in his duty would he have been to his client who had retained him to use his best endeavors to oppose Scammon's appeal, if he actually had risen before the Supreme Court and deliberately admitted away his cause already won in the lower courts, and pleaded in behalf of his adversary!

It is related that on one occasion while citing some authorities supporting his contention of law in a certain case, Lincoln inadvertently began to read a citation favoring his opponent's cause. "There, may it please the court," he was laughingly heard to say, "I reckon I've scratched up a snake, but as I'm in for it, guess I'll read it through." And read it through he did. This was but a graceful way of making the best of a heedless slip in the heat of battle. But it is unreasonable to believe that he would deliberately strengthen the opponent's case. What an unusual and insipid way that would be for a lawyer to serve his client!

A plausible explanation of this episode is that Lincoln in his appearance before the Supreme Court to argue the case of Scammon vs. Cline actually could find no authorities to support his side. It was a new and novel question for which there could be but few, if any, precedents. The case involved a problem that could arise but once in the history of any court, namely, the question of the legality of an appeal filed before the official establishment of the court itself.

Scammon, losing a case before a justice of the peace, appealed to the newly created circuit court of Boone County and filed his appeal bond a day before the statute establishing the definite time for the sitting of the circuit court in Boone County went into effect; and so the appeal was dismissed. What a rare circumstance indeed!

It is very likely that Lincoln, in opposing the appeal, argued from the facts of the case but announced that he could find no legal precedents to support his contentions. Undoubtedly he also must have argued what he thought the law ought to be to govern the situation. It is very likely that Lincoln's opponent, too, could cite very few, if any, authorities to support his case. At least the report of this case does not reveal that any citations of law were offered by the appellant, the appellee, or the court in support of its opinion.

Judge Treat's anecdote must be dismissed as just another myth about Lincoln that does not stand the test of plausibility.

Lincoln had no inherent love for technicalities, hair-splitting, and fine points of law. "If I can free this case from technicalities and get it properly swung to the jury I'll win it," he was wont to say. Clarity, conciseness, and simplicity of statement were his forte in the trial of a case. His mind was orderly. He could marshal facts in such an orderly sequence and reduce a complicated problem to such simple terms that even the dullest layman could not fail to understand.

But to picture Lincoln as refusing to avail himself of technical defenses, demurrers, and statutory limitations when his client's interests could be ethically served thereby, as many writers claim, is to belittle him as a lawyer and to brand him as derelict in his duty toward his clients.

"He never learned the technicalities, what some would call the 'tricks of the profession,' " write his secretaries Nicolay and Hay. "The sleight of plea and demurrer, the legerdemain by which justice is balked and a weak case is made to gain an unfair advantage, was too subtle and shifty for his strong and forward intelligence. He met the maneuvers sufficiently well, when practiced by others, but he never could get in the way of handling them himself."[1]

[1] Nicolay and Hay, *Abraham Lincoln: A History*, p. 12.

With very few exceptions, Lincoln's biographers, from Herndon down, represent him as a lawyer disinclined to take advantage of any technical defense. This contention is contrary to fact, and is amply refuted by available records.

Although never once did Lincoln take unfair advantage of the court or opposing counsel by unethical means, the files of a number of his cases reveal that whenever an action was subject to a technical defense or whenever it served his client's interests to plead the statute of limitations or other technical pleas, like any other wide-awake lawyer he pressed such advantage to the limit and gave his client the benefit of every favorable legitimate expediency. That he did so was a credit to his ability, diligence, and alertness as an advocate, and a commendation of his desire for justice and fair play.

Experience taught Lincoln that the pleas of limitation, infancy, usury, and other technical safeguards are absolutely necessary for a proper and equitable administration of justice. Having undertaken a case, a lawyer's duty compels him to array the facts and to present every phase of the law helpful to his client's cause. It is for the court to determine the legality, and for the jury the credibility, of the facts. A lawyer usurps the province of the judge and jury when he determines in advance the justice of his client's cause. He is unfair to his client when he fails to protect his interests with every proper device of the law.

In the case of Dorman vs. Lane, in which Lincoln was associated with Samuel D. Marshall of Shawneetown, we find the Springfield lawyer watchfully waiting for the opposition to delay a little longer in the filing of their pleading, so he could pounce upon them with a plea of limitation and forever bar them from asserting their claim.

"Friend Sam," he wrote to Mr. Marshall, "I learned today that Lane, to avoid paying the cost of taking the case between Dorman and him back from the Supreme Court, has commenced a new proceeding in your Circuit Court. Write me, if this is so; and I, together with Judge Logan, will try to frame a plea either in bar or in abatement, out of the fact of the pendency of the old case, that shall blow them up in their new case.

"By the way, if they fail for more than a year (which they have nearly done already) to take the old case down from here, I think we can plead limitation on them, so that it will stick for good and all. Don't speak of this, lest they hear it and take alarm."[1]

When the judge hearing another of Lincoln's cases refused to regard the question of the statute of limitations, raised by the Springfield lawyer, as being pertinent to the action, Lincoln insisted that he would have a hearing on the question even if he had to go to the highest court in the land for it. He wrote his clients: "Now, as to the question of Limitation, we must have a hearing on it, even if we have to go to the Supreme Court of the U.S. for it—that is, if the other question shall be decided against us—Be patient—They have not got your land yet——"

When Lincoln's client, Joel Johnson, keeper of a hotel in Springfield, was sued by a guest named Brush for money stolen from his hotel room, Lincoln unsuccessfully sought to avoid payment by raising the purely technical point that Brush's partner and joint owner of the stolen money was not made a party to the lawsuit.[2]

A judgment was taken against Frederick Pearl and Lawson Holland. Later Lincoln as their lawyer unsuccessfully tried to defeat the claim by setting up the technical defense of laches—passiveness or undue delay on the part of the successful parties in enforcing their judgment.[3]

In the case of Maus vs. Worthing,[4] Lincoln stressed a technical point and succeeded in dismissing his adversary's appeal simply because the appeal bond was not signed with due formality.

When Patrick Sullivan, a grocery-keeper, was fined ten dollars for selling liquor without a license, Lincoln carried the case to the Supreme Court and strove with all his powers as a lawyer to convince that tribunal that technically his client was not guilty because, as he claimed, the statute under which Sullivan was

[1] Dorman vs. Lane, 6 Ill. 143; Tracy, *Uncollected Letters*, p. 77.
[2] Johnson vs. Richardson, 17 Ill. 303.
[3] Pearl vs. Wellmans, II, Ill. 352.
[4] 4 Ill. 26–28.

indicted had been superseded by a later enactment. Although he lost the appeal, the complicated mess of conflicting liquor license legislation of Illinois received its first comprehensive judicial interpretation. Only by such means is the law finally settled.[1]

Although Lincoln in a law battle strove to avail himself of every legal advantage, he did not permit an adversary to overwhelm him with a technicality without putting up a stubborn resistance. His adroitness and resourcefulness in handling a difficult situation is typified by his conduct in the trial of Case vs. Snow Bros., wherein two young defendants sought to avoid the payment of an honest debt by claiming they were minors when the account was incurred.

Lincoln had been retained by the plaintiff Case, an old farmer, to sue on a note for some two hundred dollars. He had received it from the Snow brothers in payment of a "prairie team," consisting of a plow and two or three yoke of oxen. The brothers through their attorney admitted signing the note but denied their obligation to pay it, on the ground that they were minors at the time they signed it, and further because "Mr. Case knew they were at the time of the contract and conveyance." The minor act was read to the jury empaneled to hear the case in Tazewell County Circuit Court. Lincoln admitted its validity.

"Yes, gentlemen, I reckon that's so," he nonchalantly acceded.

It was a perfect legal defense; but still he wanted to ask a few questions:

"Where is the prairie team now?"

"On the farm of the Snow boys," a witness testified.

"Have you seen anyone breaking prairie with it lately?"

"Yes, the Snow boys were breaking up with it last week."

"How old are the boys now?"

"One is a little over twenty-one and the other near twenty-three."

That was all Lincoln wanted to know.

The lawyer for the youths argued that under the statute the

[1] Sullivan vs. The People, 15 Ill. 233.

Snow brothers could not be held legally liable for their contract. But Lincoln would not concede defeat.

"Are you willing to allow these boys to begin life with this shame and disgrace attached to their character?" he challenged the jury. "If you are, I am not. The best judge of human character that ever wrote has left these immortal words for all of us to ponder:

Good name in man or woman, dear my lord,
Is the immediate jewel of their souls;
Who steals my purse steals trash; 'tis something, nothing;
'Twas mine, 'tis his, and has been slave to thousands;
But he that filches from me my good name
Robs me of that which not enriches him
            And makes me poor indeed."

He admitted the defense of infancy, but he insisted that the law was never intended to sanction cheating. So, he continued, "The judge will tell you what your own sense of justice has already told you, that these Snow boys, if they were mean enough to plead the baby act, when they came to be men should have taken the oxen and plow back. They cannot go back on their contract and also keep what the note was given for.

"And now, gentlemen," he concluded, "you have it in your power to set these boys right before the world."

"He plead for the young men only," related George W. Minier, who was present in the courtroom. "I think he did not mention his client's name. The jury, without leaving their seats, decided that the defendants must pay the debt; and the latter, after hearing Lincoln, were as willing to pay it as the jury were determined they should."[1]

Despite Herndon's assertion that "Lincoln was strikingly deficient in the technical rules of the law" and that "practically he knew nothing of the rules of evidence, of pleading or practice

---

[1] George W. Minier, Statement, April 10, 1882, in Herndon and Weik, *Lincoln*, 11, 327-28; Isaac N. Arnold, *Life of Abraham Lincoln*, p. 85–87; Osborne H. Oldroyd, *The Lincoln Memorial Album Immortelles*, pp. 187–89.

as laid down in the text-books, and seemed to care nothing about them,'' we find Lincoln resorting to every legal device and utilizing every technical advantage to win his cases.

Loyal to his clients and faithful to his ideals, Lincoln fought for whatever cause he enlisted in, to the best of his ability. Ever fair and honorable to his adversaries, he was fearless and tactful, resourceful, and adroit, as he endeavored to outmaneuver them in a battle of fine points of law and technicalities. He took and he gave. He yielded a minor advantage to gain an important one. He won and he lost. But always he struck hard blows—fighting as he was to fight on a larger scale as the Nation's Chief Magistrate in the eventful days to come.

A fair view of Lincoln's career at the bar reveals that like any other honorable lawyer he accepted whatever cases came his way unless they were morally bad or manifestly a fraud against the rights of others. "In a clear case of dishonesty," according to Whitney, Lincoln "would hedge . . . so as to not himself partake of dishonesty. In a doubtful case of dishonesty, he would give his client the benefit of the doubt, and in an ordinary case he would try the case . . . like any other lawyer."[1]

He tried as hard as any other attorney to acquire business, and his conduct toward his clients and fellow practitioners was like that of any honorable, conscientious, and scrupulous member of the bar. The cases he refused were the kind that most high-minded and humane advocates would reject. He defended murderers and thieves, and fought successfully to procure the acquittal of Jane Anderson and her paramour, indicted for poisoning her husband. Now and then he refused a case that he might have won, but in which his victory would have injured innocent persons. But he did represent a slave-owner who sought to enforce his rights in accordance with the law of the land and recover his slaves, who claimed their freedom. On other occasions he strove successfully in behalf of negroes and won freedom for them by skillfully pleading their cause before the courts. He volunteered his services in behalf of a group of female temperance workers charged with malicious destruction of a saloon-keeper's stock of

[1] Whitney, *Life on the Circuit*, p. 263.

whiskey, and on another occasion endeavored to procure the acquittal of a liquor dealer indicted for selling intoxicants without a license. He represented poor individuals and powerful corporations. And though he served them all to the best of his ability, he was owned by none.

In the many hundred cases he tried during his twenty-three years of activity at the bar, not even once did he intentionally misrepresent the evidence of a witness or the argument of an opponent, nor misstate the law "according to his own intelligent views of it." Never did he yield to the temptation of gaining personal benefit at the expense of others. Never did he sacrifice his conscience for victory nor surrender his own lofty principles of justice and honor for the sake of selfish gain.

XVII. "HONEST ABE'S" HONESTY IMPUGNED

ONE day in the spring of 1853, while Abraham Lincoln was attending circuit court at Danville, a letter arrived from his brother-in-law, Ninian W. Edwards. As the lawyer read its contents, his rugged, weatherbeaten face was seen to blanch and his fingers to tremble—not from fear or trepidation, it appeared, but rather from anger and indignation.

He, "Honest Abe," whose reputation for fair dealing and integrity was to become so potent a factor in making him the President of the United States in the most perilous hour of the Nation's history, he was being charged with embezzlement of a client's funds, according to the letter.

This accusation, which came from Kentucky like the exploding crack of a bull-whip to challenge his honesty and professional conduct, became the most vexatious experience in all of Lincoln's life. The startling charge alleged that he had made some collections for his deceased father-in-law's business firm but had failed to account for the funds.

Robert S. Todd, Mrs. Lincoln's father and a member of the firm of Oldham, Todd and Company, manufacturers of cotton goods near Lexington, Kentucky, had died in 1849. When four years later his estate was ready for settlement, the money, some fifteen hundred dollars, due to the Springfield heirs, was paid to their lawyers, George B. Kinkead of Lexington, Kentucky. But before Mr. Kinkead was able to remit to Mrs. Lincoln her share of the estate, Mr. Todd's remaining partners, Oldham and Hemingway, filed suit against her husband in Fayette Circuit Court, Kentucky, claiming that the firm had sent various claims to Lincoln aggregating $472.54, for collection from Illinois customers, and that he had collected the entire sum and had converted the money to his own use.

Lincoln's ire knew no bounds as he read this aspersion. Immediately he penned a letter to Mr. Kinkead challenging the assault on his honor.

"I am here attending court a hundred and thirty miles from home, and where a copy of your letter of this month, to Mr. Edwards, reached me from him last evening," he wrote. "I find it difficult to suppress my indignation towards those who have got up this claim against me. I would really be glad to hear Mr. Hemingway explain how he was induced to swear he believed the claim to be just! I herewith inclose my answer."

Lincoln emphatically denied that he had collected any money whatsoever for the plaintiff, but asserted that he had received fifty dollars on behalf of his father-in-law which Mr. Todd had requested him to retain. Lincoln then averred that when he visited Lexington in the autumn of 1849, he explained the whole matter to Hemingway and to L. O. Todd, "and that, more recently, in the spring of 1852, he again fully stated it, in his sworn answer to a Bill filed for the adjustment of the estate of said Robert S. Todd."

"Respondent cares but little for said fifty dollars," Lincoln added indignantly. "If it is his legal right he prefers retaining it; but he objects to repaying it once to the estate of said Robert S. Todd, and again to said firm or to said Petitioners; and he particularly objects to being compelled to pay money to said firm or said Petitioners which he never received at all."

Kinkead shortly thereafter wrote Lincoln that his own brother-in-law, Levi Todd, who apparently was unfriendly to his Springfield relatives, had inspired the lawsuit by revealing to the surviving partners that Lincoln had once admitted that he actually owed the money in question. Lincoln replied that such a statement, if made by his brother-in-law, was untrue.

"I have said before, and now repeat," he wrote, "that if they will name the man or men of whom they say I have collected money for them, I will *disprove* it." "This matter harasses my feelings a good deal," he confessed to Kinkead.

Clearly the case had Lincoln worried. He realized the handicap of long distance in vindicating his honor, especially as the plaintiffs had failed to specify the names of the persons from whom they claimed he had collected the money. At this juncture came the notice that Oldham and Hemingway had filed a bill of particulars setting forth the names of the persons from whom Lincoln was alleged to have made the collections. It specified that on June 17, 1844, he had received $129.05 from Bain, Tomkins & Barrett, and $343.49 from Hawley and Edwards. This definite allegation heartened Lincoln. Now he felt certain he could refute the charges.

Having definite and concrete charges to combat, Lincoln promptly set about securing sworn statements from these parties. So completely did they refute the plaintiff's charges and exonerate Lincoln that Oldham and Hemingway caused their attorney to file a motion on January 16, 1854, to dismiss the case.

Thus ended one of the most harassing and mortifying experiences in all of Lincoln's career.

But it was not the only assault upon his honor during his busy and eventful career as a lawyer. Judges, lawyers, and other persons with whom he came in daily contact in the courts of Illinios would swear to his extraordinary unswerving moral and intellectual honesty both as a lawyer and as a citizen. His very name had become a byword for integrity. Yet on several other occasions his trustworthiness was seriously questioned. Groundless and without reason though these attacks proved to be, they caused him embarrassment and anxiety.

There were some who charged that Judge Davis unduly favored Lincoln in his courtroom. They pointed out that the two were inseparable on the circuit, constantly traveling together, eating together, and sharing the same hotel rooms, and when

Judge Davis was unable to fulfill his duties on the bench owing to illness or unavoidable absence, he frequently appointed Lincoln to serve in his stead. On account of this intimacy, it was contended, Lincoln, in Judge Davis's court, was the recipient of much favoritism and partiality at the expense of his opponents.

However, there is no actual evidence to support this accusation. Many were the adverse rulings of Judge Davis against Lincoln. Of eighty-seven cases tried by Lincoln before Judge Davis without a jury, Paul M. Angle, who examined the records, finds that in only forty cases were the decrees in favor of Lincoln's clients, while forty-seven were against them. Very frequently the Springfield lawyer was obliged to appeal to the Supreme Court in an endeavor to reverse the decisions of Judge Davis.[1]

There is nothing in the records to substantiate the claims of some of Lincoln's political opponents that he received unfair advantages in Judge Davis's court. Nothing more clearly illustrates the honesty of purpose existing between these two companions of the circuit than President Lincoln's hesitancy in appointing Judge Davis to a vacancy on the Supreme Court bench of the United States. No one had been more instrumental in procuring the Republican presidential nomination for the then comparatively unknown Lincoln than the judge of the Eighth Illinois Judicial Circuit. So when, in 1861, Justice McLean of the United States Supreme Court passed away, the friends of Judge Davis were amazed over President Lincoln's failure to appoint his loyal companion at once to the vacancy.

Lawrence Weldon wrote to Ward H. Lamon, whom Lincoln had named Marshal of the District of Columbia:

"I see Judge Mclean has departed this life. The question is, who shall succeed to the ermine so worthily worn by him. . . . Why should not Judge David Davis . . . especially when he was so instrumental in giving position to him who now holds the matter in the hollow of his hand? Dear Hill, if justice and gratitude are to be respected, Lincoln can do nothing less than to tender the position to Judge Davis. . . . I want you to suggest it to Lincoln."[2]

[1] Angle, "Lincoln, Circuit Lawyer," Lincoln Centennial Association Papers (1928), p. 38.

[2] Weldon to Ward H. Lamon, Urbana, Illinois, April 6, 1861. Lamon MSS.

Later, Hawkins Taylor, who had been a delegate from Iowa to the Chicago convention, wrote directly to the President: "But I will say that in my honest opinion, with every opportunity of knowing, that but for the extraordinary effort of Judge Davis, you would not have received the nomination at the Chicago convention. I can say to you that I consider your nomination providential. . . . Viewing the case in the light that I do, I feel that it is due to yourself as well as to Judge Davis that you should tender him the appointment of Supreme Judge."[1]

Why did Lincoln hesitate for a year and a half before naming his friend to the office? The answer undoubtedly must have been in the President's honest misgivings as to the qualifications of Judge Davis to serve on the highest judicial tribunal of the Nation. After all, his friend's judicial experience had been limited to the circuit courts of Illinois, and the judge himself, upon hearing a rumor that Thomas Drummond of Chicago, a jurist of outstanding ability, then sitting as judge of the United States District Court, would receive the appointment to the Supreme Court, declared he would prefer Judge Drummond's post to the supreme justiceship, because "I know I could discharge the duties of the one satisfactorily, but am diffident about the other."[2]

But friendship and gratitude prevailed, and in the fall of 1862 Lincoln tendered the Supreme Court appointment to Judge Davis. Lincoln's confidence in his staunch friend was well rewarded, as Judge Davis developed into an able and respected member of the Supreme Court, widely noted for his progressive views.

It was Judge Davis who, in 1866, was to deliver the opinion of the Supreme Court in the famous case of Ex parte Milligan (4 Wallace 107) which has become an outstanding pronouncement in constitutional law and deserves to rank with Marshall's most notable opinions. Strange to say, it fell to the lot of Justice Davis, during the course of this notable opinion, severely to denounce President Lincoln's limitless exercise of martial law. This decision, holding that the President has no power to institute trial

---

[1] Illinois Historical Society, *Journal*, p. 171.

[2] Illinois Historical Society Publications, No. 37, for 1930, p. 171, quoting Davis to Ward H. Lamon, Urbana, Illinois, April 14, 1861. Lamon MSS.

by military tribunal where the civil courts are open, has been placed among the landmarks of liberty.

The sensational "Peachy" Harrison murder case furnishes another instance when Lawyer Lincoln's motives and sincerity were seriously questioned. In the heat of this exciting trial, one of the prosecutors, to counteract a masterful plea by which Lincoln had apparently won the sympathy of the jury, accused the Springfield lawyer of duplicity and branded his seeming frankness and sincerity as a sham and a fake. The prosecutor, following Lincoln, realized that unless the effect of Lincoln's appeal were counteracted, the State's cause would be lost.

"Well, gentlemen," he said in the course of his argument to the jury, "you have heard Mr. Lincoln—'Honest Abe Lincoln,' they call him, I believe. And I suppose you think you have heard the honest truth—or at least that Mr. Lincoln honestly believes what he has told you to be the truth. I tell you, he believes no such thing. That frank, ingenuous face of his, as you are weak enough to suppose, those looks and tones of such unsophisticated simplicity, those appeals to your minds and consciences as sworn jurors, are all assumed for the occasion, gentlemen—all a mask, gentlemen. You have been listening to an actor, who knows well how to play the rôle of honest seeming, for effect."

Never before in open court had Lincoln's sincerity been so flagitiously impugned. He waited in silence, while the assault continued. Upon its completion, Lincoln slowly arose amid a deathly silence in the courtroom. He was deeply hurt. At length he looked squarely in the eyes of the prosecutor and spoke. His voice was sad but firm.

"You have known me for years," he said, "and *you know* that not a word of that language can be truthfully applied to me."

The prosecutor realized this was so. He had been carried away by the excitement of the trial, but he was man enough to admit, "Yes, Mr. Lincoln, I do know it, and I take it all back." He walked over to Lincoln and shook his hand. The jury, too, believed in Lincoln's sincerity. They returned a verdict acquitting his client.[1]

The most notorious aspersion against his professional integrity

[1] Rothschild, *Honest Abe*, pp. 105–07.

arose from a dramatic incident of the sensational Duff Armstrong murder case. Its baselessness was proved time and again, but for many years the story persisted that Lincoln had procured Duff's acquittal by means of fraud and chicanery.

When on Friday, May 7, 1858, Lincoln began his famous vigorous defense of his benefactor's wayward son, he was approaching a crisis in his own career. Momentous political events were following one another in swift succession. On June 6, loomed the Illinois Republican state convention, scheduled to assemble in Springfield to select the party standard-bearer to oppose Senator Douglas, candidate for re-election. Lincoln was hopeful that he would become the Republican choice.

But now he had an imperiled boy to save from the hangman's noose, and his political activities, destined to make history, must wait while the future chief actor in the great impending national drama pleaded for the life of a recreant youth. The speedy acquittal that followed brought joy to the defendant and his mother and satisfaction to the successful lawyer. But from Lincoln's sensational introduction of the almanac that destroyed the testimony of Charles Allen, the State's chief witness, arose a calumnious rumor that would not down for many years.

According to this canard, Lincoln had fraudulently exhibited to the jury an almanac, not of the year 1857, the year of the murder, but one of a previous year ingeniously made over. For a number of years there were folks in Cass County who would laugh and shake their heads whenever the almanac episode was mentioned.

How this calumny originated no one knows, but Dame Rumor's messengers were swift in spreading the story.

The best refutation of this baseless, scurrilous charge is found in the fact that a forged almanac was utterly unnecessary. A glance at an almanac for August, 1857, reveals that on the night of the murder the moon was going out of sight and was too dim to have enabled Allen to see the fight in the manner he testified.

A most complete disproof of the canard has come from Abram Bergen, who had gone to the trial shortly after his admission to the bar, because of "an intense desire to learn how good lawyers examine witnesses, and especially to see and to hear all of a trial conducted by counsel so eminent." Mr. Bergen became a prominent member of the Illinois bar and an able judge. Judge Bergen asserts that he paid particularly close attention to Lincoln and to his every word and movement from the time he entered the courtroom until his departure.

"During the entire trial I was seated in the bar behind the attorneys for the State and those for the defendant, and not more than four feet from any one of them," he said, "and noticed everything with the deepest interest, as any young lawyer naturally would.

"During the introduction of the evidence Mr. Lincoln remarked to the judge that he supposed the court would take judicial notice of the almanac; but in order that there might be no question on that point he offered it as a part of the evidence for the defense, the court accepting it and remarking that anyone might use the almanac in the progress of the argument. Lincoln, with his usual care, had brought with him from Springfield the almanac then regarded as the standard in that region. At a recess of the court he took it from his capacious hat and gave it to Sheriff Dick, with the request that it should be returned to him when he called for it. In the succeeding campaign the Democrats induced Sheriff Dick to make an affidavit that he did not notice the year covered by the almanac, and this is taken by some as conclusive evidence that Lincoln intended to deceive.

"When Lincoln finally called for the almanac he exhibited it to the opposing lawyers, read from it, and then caused it to be handed to members of the jury for their inspection. I heard two of the attorneys for the State, in whispered consultation, raise the question as to the correctness of the almanac, and they ended the conference by sending to the office of the clerk for another. The messenger soon returned with the statement that there was no almanac of 1857 in the office. (It will be remembered that the trial occurred in 1858 for a transaction in 1857.) In the presidential campaign soon following, it was even charged that Lincoln must have gone around and purloined all the almanacs in the courthouse. However, I well remember that another almanac was procured from the office of the Probate Judge Arenz, in the same building. It was brought to the prosecuting attorney, who examined it, compared it with the one introduced by Mr. Lincoln, and found that they substantially agreed, although it was at first intimated by the State's attorneys that they had found some slight difference.

"All this I personally saw and heard, and it is as distinct in my memory as if it had occurred but yesterday. No intimation was made, so far as I knew, that there was any fraud in the use of the almanac, until two years afterwards, when Lincoln was the nominee of the Republican Party for the Presidency. In that year, 1860, while in the mountains of Southern Oregon, I saw in a Democratic newspaper, published at St. Louis, an article personally abusive of Mr. Lincoln, stating that he was no statesman, and only a third-rate lawyer; and to prove the deceptive and dishonest nature of the candidate the same paper printed an indefinite affidavit of one of the jurors who had helped to acquit Armstrong, to the effect that Mr. Lincoln had made fraudulent use of the almanac at the trial. For some inexplicable reason he failed to call this pretended knowledge to the attention of the other jurors at the time of the trial, but very promptly joined in the verdict of the acquittal, and waited two years before giving publicity to what would at the proper time have been a very important piece of information.

"Soon after this I saw an affidavit made by Milton Logan, the foreman of the jury, that he personally examined the almanac when it was delivered to the jury, and particularly noticed that it was for the year 1857, the year of the homicide. I had a better opportunity than any of the jurors to see and hear all that was publicly and privately done and said by the attorneys on both sides; and know that the almanacs of 1857 now preserved in historical and other public libraries sustain and prove to the minute all that was claimed by Mr. Lincoln on that trial as to the rising and setting of the moon, although my best recollection is that the hour of the crime was claimed to be about midnight instead of eleven o'clock as stated in many of the books."[1]

[1] Judge Bergen's recollections ("Lincoln's Skill as a Lawyer," by James L. King) in *North American Review* (February, 1898), vol., 166, pp. 186, 195.

Address of Abram Bergen before the Kansas State Bar Association, 1897, p. 31.

That this foul calumny was but the outgrowth of a base desire on the part of some of Lincoln's antagonists to injure him politically, is reasonable to infer. Lincoln, whose very name had become a byword for honesty, was too big a man to stoop to such chicanery. Next to Stephen Douglas he was the most prominent man in all Illinois. He had received a large vote for the Vice-Presidency at the Republican convention of 1856. Soon, he was to become his party's "first and only choice" as the successor of the Little Giant; and the nomination for the Presidency itself was only two years away. His every act was a matter of public interest and concern. The slightest digression from the highest and most rigid ethics of his chosen profession meant political suicide. How could he have hoped to escape detection when the almanac was certain to have been inspected and scrutinized by the court, the State's attorneys, and the twelve members of the jury? In fact, according to John T. Brady, who served on the jury, "The almanac that was introduced was examined closely by the court and the attorneys for the State . . . and was allowed to be used as evidence by Judge Herriot."[1]

What could have been Lincoln's motive in attempting such an absurd fraud? A large fee? He was serving without any expectation or wish for compensation. An intense desire to assure Duff's acquittal by disproving Allen's testimony? Then a forged almanac was unnecessary, as the one for August, 1857, proved Lincoln's contention. The truth alone was needed. Besides, the importance of the almanac in the trial has been exaggerated. It did help to break down the effect of Allen's story, but the testimony of Watkins about the sling-shot, Dr. Parker's declaration that Norris's blow or the fall from the horse were probable causes of Metzker's death, and Lincoln's masterful and heart-stirring appeal to the jury actually were responsible for the jury's verdict of acquittal.

Since in politics no act or incident in a candidate's or office-

"Lincoln's Defense of Duff Armstrong," by J. N. Gridley, in the *Journal of the Illinois State Historical Society*, III, 24–44; Barton, *Life of Lincoln*, I, 506–15.

[1] Letter of John T. Brady to J. N. Gridley of Virginia, Illinois, published by the Illinois State Historical Society in 1910.

holder's life is so personal, intimate, or sacred as to escape the scandalmonger's poisonous tongue, it is certain that if this almanac canard had had the least foundation of truth it would have been told, magnified, and retold by Lincoln's antagonists to his political destruction. Although the calumny was whispered sporadically during the Douglas senatorial contest and revived during the presidential campaign two years later, it received little or no credence.[1]

As a lawyer, Lincoln, like any other active practitioner, had been unconsciously making enemies. Every time he brought an action for a client for money damages he was assailing the defendant's most tender spot—his purse. Every hard-earned victory meant another person's sore defeat—perhaps his financial ruin. No wonder then, that such persons would take advantage of every opportunity to stain the opposing lawyer's record, criticize his foibles, exaggerate his frailties, and magnify his faults. Thus, in March, 1842, Wil-

---

[1] In the index to the American edition of an English law book—*A Treatise on Facts as Subjects of Inquiry by a Jury*, by James Ram—is found this line: "Lincoln, President Abraham, how he procured an acquittal by a fraud, 269 n." The text of the note referred to is as follows:

"In Lamon's *Life of Abraham Lincoln*, page 327, an account is given to Mr. Lincoln's defense of a man named Armstrong, under indictment for murder. The evidence against the prisoner was very strong. But says the biographer, 'the witness whose testimony bore hardest upon Armstrong swore that the crime was committed about eleven o'clock at night and that he saw the blow struck by the light of a moon nearly full.' Here Mr. Lincoln saw his opportunity. He handed to an officer of the court an almanac of the year previous to the murder. Mr. Lincoln made the closing argument for the defense, and in the words of Lamon 'in due time he called for the almanac and easily proved by it that at the time the main witness declared the moon was shining in great splendor, there was in fact no moon at all, but black darkness over the whole scene. In the roar of laughter and undisguised astonishment succeeding this apparent demonstration, court, jury and counsel forgot to examine that seemingly conclusive almanac and let it pass without question concerning its genuineness.' "

In the St. Louis *Globe-Democrat* of September 15, 1895, a correspondent writing from the town of Virginia, Illinois, said: "The old courthouse in Beardstown still stands. It was in this edifice that Lincoln used a doctored almanac in the defense of Duff Armstrong for murder." This item was republished in the Virginia *Gazette*, and widely copied in the country press.

liam Darmody retained Lincoln to sue John S. Bradford, state printer for slander, claiming the latter had publicly called him a "damned rogue." Although Lincoln lost the case, Bradford never forgave him for participating in the suit against him and never thereafter lost an opportunity, especially during political campaigns, to belittle and denounce the Springfield lawyer.

No one was more vociferous in spreading the canard about the doctored almanac in the Armstrong case than a Mr. Carter, a lawyer of Beardstown, who was present but not engaged in the case. This Mr. Carter claimed to be satisfied that the almanac was of the previous year, and thought that he had examined it at the trial. But, says Judge Bergen, "This man Carter, who was Buchanan's village postmaster, had one case for jury trial at that term. Mr. Lincoln, for a five-dollar fee, had run Carter's worthless, litigious client out of court on a motion for security for costs. Of course, it was easy to satisfy Carter that Mr. Lincoln had done almost anything diabolical."

Lincoln himself never dignified the calumny with his notice, and if it was called to his attention at all he ignored it entirely. Judge Bergen truly said, "If his public and private conduct and his reputation as a citizen and lawyer were not sufficient to refute the charge, his personal denial would have been of little avail."

How futile and baseless these aspersions proved to be is evidenced by the almost universal confidence the general public always had in Lincoln. A correspondent of the Chicago *Tribune*, reporting a political address by the Springfield lawyer at Danville, September 27, 1858, wrote:

"Such has become the established integrity of Lincoln with us that let a jury be empanelled from any part of our populous county, to try a cause, and they will take his exposition of the law and the facts of a case without a scruple; for they know that as Lincoln has never misconstrued the law nor perverted the evidence, they can follow him and do no wrong. And when a man brings that kind of a reputation on the hustings, his power with the people is almost omnipotent."

XVIII. FEES AND INVESTMENTS

JOHN SCOTT, a client of the firm of Lincoln & Lamon, was pleasantly surprised when Lamon called him over and without warning or explanation refunded to him one half of a two-hundred-and-fifty-dollar fee Scott had cheerfully paid to Lamon but a few moments before.

Scott had retained Lincoln & Lamon to protect an estate valued at about ten thousand dollars belonging to his feebleminded young sister, for whom Scott was acting as conservator or guardian. A certain designing adventurer was seeking to marry the girl, and because of Scott's opposition to the marriage, filed a motion in court to have the brother removed as guardian. Scott insisted upon fixing in advance the fee Lincoln & Lamon would charge for attending to the matter. Lamon suggested the sum of two hundred and fifty dollars and the guardian assented at once, as he expected a hard contest over the motion. In court Lincoln took full charge of the case and so well did he argue the motion that in less than an hour the presiding judge dismissed the entire proceedings.

"Our success was complete," says Lamon. "Scott was satisfied and cheerfully paid over the money to me inside the bar, Lincoln looking on. Scott then went out and Mr. Lincoln asked, 'What did you charge that man?' I told him two hundred fifty

224

dollars. Said he, 'Lamon, that is all wrong. The service was not worth that sum. Give him back at least half of it.'

"I protested that the fee was fixed in advance, that Scott was perfectly satisfied and so expressed himself. 'That may be,' retorted Mr. Lincoln, with a look of distress and undisguised displeasure, 'but I am not satisfied. This is positively wrong. Go call him back and return half of the money at least, or I will not receive one cent for my share.' "

The animated conversation between Lincoln and Lamon attracted the attention of Judge Davis and several lawyers present in the courtroom. And it was in their presence that Lamon paid back the one hundred and twenty-five dollars to the astonished client.

This affair soon became the topic of conversation of many of the lawyers of the circuit. They urged Judge Davis to rebuke Lincoln for attempting to pauperize the profession. So to one of the night sessions of a moot tribunal called the Orgamathorical Court, Lincoln was summoned, and the charge was read to him.

"Lincoln, I have been watching you and Lamon," thundered Judge Davis, trying to maintain his gravity. "You are impoverishing this bar by your picayune charges of fees, and the lawyers have reason to complain of you. You are now almost as poor as Lazarus, and if you don't make people pay you more for your services you will die as poor as Job's turkey!"

Though the lawyers applauded the court's "denunciation," and amid the uproarious laughter saw to it that Lincoln was found guilty and properly fined for his crime against their purses, Lincoln, in all seriousness, arose and said: "That money comes out of the pocket of a poor demented girl and I would rather starve than swindle her in this manner."

Never would he consent to be a member of a firm, said Lincoln, that would deserve the reputation "enjoyed by those shining lights, 'Catch 'em and Cheat 'em.' "[1]

Owing to such incidents as the Scott case, efforts have been made to show that Attorney Lincoln's fees, for the most part, were trivial and that very often he refused proffered compensation and gave his services free of charge. These altruistic attri-

---

[1] Lamon, *Recollections of Abraham Lincoln*, p. 17.

butes have been greatly exaggerated. Although in some instances his fees were inadequate for the services rendered, yet for the most part they were normal and compared favorably with the compensation received by other lawyers of the same region.

To Gustave Koerner, a successful lawyer of Belleville, who later became Lieutenant-Governor of Illinois, Lincoln wrote after they had opposed each other in the important case of Clark & Morrison vs. Page & Bacon in Macoupin Circuit Court: "You left here sooner than I expected; else I should have asked you on what terms you settled your fee in the case in connection with which we met at Carlinville last fall. . . . I wish to regulate my claim somewhat by yours."[1]

When Lincoln thought a client could afford to pay a large fee he showed no such generosity as he did in the Scott affair. Even during the early days of his partnership with Stuart, he made a charge of five hundred dollars in one case, and when the client was unable to pay cash he took some notes secured by a mortgage on a farm.

A fee of $1500 was the share received by Lincoln & Herndon of a total of three thousand dollars paid them and another law firm for successfully representing the defendants in the case of Beaver vs. Taylor & Gilbert in the United States District Court. The plaintiff had endeavored to recover from Lincoln's clients sixty-five acres of land adjoining the city of Cairo, Illinois. The lucrative fee was paid to the successful lawyers in three installments.

In the McCormick Reaper case Lincoln received a fee of twenty-five hundred dollars, and this was exceeded only by the Illinois Central fee of five thousand dollars. However, fees like those were extraordinary, and charges of from five to twenty-five dollars were generally the rule with Attorney Lincoln. And after a career of twenty-three years at the bar, with a practice surpassed in volume by that of few lawyers in the State, Lincoln closed his professional life a comparatively poor man. "I question whether there was a lawyer in the circuit who had been at the bar as long a time whose means were not larger," was Judge Davis's opinion.

The judge, Stephen T. Logan, and a number of other of Lin-

---

[1] Tracy, *Uncollected Letters*, p. 65.

coln's close associates became independently wealthy, but their affluence came chiefly from successful land speculations and not from income at the bar. Lincoln had little taste for real-estate speculation. When Gillespie told him, "You might have made money entering land at a dollar and a quarter an acre," he answered, "Yes, that is true—but I never had any money sense."

"He never speculated in lands or anything else," said Herndon. "In the days of land offices and 'choice lots in a growing town' he had many opportunities to make safe ventures promising good returns, but he never availed himself of them. His brother lawyers were making good investments and lucky turns, some of them, Davis for example, were rapidly becoming wealthy; but Lincoln cared nothing for speculation, in fact there was no venturesome spirit in him."[1]

But to infer from this that Lincoln was indifferent as to fees and shiftless in money matters is without foundation in fact. "While Mr. Lincoln was no financier and had no propensity to acquire property—no avarice of the get—yet he had the capacity of retention, or the avarice of the keep," was Herndon's observation. Lincoln was far from being the indigent country lawyer, artless almost to the point of incompetency in financial matters, as he has often been pictured.

When twenty-nine years of age he made a speech on a banking bill, then pending before the Illinois legislature, that reveals that he had far more than a mere superficial understanding of money questions. Then, too, he appeared in a number of important corporation cases that required a thorough knowledge of business and financial principles. His field of endeavor was law, and he strove as hard as any other lawyer to get business; and having completed his services he made every effort to have his fees paid promptly. Generally, he was rather punctilious about this matter.

"Judge Logan and myself are doing business together now; and we are willing to attend to your cases as you propose," he wrote C. B. Sheledy, on February 16, 1843. But he hastened to

---

[1] Judge Davis and Clifton H. Moore owned in partnership in 1865 over fourteen thousand acres of land. *Transactions* of Illinois Historical Society, 1930, p. 160.

impress that lawyer that he would prefer to have his fees in advance. For he adds: "As to terms we are willing to attend each case you prepare and send us for ten dollars (when there shall be no opposition) to be sent in advance, or you to know that it is safe."

"Money is always acceptable to me," he wrote Attorney C. Ballance of Chicago, in acknowledging receipt of a fee of twenty dollars. "But when I left Chicago I was not in 'extremis' on that subject," he added.

In a lecture to law students, Lincoln expressed his attitude regarding the question of compensation frankly and unblushingly. "The matter of fees is important, far beyond the mere question of bread and butter involved," he declared. "Properly attended to, fuller justice is done both lawyer and client. An exorbitant fee should never be claimed. As a general rule never take your whole fee in advance, nor more than a small retainer. Settle the amount of fee and take a note in advance. Then you will feel that you are working for something and you are *sure* to do your work faithfully and well. Never sell a fee note—at least not before the consideration service is performed. It leads to negligence and dishonesty—negligence by losing interest in the case, and dishonesty in refusing to refund when you have allowed the consideration to fail."[1]

Lincoln practiced law in Illinois at a time when none were rich; when dignified and eminent judges were receiving less than twenty dollars a week for their arduous services on the circuit; when workingmen were being paid seventy-five cents to a dollar for a twelve-hour day of labor. Good farm land in central Illinois was current at five dollars an acre, and some as low as a dollar and twenty-five cents an acre.[2] A circuit-riding lawyer could get his lodging and meals at a country tavern, and also feeding and stabling of his horse, for a trifling amount, probably not more than fifty cents a day. In fact, after Lincoln's marriage to Mary Todd

---

[1] *Works*, II, 142.

[2] In a letter to William Fithian, dated February 16, 1850, Lincoln writes of land in Menard County "worth about $3.25 per acre . . . and probably would bring $4 per acre, if it could be sold on a credit." Angle, *Letters*, pp. 63–64.

they went to live at the Globe Tavern, where they received both room and board for only four dollars a week.[1] Two-dollar and five-dollar fees were, therefore, not uncommon, and it was not unusual for Lincoln to handle a case in the lower court and then carry it through an appeal in the Supreme Court for ten dollars.

It was a time when the income of such contemporary legal giants of the national bar as Webster and Wirth rarely exceeded four and five thousand dollars a year. Professional men were being paid fees commensurate with the standard of living of the period. In general Lincoln's fees compared favorably with those received by other lawyers.

A schedule of fees adopted by the bar of Chicago in 1852, although intended merely as a guide for minimum charges, undoubtedly reflects the compensation that lawyers throughout the State of Illinois were asking for their services. Thus, in common law cases the usual charge for counsel or advice was two dollars. A written opinion cost ten dollars. The client had to deposit five dollars at the commencement of a suit, and an additional five dollars if the attorney was to become security for the costs. In a large number of cases Lincoln bound himself for the costs and signed the bond to guarantee payment.

The schedule further provided a minimum fee of ten dollars for drawing a special declaration, one dollar for drawing a rule to plead, and five dollars for each of the following: term fee when suit is disposed of, drawing, filing, and arguing a motion for continuance, drawing demurrer, plea or notice of defense, arguing a demurrer, if sustained; arguing plea in abatement or drawing an affidavit for attachment. The charge for the trial of a cause in a court of record was ten dollars, and the same was demanded as the minimum fee in the State Supreme Court or in the United States District Court. The retainer for arguing the cause in the Supreme Court was twenty-five dollars, one half to be paid in advance. But when the amount in controversy did not exceed the jurisdiction of a justice of the peace, a sum deemed

[1] In the divorce case of Cowls vs. Cowls, 8 Ill. 435, Lincoln for the husband argued that thirty dollars a year for the support of each of two children was an excessive allowance.

reasonable was charged. It appears that when a *per diem* arrangement was made the usual fee was ten dollars a day.

Fees in chancery cases were slightly higher, and the charge for drawing a bill of divorce, or making and arguing an application for receiver, and similar actions was fifteen dollars.

In the collection of accounts the schedule called for a fee of 10 per cent of the first one hundred and fifty dollars, 5 per cent on the excess over one hundred fifty dollars, and 2 ½ per cent on the excess over two thousand dollars. The same commissions were charged on the amounts collected by foreclosure of mortgages.

In conveyancings the usual fee for drawing an ordinary deed, mortgage, power of attorney, bill of sale, or other instrument where a printed blank form was used was two dollars; a lease in duplicate or an agreement to sell real estate, or a chattel mortgage, cost three dollars. The ordinary charge for special deeds and mortgages, for articles for co-partnership, building contracts, opinions on abstracts of title, and for indentures of apprenticeship was five dollars.[1]

Of course this schedule of fees was not inflexible, and the actual compensation in each case depended largely on the peculiarity of the services rendered, the amount of money and responsibility involved, and the time consumed. Very few lawyers became rich by their practice. Even then it was recognized that considering the great amount of time required to prepare them for their profession, the intellect necessary for a successful practice, and the hardships connected with extensive circuit riding, lawyers were notoriously underpaid for their services.

Although Lincoln's charges did not differ much from the general run of fees received by his fellow practitioners, now and then he was prone to underrate his services and surprise his client by the smallness of his bill.

Thus George W. Nance relates that he engaged the Springfield lawyer to handle a legal matter for him, and when it was successfully completed he was amazed that Lincoln charged him only two dollars and fifty cents for his services. "I had no idea of paying less than ten dollars," he said.

[1] *Chicago Legal News*, February 13, 1869.

John W. Bunn, the Springfield banker who was a client and intimate friend of Lincoln, entrusted an attachment suit to him in behalf of George Smith & Co., a Chicago banking firm. The case involved several thousands of dollars. Lincoln collected the money and deducted twenty-five dollars as his compensation. The Chicago bankers wrote to Bunn: "We asked you to get the best lawyer in Springfield and it certainly looks as if you had secured one of the cheapest."

Lincoln charged only three dollars and fifty cents for collecting nearly six hundred dollars from his political rival Stephen A. Douglas. His reason for this small fee was that he had so little trouble with the collection. "I sent it to my friend in Washington, and was only out the postage," he explained.[1]

Isaac Hawley of Springfield was prepared to pay him fifty dollars for his services in saving his farm in Brown County. But he was pleasantly surprised when Lincoln said, "Well, Isaac, I think I will charge you about ten dollars."[2]

Father Curtis Chiniquy, the Kankakee clergyman whom Lincoln successfully defended against a criminal charge, believed the lawyer's services were worth "at least two thousand dollars." He was amazed when Lincoln informed him that he would be satisfied to accept Chiniquy's note for fifty dollars as payment in full.[3]

John W. Bunn relates that "One morning he was telling me about a suit the day before in which he succeeded in gaining possession of a farm for one of his clients. For his services he made a charge of two hundred dollars, but said he had been thinking the matter over and was beginning to wonder if that wasn't after all rather too stiff a fee. He asked my opinion, but before I could answer we espied a short distance ahead of us Ben Edwards, the lawyer who represented the other side of the case and lost it. When we overtook him Lincoln, curious to learn

---

[1] Curtis William Eleroy, *The True Abraham Lincoln*, p. 75; Tarbell, *Life of Abraham Lincoln*, 1, 267–68; Thomas Lewis in *Leslie's Weekly*, February 16, 1899.

[2] Browne, *Abraham Lincoln and the Men of His Time*, p. 224.

[3] Whitney, *Life on the Circuit*, pp. 53–55, 136; Chiniquy, *Fifty Years in the Church of Rome*, pp. 566, 620–67.

whether the fee he charged equalled or exceeded that of his opponent, ventured to inquire how he fared in settling with his client. 'Very well,' answered Edwards. 'My man said that inasmuch as we had lost he hoped I would be proportionately merciful when I fixed my fee, and I was, for I let him off with three hundred dollars.' "

A dark-complexioned Portuguese, William Dungey by name, claimed his brother-in-law, Joe Spencer, slandered him by calling him a "nigger." It was a crime in Illinois for a negro to marry a white woman. So Dungey had Lincoln sue his wife's brother for damages. After a very bitter and long drawn out trial Lincoln succeeded in winning a verdict of six hundred dollars for his client. He suggested that Dungey remit four hundred of this amount to his brother-in-law on condition that the latter pay his fee. When asked what his charge would be, he replied to Lawrence Weldon and C. H. Moore, attorneys for the defendant, "Well, gentlemen, don't you think I have honestly earned twenty-five dollars?" These lawyers were astonished by the moderateness of his request.[1]

George P. Floyd of Quincy, Illinois, engaged him to draw up a lease for a hotel and sent him twenty-five dollars for his services. Lincoln wrote back: "I have just received yours of the 16th with a check on Flagg & Savage for twenty-five dollars. You must think I am a high-priced man. You are too liberal with your money. Fifteen dollars is enough for the job. I send you a receipt for fifteen dollars and return to you a ten-dollar bill."[2]

When asked why he failed to make a charge for acting as an arbitrator in a dispute Lincoln laughingly replied: "They wouldn't want to pay me. They don't think I have earned a fee unless I take the case into court and make a speech or two."[3]

At times after completing a case, if not in immediate need of cash, Lincoln would defer the question of his compensation to a

---

[1] Weik, *The Real Lincoln*, pp. 162–64.

[2] George P. Floyd in *McClure's Magazine*, January 1908, p. 303.

[3] Gibson W. Harris in Browne, *Abraham Lincoln and the Men of His Time*, p. 220.

future date. But when he became short of money he would make a strenuous effort to collect the fee at once.

"I am short of funds and intended to ask Col. Dunlap for my fee in the case in the United States District Court, but he left sooner than I expected," he wrote to David A. Smith. "He is in no default with me for he once mentioned the subject to me and I passed it by. But now I need the money and I will take it as a favor if you will show him this note and get him to send it to me. We never agreed on the account; but I claim $50, which I suppose neither he nor you will think unreasonable."[1]

He speaks again of his need for money in a letter to Harry E. Dummer and urges him to collect a fee for him. "When I was in Beardstown last spring, Dr. Sprague said if I would leave a bill, he would pay it before long," he wrote. "I do not now remember that I spoke to you about it. I am now in need of money. Suppose we say the amount shall be $50. If the Dr. is satisfied with that, please get it and send it to me."[2]

In a like vein, in a letter to Samuel D. Marshall of Shawneetown concerning some cases in which they were jointly interested, he adds: "At the request of Mr. Eddy, I attended a case in the Supreme Court of Rawlings against Field, your father, Mr. Eddy and some others, and got the judgment reversed. This is no business of yours, and I now only ask as a favor of you, that if Mr. Eddy is well, you say to him I would like to have the little fee in the case if convenient."[3]

The question of fees was no secondary matter to him. It meant his bread and butter. When his work was finished he wanted his money. Whitney relates that during a term of court in the summer of 1856 at Urbana, Lincoln "had collected twenty-five or thirty dollars for that term's business thus far, and one of our clients owed him ten dollars which he felt disappointed at not being able to collect. So I gave him a check for that amount and went with him to the bank to collect it. I do not remember to have seen him happier than when he got his little earnings together,

---

[1] Angle, *Letters*, p. 78.
[2] Tracy, *Uncollected Letters*, p. 90.
[3] *Ibid.*, p. 14.

being less than forty dollars as I now recollect, and had his carpet bag packed ready to start home."[1]

To Andrew McCallen, he wrote this characteristic note: "I have news from Ottawa that we won our Gallatin and Salin county case. As the Dutch justice said when he married folks, 'Now vere ish my huntred tollars?' "

He had trouble collecting fees from out-of-town clients, so he wrote James S. Irwin: "Whatever fees we earn at a distance, if not paid before, we have noticed we never hear after the work is done. We, therefore, are growing a little sensitive on that point."[2]

Again, in advising Richard S. Thomas to accept a hundred and ten dollars in settlement of a claim, he did not forget the matter of his fee. "As to the amount of the fee," he wrote, "take ten dollars, which you and I will divide equally."

In a letter to Cornell, Waite & Jameson of Chicago, apprising them of the manner in which he was taking care of a land deal for them, he wrote, "Now, if you please, send me ten dollars as a fee."[3]

A client, Benjamin Kellog, Jr., sent fifty dollars for services rendered him by Lincoln. When the lawyer checked his files he found that Kellog did not owe him quite that amount. So he gave him a receipt reading: "Received May 11, 1855, of Benjamin Kellog Jr. fifty dollars in full balance of all fees up to this date, and also one dollar and a quarter to be applied on the next fee."

He charged Nicholas H. Ridgely, Springfield capitalist, a fee of five hundred dollars for "services in the Gas Light Works and in defending the same at Law vs. Gibson." "We may want to draw on you or get the money in a day or two," he wrote at the end of his bill.[4]

Not infrequently when his sympathies were aroused by the poverty of a client, Lincoln refused compensation. He would not accept any fee from the Wright widow in her claim against the

---

[1] Whitney, *Life on the Circuit*, p. 81.
[2] *Works*, XI, 98–99.
[3] Tracy, *Uncollected Letters*, p. 76.
[4] Angle, *Letters*, pp. 203–04.

unscrupulous pension agent, nor from Hannah Armstrong for winning the acquittal of her son Duff on a charge of murder.

When back in 1843 Isaac Cogdal, a quarryman of Rock Creek, was beset with financial difficulties, he employed Lincoln as his legal counsel. He could not pay the fee in cash, but he delivered to Lincoln his promissory note for the agreed amount. Some weeks later the lawyer saw Cogdal on the steps of the State House in Springfield and was dumbfounded to observe that one of his arms had been amputated. Upon inquiry he learned that the luckless fellow, while making a blast, had met with a serious accident resulting in the loss of his arm.

"I have been thinking about that note of yours," Cogdal said.

"Well, you needn't think any more about it," Lincoln replied. And from his wallet he took out the note and handed it to the crippled quarryman. "If you had the money, I could not take it," he said sympathetically as he hurried away.[1]

With the exception of the Illinois Central case, never once did a client complain of being overcharged. And yet Lincoln had considerable trouble in collecting his modest fees. Contrary to Herndon's statement that his senior partner would rather be swindled than sue for his fees, we find Lincoln, in at least five instances in addition to the Illinois Central case, resorting to court action to compel clients to pay him for legal services he had rendered in their behalf. He had fought for justice and equity for them. Now, his work completed he demanded a square deal for himself.

On May 30, 1840, Spencer Turner and William Turner delivered their note to Lincoln for two hundred dollars for legal services rendered in their behalf. It was to have been paid within ninety days. But when nearly a year and a half after its delivery the note remained unsatisfied, Lincoln during the October term, 1841, of the De Witt Circuit Court filed suit. Service was procured only on Spencer Turner, and that defendant set up the plea that he was a minor when he signed the note. However, a judgment was rendered in the lawyer's behalf for the amount of the note plus thirteen dollars and fifty cents costs. Almost five years

[1] Holland, *Life of Abraham Lincoln*, p. 93.

later papers were served on William Turner and a judgment was entered against him as well.

The Trailor brothers failed to pay the modest fee of one hundred dollars for all of Lincoln's work in defending them against a charge of murdering one Fisher back in May, 1841. So at the July term, 1845, of the Sangamon Circuit Court Lincoln filed suit for himself and his former partner Logan, against James D. Smith, executor under the will of William Trailor, and recovered a judgment for the amount claimed plus court costs.

John Atchinson was another client of the Logan & Lincoln firm who refused to pay a fee. Lincoln sued him for two hundred dollars, but the jury allowed him and his partner only a hundred dollars.

The partnership of Lincoln & Herndon appears as plaintiff in a suit filed at the March term, 1850, of the Sangamon Circuit Court against John B. Moffett for services rendered attending "suit with Lewis and others" in the Circuit and Supreme Courts. Lincoln claimed a hundred and fifty dollars, but settled the suit when the defendant paid seventy-five dollars and the court costs.

Samuel Short, a farmer living near Taylorville, showed his appreciation of Lincoln's loyal services in successfully defending him against a charge of maliciously firing a shotgun at some boys prowling in his melon patch, by completely ignoring his requests for compensation. Lincoln, losing all patience, sued for his fee in the court of a justice of the peace.

When Samuel Sidner was unable to pay a fee of five hundred dollars, Lincoln took his note, secured by a mortgage on real estate located in Springfield. After the obligation became due, the lawyer procured judgment against Sidner for $594.80, levied upon the property, and bought it at the sheriff's sale for $628.54.[1]

During Lincoln's most prosperous years at the bar, his income averaged from two to three thousand dollars a year. He carried an account with the Springfield Marine Bank, with which institution his friend John Bunn later became associated. But he did not deposit all his earnings in the bank. Apparently his dealings were largely in cash, and when he collected a fee he would

[1] Lincoln Centennial Association, Bulletin No. 8, September 1, 1927, p. 4.

ordinarily carry his share of the fee in his pocket and make his purchases with cash.

The records of the bank show that in 1854 Lincoln deposited $710 and drew it all out during the course of the year. In 1855, he deposited only $198 and had a balance of $54.64 at the end of the year. On November 13, 1856, he deposited $970 dollars and withdrew it about a month later, probably to make an investment. His largest deposit was on August 12, 1857. It totaled $4800 and undoubtedly included his share of the Illinois Central and McCormick cases. This money remained in the bank but a short time, as in nineteen days he drew it out for investment at a better rate of interest than offered by the bank. During 1858, the year of his historic debates with Douglas, he deposited less than $500. Although during this year his earnings were practically negligible—not even enough to pay his household expenses—he was fortunate in having laid aside some money for just such an emergency.

Lincoln was simple and frugal in habits and not very fastidious as to food or dress. The steady flow of trifling and ordinary fees, augmented now and then by an extraordinary fee, enabled him to save a portion of his earnings and occasionally to make some profitable investments in the form of loans to responsible individuals. Banking facilities were then inadequate, and persons requiring funds for real-estate purchases or business enterprises were often compelled to borrow from private sources. Lincoln made a number of such loans, charging as a rule 10 per cent interest and sometimes as high as 12 per cent. A first mortgage on real estate was the usual security he demanded, although now and then he waived this requirement and accepted the borrower's personal note alone.

Shortly after his return from Congress, he loaned five hundred dollars to John Hay, an early settler and the grandfather of the young man who was to become one of Lincoln's secretaries in the White House. A first mortgage on the borrower's one hundred-and-sixty-acre farm near Springfield secured this loan. For six months Hay paid 6 per cent interest and thereafter for an additional two years until the mortgage was satisfied, 10 per cent.

On August 15, 1851, August Ruckel and his wife delivered their note to Lincoln for three hundred dollars bearing 10 per cent interest for a loan in that amount. They also gave him adequate real-estate security to protect him against default in payment. Six years later the obligation was paid in full. Then Ruckel borrowed five hundred dollars on another property. Lincoln next loaned six hundred dollars to Thomas Cantrall and his wife, charging the usual interest of 10 per cent and receiving a first mortgage on their farm of eighty acres for security.

Ritta Angelica da Silva, "a Portuguese woman" of Springfield, made two separate loans of one hundred and twenty-five dollars each, and executed in Lincoln's favor a first and second mortgage, pledging her Springfield land as security. To Isaac Lindsey he loaned six hundred dollars, and to William Cline seven hundred and fifty dollars, in each case receiving 10 per cent interest and adequate real-estate security.

To Norman B. Judd, who was to become instrumental in fostering Lincoln's political fortunes, the latter made his largest loan—one of three thousand dollars. But Lincoln did not permit friendship to interfere with business, and took adequate security for this loan. In addition to a note bearing 10 per cent interest, Judd and his wife gave Lincoln their quitclaim deed for two separate properties in Council Bluffs, Iowa, which were reconveyed only after the loan was paid in full.

Lincoln made a number of unsecured loans ranging in amounts from fifty dollars to four hundred dollars. One such loan was in the sum of two hundred dollars to Nathanial Hay, a brick-maker of Springfield.

Frequently Lincoln accepted interest-bearing notes from clients in payment of law fees, and if he could buy good outstanding accounts at a profit to himself, he would do so.

When during the midst of his political activities an aunt requested him to collect some accounts for her, Lincoln wrote to her January 3, 1859: "It annoys me to have to say that I can not collect money now—I now believe the quickest way I can get your money is for me to buy the debts off you, as soon as I can get in any money of my own to do it with. I keep some money loaned at ten per cent; and when I can get hold of some, it would be a ready investment for me just to take these debts off your hands; and I shall try to do so—I think it will be better all round than to resort to the law.''

The Alton & Sangamon Railroad retained Lincoln as counsel in a number of lawsuits. When the company launched a campaign to sell its stock, Lincoln purchased six shares, paid five dollars cash on each share, and agreed to pay the balance in installments as fixed by the board of directors.

Despite Lincoln's aversion to speculation in lands, he became the owner of considerable real estate. In addition to his home in Springfield, he owned a lot in Lincoln, Illinois, given him for services in incorporating the town. He also acquired title to farms of one hundred and twenty acres in Crawford County, and forty acres in Tama County, Iowa, granted by the United States Government as ''bounty lands'' for his military services in the Black Hawk War. Another lot in Springfield came into his possession when James Primm of Logan County, for whom he had endorsed a note for four hundred dollars, conveyed the property to him, because Lincoln had been compelled to pay the obligation when Primm defaulted.

In 1851, Lincoln purchased two lots in Bloomington for four hundred dollars, and after holding them for nearly five years resold them for the same price.[1]

Previously he had owned and sold a lot in New Salem, four lots in Springfield, and a fifth one in that town acquired jointly with Stephen T. Logan. This latter parcel he used as part of the purchase price of his home. He also took title to forty acres of farm land in Coles County, in which he allowed his father and stepmother a life estate. His father-in-law deeded eighty acres, about three miles southwest of Springfield, to Mrs. Lincoln as a gift. In 1854, they sold this land for twelve hundred dollars.[2]

Lincoln once declared, ''I don't know anything about money. I never had enough of my own to fret me.'' To him worldly wealth was ''simply a superfluity of things we don't need.'' His

[1] Abraham Lincoln Association, Bulletin, December 1, 1929.
[2] *Ibid.*, September, 1919.

wants never being large, he took no delight in accumulating money for its own sake.

Yet through frugal living and careful small investments his worldly goods increased steadily, so that when his career at the bar was ended and he was entrusted with the business of a great nation, his personal estate had risen to the modest yet respectable sum, for the period, of ten to fifteen thousand dollars.

Apparently little of this was in cash at any one time, and frequently he was stressed for ready money to meet his obligations.

The unsuccessful campaign against Douglas in 1858 wrought havoc with his personal finances. Active on the stump for more than six months of the year, he found his income from the practice of law stopped almost completely, and the expenses of the canvass drained heavily upon his savings. He wrote Norman B. Judd that he was then without ready cash "for even household expenses."

And in a moment of financial distress he reminded his friend, A. Campbell, that in 1857 he had given Lincoln authority to draw on him for any sum not exceeding five hundred dollars, and that now he would like to exercise that privilege. "Please write me at all events," he pleaded, "and whether you can do anything or not, I shall continue grateful for the past."

"I could not raise ten thousand dollars if it would save me from the fate of John Brown," he wrote on March 17, 1860, in reply to a friend's question whether he would be willing to risk that amount on his chances for the Presidency.

When Judge Davis entered upon the sad duty of administering the estate of his martyred friend in 1865, he found Lincoln's personal wealth had increased considerably during his occupancy of the White House. His estate then totaled over one hundred thousand dollars, approximately two thirds of which he had providently invested in United States Government bonds.

XIX. A LEADER OF THE
ILLINOIS BAR

It is no easy task for us, many years removed from the days of Lincoln's prime at the bar, to pass judgment on his ability and standing as a lawyer. The cold, mute trial records of courtroom victories and defeats, his entry books of earnings and fees, and the dry-as-dust law briefs found in the musty files of the court-houses where he practiced give a most inadequate picture of his ability and genius as an advocate. To reanimate the power, persuasiveness, and personal magnetism that distinguished Lincoln and caused some to describe him as the "best all-around jury lawyer of his day in Illinois," to recall that rare combination of qualities, moral and intellectual, essential to the making of a good lawyer, to recapture his deep reverence for the law and the high professional standard, it is necessary to call as witnesses his colleagues at the bar who saw him in action, and heard him argue and plead his cases before judges and juries.

As our first witness it is proper that we call Judge David Davis, probably the most intimate of all of Lincoln's associates. It was Judge Davis who presided over most of the cases Lincoln tried in court. For many years, six months out of the twelve, he

241

traveled with the Springfield lawyer over his native circuit, the two spending the nights together in the same hotel room.

Judge Davis testifies that although Lincoln did not conform to the simple and technical rules of the profession, and although he read law books only when the cause in hand made it necessary, yet "In all the elements that constituted a lawyer he had few equals. He was great at *nisi prius* and before an appellate tribunal. He seized the strong points of a cause and presented them with clearness and great compactness. In order to bring into full activity his great powers it was necessary that he should be convinced of the right and justice of the matter which he advocated. When so convinced, whether the cause was great or small he was unusually successful."

Our next witness must naturally be William Herndon, for more than sixteen years Lincoln's law partner and loyal friend. He testifies:

"Nothing in Lincoln's life has provoked more discussion than the question of his ability as a lawyer. I feel warranted in saying that he was at the same time a very great and very insignificant lawyer.

"I early realized that Lincoln was strikingly deficient in the technical rules of the law. Although he was constantly reminding young legal aspirants to study and 'work, work,' yet I doubt if he ever read a single elementary law book through in his life. In fact, I may truthfully say, I never knew him to read through a law book of any kind. Practically he knew nothing of the rules of evidence, of pleading, or practice, as laid down in the textbooks, and seemed to care nothing about them. He had a keen sense of justice, and struggled for it, throwing aside forms, methods, and rules, until it appeared pure as a ray of light flashing through a fogbank. He was in every respect a case lawyer, never cramming himself on any question till he had a case in which the question was involved. He thought slowly and acted slowly; he must needs have time to analyze all the facts in a case and wind them into a connected story. He was greatest in my opinion as a lawyer in the Supreme Court of Illinois."[1]

[1] Herndon and Weik, *Lincoln*, II, 335.

Similar testimony is given by Samuel C. Parks, another attorney who knew Lincoln the lawyer. He says: "Lincoln's conscience, reason, and judgment worked out the law for him. It would not do to call him a great lawyer, for he was not; but it is fair to state that he was a good lawyer under conditions. He was not as quick as some men—in fact required more time to study his case and thus arrive at the truth. But above all things he must feel that he was right. For a man who was for a quarter of a century both a lawyer and a politician he was the most honest man I ever knew. He was not only morally honest, but intellectually so. At the bar he was strong if convinced that he was in the right, but if he suspected that he might be wrong he was the weakest lawyer I ever saw."

The distinguished jurist, Sidney Breese, Chief Justice of the Illinois Supreme Court, testifies emphatically: "For my single self, I have for a quarter of a century regarded Mr. Lincoln as the finest lawyer I ever knew and of a professional bearing so high-toned and honorable as justly and without derogating from the claims of others to entitle him to be presented to the profession as a model well worthy of the closest imitation."

Judge Thomas Drummond, who while presiding over the United States District Court at Chicago, heard Lincoln argue many cases, gives this characterization of Lincoln as a lawyer:

"He was not skilled in the learning of the schools, and his knowledge of the law was acquired almost entirely by his own unaided study and by the practice of his profession.

"He could hardly be called a very learned man in his profession, and yet he rarely tried a cause without fully understanding the law applicable to it. I have no hesitation in saying he was one of the ablest lawyers I have ever known. If he was forcible before the jury he was equally so with the court."

Lawrence Weldon, who from 1854 on was closely associated with Lincoln in the trial of cases, testifies that when he became acquainted with the Springfield lawyer that year, "he had a very strong hold upon popular affection, and stood high in the confidence of the people of the State. He was the leader of the bar, Judge Logan having substantially retired from the active practice.... In and among 'itinerant lawyers' Mr. Lincoln was the star; he stood above and beyond them all.... He could not be called a great lawyer measured by the extent of his acquirement of legal knowledge; he was not an encyclopedia of cases, but in the text-books of the profession and in the clear perception of legal principles, with natural capacity to apply them, he had great ability. He was not a case lawyer, but a lawyer who dealt in the deep philosophy of the law. He always knew the cases which might be quoted as absolute authority, but beyond that he contented himself in the application and discussion of general principles."[1]

Leonard Swett and Isaac N. Arnold, Lincoln's colleagues at the bar, often engaged with him in litigation either as associates or as opponents, regarded Lincoln as one of the most successful jury lawyers in the history of the Illinois bar. Arnold placed him at the very forefront of all jury pleaders of that State. "On the whole, Lincoln was the strongest jury lawyer we ever had in Illinois," he wrote. Arnold knew of no advocate who could so expertly examine and cross-examine witnesses. "He excelled all I ever heard in the statement of his case. However complicated, he would disentangle it and present the turning-point in a way so simple and clear that all could understand. Indeed his statement often rendered arguments unnecessary and often the court would stop him and say: 'If that is the case, Brother Lincoln, we will hear the other side.' He had in the highest possible degree the art of persuasion and the power of conviction."[2]

Leonard Swett, who knew Lincoln the lawyer as intimately and as well as any person, testifies that as a jury lawyer he had few equals and no superiors. "He was as hard to beat in a closely contested case as any lawyer I have ever met." Swett points out that in his days he had listened to Tom Corwin, Rufus Choate, and other luminaries of the American bar, but that Lincoln at his best was more sincere and impressive than any of them. If Lin-

---

[1] Lawrence Weldon, in A. T. Rice, *Reminiscences*, revised edition, 1909, p. 128.
[2] Arnold, *Life of Abraham Lincoln*, p. 84.

coln had a superior before a jury—and the more intelligent the jury the more he was pleased—he, Swett, did not know him.

The testimony of these distinguished colleagues of the circuit scarcely settles the vexing question of Lincoln's capacity as a lawyer. The opinions of his contemporaries are too divided—no two agreeing in their estimates of his ability. But from their conflicting views and from our own study of his career it is evident that Lincoln was not a great lawyer through profound knowledge of the law. In the first place, he lacked the broad education. He was not in any academic sense a student. His mind was not a storehouse of knowledge. He was not brilliant nor by nature industrious. The knowledge he acquired came as a result of hard plugging. But that which he learned, he learned well and never forgot.

In the second place, he lacked the "soldier of fortune conscience" that enables a man to fight on the one side of a cause as well as on the other, and on a bad as well as on a good one. He was not unusually successful in winning the lawsuits entrusted to him. His victories, at least in his Supreme Court cases, did not far exceed his defeats. Of the one hundred and seventy-eight cases in which he participated in that high tribunal, either alone or in association with other lawyers, he won ninety-four, not much more than half. Of three cases he tried in the Supreme Court of the United States, he won two. Of a number of cases in the federal district and circuit courts for which the records have been found, he appears to have been victorious in about 70 per cent.[1]

Lincoln's fellow circuit rider and intimate friend, Henry C. Whitney, testifies that "when it came to cases with no well defined precedent, then it was that Lincoln had a powerful advantage [over his adversaries], for he had no superior, certainly, and but very few equals, at our bar in original reasoning. Take it all in all, he had probably only one superior as a lawyer in our circuit—viz: Stephen T. Logan."[2]

It is impossible to determine his record of victories and defeats

---

[1] Weik, *The Real Lincoln*, p. 145.
[2] Whitney, *Lincoln the Citizen*, p. 172.

in the circuit courts, where he must have tried two thousand or more cases during his long career. But we have the statement of Whitney that Lincoln "was not more than ordinarily successful for a first-class lawyer; he certainly did not succeed in every case . . . he was sometimes defeated, like other lawyers, even in cases that he believed in and did his best to succeed in."[1] Lincoln himself told Bunn, the Springfield banker, that on one trip around the circuit he lost every case he tried, and he overheard someone remark, "Well, he isn't lawyer enough for it to hurt him."

His partner Herndon declared: "I have seen him lose cases of the plainest justice, which the most inexperienced member of the bar would have gained without effort. Two things were essential to his success in managing a case. One was time; the other a feeling of confidence in the justice of the cause he represented. . . . If either of these essentials were lacking, he was the weakest man at the bar."[2]

Of eighty-seven cases for which the records are available and that Lincoln tried before the court without a jury, decrees were rendered in favor of his clients in forty and against them in forty-seven. Of eighty-two actions argued before a jury, verdicts favorable to his clients were returned in forty-three.[3]

Competing with a coterie of legal giants battling for supremacy at the bar, Lincoln's standing among them was always of a high order. In certain respects he led them all. In others he trailed behind. In the right kind of case he was a great advocate, and in the wrong kind only ordinary or very weak. This lack of consistency is doubtless responsible for the conflicting testimony of his contemporaries. For, as Herndon points out, justice and truth, rather than the desire to win at all cost, were paramount with Lincoln the lawyer. "If to him a thing seemed untrue he could not in his nature simulate truth," said the junior partner. "The extreme conscientiousness and disregard of the alleged sa-

---

[1] Whitney, *Life on the Circuit*, p. 255.

[2] Herndon and Weik, *Lincoln*, II, p. 337.

[3] "Abraham Lincoln; Circuit Lawyer," paper delivered by Paul M. Angle before the Lincoln Centennial Association, February 11, 1927.

credness of the professional cloak robbed him of much so-called success at the bar.''

But Lincoln lost no greater portion of his cases than other leaders of the bar. In the numerous trials in which he was opposed by Judge Stephen T. Logan, regarded as the greatest *nisi prius* lawyer of Illinois, Lincoln more than held his own. In fact, his victories in these instances exceed his defeats. In a number of Lincoln's court reversals Logan or some other leader of the bar was associated with him. Some other defeats were on purely technical grounds of procedure. A pioneer of the profession, handling whatever cases came his way, he had few precedents to guide him in his work. He could not with any degree of certainty tell a client in advance the outcome of the litigation. In some instances his own logic and reasoning created the law for the immediate case. In others the equities were against his side and naturally he lost.

Some defeats could not be helped. To Charles Hoyt, Lincoln writes on one occasion: ''Our case is decided against us. . . . Very sorry, but there is no help. . . . I made every point and used every authority, sent me by yourself and by Mr. Goodrich; and in addition all the points I could think of and all the authorities I could find myself. . . . I do not think I could ever have argued the case better than I did. I did nothing else, but prepare to argue and argue this case from Friday morning till Monday evening. Very sorry for the result; but I do not think it could have been prevented.''

Defeats and victories in legal contests, depending as they do upon other antecedent facts and circumstances, are those ultimate results that may or may not prove anything in so far as the respective abilities of the contesting lawyers are concerned. Neither unusual success in winning cases nor profound knowledge of the law alone suffice to make a great lawyer. Each is an element; but there are other factors equally important. Lord Coke said substantially that the sages of the law had been men who had not only acquired a superior knowledge of the law but had also ''sucked from the breasts of that divine knowledge, honesty, gravity, and integrity.''

This essential qualification of the great lawyer, Lincoln possessed to an eminent degree. His keen, unique intellect, hating quibbles and evasions, could tolerate dishonest reasoning no more than unscrupulous dealing. The same conscience that marked his own life is found in the advice he had given to his clients. He was honest with them, with the court and jury, and with himself. A faithful adviser, a fearless defender ready to use his skill and every opportunity for his clients' protection, he never forgot his duty as a citizen and remained ever honest with the public. He shunned success that comes only at the expense of justice.

No one appreciated more than he the handicap of a defective education, and he strove mightily to overcome it. And though his brain was no compendium of legal precedents and adjudicated cases duly digested, arranged, and labeled, he possessed something greater than the mere abstract knowledge of law. He possessed these essential characteristics of the great lawyer: the ability to reason from a general principle, clearness of exposition, and a style of expression distinguished by its rare simplicity. He possessed a profound knowledge of the men and women with whom the law deals. He possessed a genius that enabled him to brush aside all non-essentials of a case and instinctively determine the vital and controlling principles.

Logic was his constant companion, and only infrequently did he permit himself to be drawn away from the mathematics of his profession. He sought to win his cases on prosaic ground of hard practical sense and logical demonstration. He could state his case in a manner that frequently made argument unnecessary. All his colleagues agree that for lucidity of statement, clear reasoning power, and analogy Lincoln had no superior at the bar of Illinois. His mental aptitude was to comprehend not only the techincal rules of the law, but to discern the philosophy and the spirit which undergirds those rules.

He had that most uncommon of possessions—common sense. In the varying and unexpected contingencies of a trial, a rich fertility in resources, coupled with a keen understanding of the moral value of the facts, enabled Lincoln to take the prudent course and without misgivings pursue it more successfully than a thorough knowledge of the law alone would have enabled him to do.

He possessed to an eminent degree the essential and indispensable qualities of the great jury pleader—a strong personality, a readiness of wit and invention, and a strong dramatic sense. His was the ability to repress his identity as the paid advocate and to assume instead virtually the rôle of juror, counselling and pleading with his fellows in the jury-box. He possessed the knack of making the jury feel that they and not he, were trying the case. He shunned always the appearance of the advocate trying too hard to protect a client's interests. He avoided giving the impression that by every means at his command he was attempting to prevent the guilt of his client from becoming known. The atmosphere he created at the very outset of the case was one of honesty, candor, and fair dealing.

He could look a jury squarely in the eyes during his defense of a tramp accused of murder by reason of circumstantial evidence, and say: "While I concede that the testimony bears against my client I am not sure that he is guilty. Are you?" Thus did he plead the existence of a reasonable doubt. The jury believed him and acquitted his client. He never tried to impress upon the jury that the opposition had not even the shadow of a leg to stand on. On the contrary, it seemed often that he was giving his own case away by yielding point after point claimed by the adversary. He refrained from quibbling over trifles, and at times admitted issues that other lawyers would have disputed violently. Often his clients and associates trembled with apprehension as he nonchalantly drawled: "I reckon it would be fair to let that in," or, "We will give them that point." "I reckon they were right there," or, "Oh! I'll freely admit that. But that is not the gist of the matter anyway," he would say.

"Here, gentlemen, is the real point in this case, and on it we rest our defense." Then with candor, clearness, and adroitness he would state what he regarded as the real issue, and finally, "Now, this much we may ask, and when I state it, it will be a reasonable demand."

At the outset of the trial, having instinctively seen the kernel of the case, he never lost sight of it and never permitted it to escape the jury. "This is the real point," he would declare, and with the husk brushed away, with tenacious determination he kept the judgment of the jurors constantly fixed on the vital issue upon which the case depended; just as years later as the Nation's Chief Magistrate he was to focus the people's attention upon the issue of the preservation of the Union as the paramount and supreme issue and never for a moment would permit them to digress from it.

In his summation he seemed to be speaking to each juror individually, taking each and every one into his confidence. They were invariably convinced that this homely, gawky barrister speaking their own language was really one of their own kind— a fair-minded noble man whom they could trust implicitly.

During trial of a case, with rare exceptions, Lincoln was calm, placid, and benign. Nothing disturbed or excited him. Soberly and discreetly he would go about the business of the litigation in a matter-of-fact way. No matter how eventful the case, no matter whether disaster impended or victory smiled, he displayed no enthusiasm nor revealed the slightest trace of trepidation. This disturbed Herndon, who was accustomed to the thrilling and ear-splitting oratory and fiery rhetoric for which the courts were then famed, and therefore failed to appreciate as Lincoln did that results could be obtained with less noise. Lincoln's art of persuasion was different than that of most of the lawyers of his day. He was a courtroom strategist who fought his legal battles with a light brigade, as it were, calling upon his heavy artillery only when absolutely necessary. Whenever that occasion arose he had the forces behind him. He could charm men from their determination, magnetize them, and work a spell about them. Under provocation his onslaught was simply irresistible.

His arguments to the juries were like his later speeches to the people—clear, lucid, fair in statement, and marked by logic and accurate reasoning power. He never spoke over the heads of the jury. His speeches were never wearisome. His quaint expressions were the people's own homely language, abounding in native wit, figures of speech, and telling illustrations. He used the catch words of the farmers and the common words of the tradesman who composed the jury. His simple, candid words so wonderfully clear and persuasive often made the members of the jury feel that they themselves were speaking.

The counterpart of Lincoln the trial lawyer and jury pleader is found in Lincoln the stump-speaker of the Douglas campaigns, in the statesman making clear to the people the great issues of the day, in the orator who electrified the multitudes by his inaugural and Gettysburg addresses. He spoke to the juries of the Illinois circuits as he was to speak later to the masses. He came from their ranks and he talked their language. He knew them well.

In a case in Coles County involving the disputed ownership of a colt, Lincoln took great pains to make the jury understand the meaning of the phrase, "preponderance of the evidence." He realized they were puzzled and he decided to give them a simple test by which they could arrive at an intelligent conclusion. "Now," said he, "if you were going to bet on this case on which side would you be willing to risk a picayune? That side on which you would be willing to bet a picayune, is the side on which rests the preponderance of evidence in your minds. It is possible that you may not be right, but that is not the question. The question is as to where the preponderance of evidence lies, and you can judge exactly where it lies in your minds, by deciding as to which side you would be willing to bet on."[1]

Of course the jury understood this simple yet ingenious explanation of a difficult legal proposition. He succeeded in convincing them that the verdict should go to the side in whose favor the evidence balanced "even if the preponderance should only be a hair's weight."

Speaking "horse sense" after this fashion was mainly responsible for the jury's verdict's going in favor of Lincoln's client.

This rare faculty to make the most intricate matter clear and understandable, developed and perfected in the hundreds of cases before the farmers, laborers, and tradesmen who composed the

[1] Holland, *Life of Abraham Lincoln*, p. 80.

juries in the Illinois courts, later was to enable him to explain to all the people the larger controversies that precipitated the Civil War.

Well might Lincoln's rank as a lawyer be epitomized in the words of Judge Samuel C. Parks: "He was a great advocate, and more successful at the bar than many men who knew more law than himself."[1]

The greatest professional standard and the deepest reverence for the law ever marked Lincoln's activities as a lawyer. Fellow practitioners and clients recognized the rare combination of qualities moral and intellectual, and were almost unanimous in ascribing to him a prominent place among the leaders of the Illinois bar.

It is significant that Lincoln's enviable reputation as a lawyer came to him without the aid of political prestige, for he argued nearly all his great cases before the contest with Senator Douglas brought him national prominence.

The retainers from the railroad, business, and municipal corporations, and other interests and individuals financially able to employ the finest legal talent in the Nation, constitute an eloquent yet practical evidence of the eminence he attained in the legal circles of his State.

But even more conclusive of his high regard and recognition of his qualifications as a lawyer is the fact that so many other members of the bar—competitors, if you please—employed him, of all the thousand or more barristers then practicing in Illinois, to become associated with them in the trial of cases in the lower courts or argument of appeals in the Supreme Court. Who is better qualified to pass upon the capabilities of a professional man than his fellow practitioners? When a physician must call an associate or consultant into a difficult case, he turns only to him who has achieved success and stands high for merit in the profession. So in the confidence expressed by Lincoln's competitors in selecting him so often to serve as their associate or consulting counselor is found the highest compliment and finest recognition of the true worth of Lincoln the lawyer.

[1] Samuel C. Parks, in a lecture before the University of Michigan.

XX. LINCOLN, DOUGLAS, AND THE DRED SCOTT DECISION

THE eminence that Lawyer Lincoln attained in his chosen profession brought him a certain solace and peace of mind that partly dispelled the political frustration he experienced following his disillusioning and unfruitful term in Congress. He had buried himself in the law, practically to the complete exclusion of politics. And he was contented in his work and as happy as one of his restless and melancholy nature could be.

All of a sudden an alarm was sounded at the national capital that agitated Lincoln as well as all other anti-slavery men as nothing before had done. Like a sleeping lion suddenly aroused, he sprang form his political lethargy into the national vortex, and was soon on the path that fate or destiny had intended for him. And strange to say, the man who brought this supreme opportunity and marked the path was none other than his old political rival, Stephen A. Douglas.

On January 4, 1854, without previous warning or preliminary agitation, without a demand from either the North or the South, Senator Douglas, virile advocate of territorial home rule, as chairman of the powerful Committee on Territories, recommended the startling innovation of permitting the inhabitants of the Territory of Nebraska, whenever it should be admitted to statehood, to decide for themselves whether they desired to allow or prohibit slavery. To make matters worse, Senator Archibald Dixon of Kentucky offered an amendment to Douglas's bill that expressly repealed the Missouri Compromise; and though Douglas at first remonstrated, he finally yielded to Senator Dixon's theory that the Missouri Compromise was unconstitutional and should be nullified. A vast region long consecrated to freedom was ruthlessly to be thrown open to slavery. The wounds partly healed by the compromises of 1850 were to be torn open.

The storm of angry protest that arose throughout the outraged North in denunciation of Douglas and his bill stirred in the heart of the awakening lion of Springfield certain solemn resolves. "I tell you, Dickey," he declared to his circuit companion when the news of the legislation was first brought to his attention, "This nation cannot exist half-slave and half-free." That night he hardly slept. His return to politics was now a matter of course. He permitted his name again to be put up for the General Assembly, and was elected by a large majority.

But without even taking office, he resigned to make the race for the United States senatorship as a Whig on an anti-Nebraska platform. Leading in the early balloting and with victory nearly in his grasp, he was finally forced by political expediency to sacrifice himself in favor of Lyman Trumbull in order to defeat Governor Joel Matteson, a Nebraska Democrat and Douglas's protégé. The venerable Judge Stephen T. Logan, in charge of Lincoln's candidacy, actually shed tears when, at Lincoln's earnest request, he withdrew his name.[1]

"When I received the bond I was dabbling in politics, and of course neglecting business. Having since been beaten out I have gone to work again." So wrote the disappointed Lincoln to a client.[2]

Politically he had failed again. But though he wearily returned to his neglected law practice, his heart and thoughts remained with the seething political events which, unknown to him, were even then shaping his destiny.

---

[1] *Works*, II, 272–77.
[2] Lincoln to Sanford, Porter and Striker, March 10, 1855. *Works*, II, 278.

Until now the career of the Sangamon County lawyer had consisted largely of bitter disappointments. But in Douglas's life-vocabulary there had been no such word as "fail." His career had been one steady march of brilliant successes and triumphs. Admitted to the bar before he was twenty-one, he became Attorney General of Illinois just a few months later. Then in rapid succession came his elections or appointments as a member of the state legislature, Registrar of the Federal Land Office at Springfield, Chairman of the Democratic State Committee, Secretary of State, and when only twenty-seven, as a member of the bench of the Supreme Court of Illinois. The conservative profession of law records but few such meteoric rises. Then followed his triumphant career at Washington and his advance to the national leadership of his party. Thereafter no list of potential candidates for the Presidency was complete without the name of Stephen A. Douglas.

Lincoln, on the other hand, was still undergoing the training and discipline that were preparing him for the epoch-making last four years of his life.

Disappointed but undaunted, with an admonition to his friends and loyal followers to stand firm for the principles of their cause, he returned to his law practice to try some of the most important and famous cases of his entire career. But though he temporarily withdrew from the political arena, he did not abandon the battle. The "monstrous injustice" of the Kansas-Nebraska Act would not let him rest. He never stopped talking about its iniquity. He watched the development in "bleeding" Kansas, where a pro-slavery mob had gained control. He waxed indignant over the outrages committed there. He attended the Bloomington Convention and helped found the Republican Party in 1856. A few months later the Republicans, in national convention assembled in Philadelphia, cast 110 votes for Lincoln as Vice-President. He was growing in political power every day.

Then on March 7, 1857, to a large audience assembled in the Supreme Court of the United States, the aged and venerable Chief Justice Roger B. Taney, in a low voice almost inaudible, delivered the long-awaited, subtly reasoned, epoch-making decision in the Dred Scott case. Dred Scott, a negro slave who had been taken into free territory, was not entitled to his freedom by reason of such residence, the Chief Justice said on behalf of the majority of the Court. A negro could not become a citizen, had no rights, and therefore could not sue.

Moreover, slaves are property, and Congress has no more power over slave property than over chattels of any other description. Therefore, the Missouri Compromise, which prohibited a citizen from holding and owning slaves in a territory of the United States, is unconstitutional and void.

Thus were the most radical views of the Southern slave-powers given judicial ratification by the highest tribunal in the land.

Following so close upon the heels of the Kansas-Nebraska Act, the pronouncement filled Lincoln with horror and apprehension. The cruel decision that eternally doomed the negro by the worm-eaten standards of centuries past now deprived Congress and the territories of the right to forbid slavery within their boundaries. How long, he wondered, before free territories and even free States would also be opened to slavery by judicial decree? As a lawyer he believed that the Dred Scott decision was contrary to law and fact and an outrage to precedent, history, and justice. He resolved that it should never become binding upon the political consciences of the people.

Lincoln found comfort in the vigorous dissenting opinion of Justice Benjamin R. Curtis, who denounced the majority pronouncement as unwarranted by the Constitution. Categorically the great dissent refuted every one of Taney's arguments. Challenging the contention that no negroes had ever been citizens in any of the States, Justice Curtis declared that as a matter of fact negroes were citizens in several of the northern States at the adoption of the Constitution, and that the language of the Declaration was applicable to them. Congress, he insisted, through its constitutional power "to make all needful rules and regulations" for federal territories, had the power to exclude slavery from a territory, and therefore the Missouri Compromise was constitutional.

Lincoln secured a copy of Curtis's dissent, and drew from it a number of arguments he was to use in his coming senatorial battle with Douglas. Of all the discussions of the Dred Scott decision, either in Congress or elsewhere, none were to have such a powerful effect upon the people as the opinions uttered by Lincoln and Douglas during their memorable campaign of 1858.

The extension of slavery as affected by the fateful Supreme Court pronouncement was the chief issue of the impending contest. The candidate best able to discuss and interpret this "decisive battle of the law" would now have a great advantage. Only a trained lawyer could fathom the subtle reasoning of the Dred Scott case and explain the logical contradictions between its principles and those of Douglas's pet doctrine of "popular sovereignty."

But Lincoln was prepared. For twenty-one years as a practicing lawyer he had been studying law cases, reading, analyzing, and interpreting court decisions and the enactments of legislatures.

The same experience that had enabled him so successfully to explain and interpret dry points of law to the juries of the Eighth Circuit now qualified him to make clear to the people the legal bearing of the intricate Supreme Court decision and explain the matter so that the average voter could understand.

Although Douglas had left the Sangamon County lawyer far behind in his rapid ascent to fame and power, Lincoln had not been standing still. While Douglas was becoming more adroit in political manipulations, Lincoln was developing to a higher degree in legal skill.

A popular saying among the lawyers of Illinois asseverated that "With a good case, Lincoln is the best lawyer in the State, but in a bad case, Douglas is the best lawyer the State can produce." In general, Lincoln possessed greater all-round knowledge of law and better grounding in legal argument and reasoning than his more famous rival. Though both were strong jury lawyers, and skilled in presenting clearly and distinctly the real points of a case to a body of average laymen, Lincoln surpassed Douglas as a cross-examiner.

Lincoln was also clearer in statement than Douglas, and in the use of apt and appropriate language that everyone could understand he ranked higher. The homeliness and force of his illustrations and their effective pertinence gave a novelty and freshness to his style that was most persuasive.

"A house divided against itself cannot stand," Lincoln declared in sounding the keynote of the campaign at Springfield, June 17, 1858. "I believe this government cannot endure permanently half slave and half free. I do not expect the house to fall, but I do expect that it will cease to be divided. It will become all one thing or all the other."

The lawyer who so aptly illustrated his law arguments in the courtroom by appropriate anecdotes, now had crystallized the entire issue with this remarkable phrase. A clearer, truer, apter comparison could not have been conceived; and it produced a nationwide effect that was electrifying.

After its powerful opening paragraph, the address, so pregnant with prophecy, launched into a history, discussion, and analysis of the Dred Scott decision in relation to the spread of slavery.

Again Lincoln demonstrated his genius for argumentative statement when in a single sentence he summarized the entire issue presented by the Dred Scott decision, with these convincing words:

"If any man choose to enslave another, no third man shall be allowed to object."

This speech more than any other of his addresses established him as the man of the hour. More than any other speech it "made" Lincoln. It was the foundation for his debates with Douglas. Together with his Cooper Union speech, it established him as the Republican Party's most available candidate for the Presidency. It was Lincoln the lawyer at his best—Attorney Lincoln pleading for a favorable judgment in the greatest of all his law appeals.

Almost in its entirety the speech dealt with the Dred Scott case and how it squatted Douglas's pet theory of "popular sovereignty" out of existence.

In due time Douglas characterized his speech as a dangerous utterance "advocating boldly and clearly a war of sections," and denounced Lincoln's "warfare upon the Supreme Court of the United States, because of their decision in the Dred Scott case."

Lincoln replied: "We believe as much as Judge Douglas (perhaps more) in obedience to and respect for the judicial department of government. But we think the Dred Scott decision is erroneous. We know the Court that made it has often overruled its own decisions, and we shall do what we can to have it overrule this.''

The great underlying truth of Lincoln's structure—that slavery was wrong and should be extirpated—Douglas could not shatter. ''Be slavery right or wrong,'' he thundered, ''the people of every State have a right to choose.'' Even though the Dred Scott decision had declared that the Missouri Compromise was unconstitutional and that Congress could not destroy the right of the master to his slave, it was ''a barren and worthless right, unless sustained, protected, and enforced by appropriate police regulations and local legislation, prescribing adequate remedies for its violation.''

Here was Douglas's attempt to reconcile his famous principle of ''popular sovereignty'' with the Dred Scott decision. The whole issue between himself and Lincoln he epitomized in this manner: ''He [Lincoln] says that he looks forward to a time when slavery shall be abolished everywhere. I look forward to the time when each State shall do as it pleases.''

Douglas held, as did many able Republican lawyers, that the Supreme Court had decided only the question of jurisdiction in the Dred Scott case and that all else was mere *obiter dictum*. He refused to admit that the Dred Scott pronouncement decided that slavery could go into a territory against the express wish of the inhabitants of that territory. The *obiter dictum* of the court was not decisive on that point at all, he insisted. ''With or without that decision, slavery will go just where the people want it, and not one inch further.''[1]

Lincoln shot back: ''The court did pass its opinion ... If they did not decide, they showed what they were ready to decide whenever the matter was before them. They used language to this effect: That inasmuch as Congress itself could not exercise such a

[1] When several Southern Senators at the Thirty-Sixth Congress accused Douglas of refusing to accept the Supreme Court's ruling in the Dred Scott case after agreeing to do so, he answered, ''But I deny that the point now under consideration has been decided in the Dred Scott case.''

power (i.e. pass a law prohibiting slavery in the Territories), it followed as a matter of course that it could not authorize a territorial government to exercise it; for the territorial legislature can do no more than Congress could do."

In reply, Douglas could only reiterate: "I assert that under the Dred Scott decision (taking Lincoln's view of that decision) you cannot maintain slavery a day in a territory where there is an unwilling people and unfriendly legislation. If the people are opposed to it, our right is a barren, worthless, useless right; and if they are for it, they will support and encourage it."

Although Douglas intended to place Lincoln on the defensive, the latter took the offensive as he relentlessly tore into the Senator's favorite doctrine of "popular sovereignty." He pointed out the inconsistency between that principle and the Dred Scott judgment, and explained to the voters that "squatter sovereignty"— the right of a people of a territory to govern themselves—had been wiped out by that Supreme Court judgment. For, said he, if the Dred Scott decision is good law, of what value is the vote of the population of a territory, whether for or against slavery? Why, any one man may take slaves into a territory, he pointed out, and all the other men in the territory may be opposed to it, and yet by reason of the Dred Scott decision they can not prohibit it. "When that is so, how much is left of the vast matter of squatter sovereignty?" he challenged.

Having demonstrated that "squatter sovereignty" was nothing but a fallacy, a sham, and an absurdity—a principle completely repudiated by the Dred Scott judgment—Lincoln soon had Douglas on the defensive vainly endeavoring to save his pet theory from judicial destruction. With relentless skill Lincoln pursued him with questions: "If Congress could not prohibit slavery from a territory, how could a territorial legislature, the creation of Congress, prohibit it?"

Repeatedly Lincoln attacked the soundness of the legal principles of Taney's pro-slavery pronouncement. Why, decisions apparently contrary to that decision have been made by that very court before, he asserted. Although the opinion settled the fate of one helpless betrayed negro, it was based upon falsehoods in the main as to the facts; it was false in principle and an atrocity in morals. A decision made under so many unfavorable circumstances had never been held binding by the profession as law, Lincoln declared. Without additional confirmation it should not be regarded as settled law. Of course, so long as the decision remained unreversed it should be obeyed. In this he was in full accord with Senator Douglas. But "somebody has to reverse that decision ... and we mean to do what we can do to have the court decide the other way."

Again and again he brought home to the people the fact that the Dred Scott decision involved not a mere abstract legal principle, but an imminent jeopardy that might result in making slavery a national institution.

He warned the voters of Illinois that the Dred Scott pronouncement was part of a great conspiracy to extend slavery, and that unless they repudiated the decision they should not be surprised if a later Supreme Court edict declared that the Constitution did not permit even a State to exclude slavery from its limits.[1]

There was no escape from Lincoln's constant attack against the Dred Scott infamy. And at one of the meetings an Irish adherent of Douglas, weary of the prodding, was heard to shout, "Give us something besides Dred Scott."

The canvass was already attracting national attention when, toward the end of July, Lincoln challenged Douglas to a series of joint debates. Reluctantly this "best off-hand, tit-for-tat debater in America, perhaps in the world," accepted the challenge. Thus were these two perennial rivals brought face to face in the contest that was making history.

When these two products of the Illinois circuits came together in verbal combat at the first of their joint debates in Ottawa, August 21, 1858, they formed a most striking contrast standing

[1] Sparks, *Debates*, pp. 110–13, 359–63, 430, 446–67.
Carl Russel Fish, *Development of American Nationality*, p. 351.
"Already in New York State the Lemmon case, which involved the status of slaves accompanying persons passing through a free state, was on the way to the Supreme Court. It can scarcely be doubted that the Court would have decided as Lincoln feared."

side by side on the high platform, silhouetted against the late summer prairie sky. On one hand was the jolly, rubicund Little Giant, slightly over five feet tall, stocky, broad-shouldered, deep-chested, at the full measure of his extraordinary power at the age of forty-five. His massive head and mane of abundant dark hair, his deep-set, flashing eyes and shaggy brows gave an appearance of intellectual power to his masterful, resolute, and fearless countenance. Aggressiveness, combativeness, defiance, and a never-say-die spirit seemed to be written on his every feature. Carefully and immaculately groomed in a well-fitting suit of broadcloth, he was the very embodiment of self-confidence, audacity, and personal force.

Beside him contrasted the tall, gawky, ungainly lawyer from Springfield, towering a foot and a half above the compact, manful Little Giant. He might have been called the Big Giant in comparison, despite his drooping shoulders, narrow chest, and small head. He was four years the senior of his more famous rival. His countenance was sallow and hollow-cheeked. In his benignant eyes was the look of sadness.

He was clad in a frock coat of rusty black; the sleeves missed his wrists by several inches, and the baggy trousers were too short to reach the tops of his rough shoes.

The reputation of Douglas for forensic skill far overshadowed that of his adversary. He was the most dextrous, the most heartily feared, and the most resourceful stump-speaker in American politics. A master in all the tricks of rough-and-tumble debate, he was excelled by none for fluency in speech and facility in logic, vehemence in attack, and bitterness in denunciation. He could be evasive when to his advantage and becloud the issue if it suited his purpose. Douglas's voice was more powerful and melodious than the high-strained voice of Lincoln, which often rose to a shrill treble in moments of excitement. His gestures were more forceful and graceful than those of his awkward opponent. He was indeed a stump-speaker whom very few men would have dared to encounter in verbal battle.[1]

[1] In the acrimony and bitterness of partisan strife much has been written about Douglas that is unjust and ungenerous. Extreme contemporary critics have pictured him as a blustering and unscrupulous demagogue and a master

All in all, men who knew them both had not yet recognized the divine spark in Lincoln, and blinded by the glare of Douglas's well-deserved fame, rated the shrewd, able, and resourceful rival far above the unassuming, sad-visaged barrister from Sangamon County.

And so they began—these two Western lawyers—pleading their most important cause before a jury of all the voters of their State, with the prairie as their courtroom, with the Constitution of the United States as their law book and authority, with the validity of the Dred Scott decision as the pivotal question to be determined. Upon the outcome hung the fate of a nation.

At Ottawa, Douglas asked a series of searching questions. Lincoln answered them in his next address at Freeport, clearly, adroitly, explicitly. Here Lincoln, the experienced courtroom strategist, became the questioner, and propounded four interrogatories for Douglas to answer. The second question was shrewdly framed:

"Can the people of a United States territory, in any lawful way, against the wishes of any citizen of the United States, exclude slavery from its limits prior to the formation of a state constitution?"[1]

Although this question turned out to be by far the most important of the series in so far as national results were concerned, the third interrogatory was probably more effective and of greater immediate interest to the voters of Illinois. It read: "If the Supreme Court of the United States shall decide that States cannot exclude slavery from their limits—are you in favor of acquiescing to adopting, and following such decision as a rule of political action?"

In other words, what is there to prevent the Supreme Court at some future day, by a new Dred Scott decision, from making the free and liberty-loving commonwealth of Illinois a slave State?

of the art of evasive and fallacious argument. For a fair portrayal of this foremost American statesman of his day, see such works as George Fort Milton's *The Eve of Conflict*, Clark E. Carr's *Stephen A. Douglas*, Gustave Koerner's *Memoirs*, and Louis Howland's *Stephen A. Douglas*.

[1] *Works*, II, 279; Sparks, *Debates*, p. 152.

Lincoln the great trial lawyer had begun the greatest of all his cross-examinations.

Douglas evaded this third question completely. He declared it was absurd and an aspersion against the Supreme Court and an attempt "to destroy public confidence in the highest judicial tribunal on earth."[1]

But he could not evade the fateful second interrogatory. If Congress, under the Dred Scott decision, could not exclude slavery from a territory, how could a territorial legislature with only such powers as Congress granted it have such authority?

It was Lincoln the lawyer asking, in other words, a question he already had answered many times himself. Briefly this adroit question could have been paraphrased: "Is the Dred Scott decision good law?" The answer once again called for an unequivocal interpretation of that famous Supreme Court judgment.

Of course Lincoln knew how Douglas would answer his query. He would answer in a way that promised the most votes in the present election. He would endeavor to evade the inevitable conclusion that since by the Dred Scott decision Congress had no power to prohibit slavery in a territory, then surely no territorial legislature possessing only such authority as is delegated by Congress could have that power. Instead he would somehow endeavor to reconcile his popular sovereignty doctrine with the Dred Scott ruling; he would answer the question so as to reassure the voters of Illinois, sorely puzzled over the Dred Scott case, that they had nothing to fear from it. He would try to avoid the trap set for him by Lincoln, and answer in a manner pleasing to his Illinois constituency that slavery could never exist where it was not wanted.

Lincoln's friends, to whom he confided his purpose, urged him not to ask this question. They warned him it would surely lose him the senatorship. But Lincoln, the masterful courtroom strategist who had so often in the course of exciting legal battles given away several minor points to win a big one in the end, was willing to risk immediate defeat to gain a larger principle. "Gentlemen," he said to his fearful friends. "I am killing larger game;

[1] Sparks, *Debates*, 163–64.

if Douglas answers, he can never be President, and the battle of 1860 is worth a hundred of this.'' Whether or not this momentous declaration, revealing almost divine foresight, was actually made by Lincoln, events certainly proved its truth.

Lincoln sought to force Douglas to take a definite stand and again compel him to interpret the Dred Scott decision. From this dilemma there could be no escape for the Little Giant. If he answered the question as Lincoln believed he would—to retain the favor of the Illinois voters—he would forever lose the support of the South and virtually tear the Democratic Party asunder. If he answered it in a way to please the Administration and the slave-power, his defeat at the hands of his constituents was inevitable.

Desperately Douglas tried to extricate himself from this trap. As Lincoln's friends had feared, here is how the Senator answered the fateful question:

"I answer emphatically, as Mr. Lincoln has heard me answer a hundred times from every stump in Illinois, that in my opinion the people of a territory can, by lawful means, exclude slavery from their limits prior to the formation of a state constitution. . . . It matters not what way the Supreme Court may hereafter decide as to the abstract question whether slavery may or may not go into a territory under the Constitution, the people have the lawful means to introduce it or exclude it as they please, for the reason that slavery cannot exist a day or an hour anywhere unless it is supported by local police regulations. Those police regulations can only be established by the local legislature; and if the people are opposed to slavery they will elect representatives to that body who will by unfriendly legislation effectually prevent the introduction of it into their midst. If, on the contrary, they are for it, their legislation will favor its extension. Hence, no matter what the decision of the Supreme Court may be on that abstract question, still the right of the people to make a slave territory a free territory is perfect and complete under the Nebraska Bill. I hope Mr. Lincoln regards my answer satisfactory on that point."[1]

Douglas, the father of "squatter sovereignty," had made his

[1] Sparks, *Debates*, pp. 61–62.

last desperate effort to save his pet theory from judicial destruction.

His answer was satisfactory to Lincoln only in so far as it made the rift between Douglas and the relentless leaders of the South irrevocable. But as an explanation of the power of a local legislature to nullify and override a decision of the Supreme Court it was not satisfactory. It was ridiculous. Lincoln's training as a lawyer at once recognized the absurdity of a proposition that "a thing may lawfully be driven away from a place where it has a lawful right to be." Here was Douglas, a former judge, saying in so many words that the Dred Scott decision, specifically ruling that Congress had no authority to exclude slave-holding from the Territories, was a mere "abstraction" which the people of any territory might properly disregard through the simple expediency of "unfriendly legislation." Here was a United States senator, professing to defend the Supreme Court, demonstrating to the voters how by political maneuvering they could go through the gesture of obedience to the Court while actually defeating the spirit and intention of its decision. "There has never been as outlandish or lawless a doctrine from the mouth of any respectable man on earth," Lincoln charged. "How is it possible to exclude slavery from the territory unless in violation of that decision?" Again and again he hurled his unanswerable challenge.

Clearly, the Dred Scott decision had repudiated the Little Giant's brain-child. But somehow he never fathomed the real significance of this fateful edict as it bore on his pet principle of home rule.

Lincoln, his superior as a constitutional lawyer, was enouncing a sounder jurisprudence.

With remorseless logic, with trenchant analysis, until the last day of the campaign he continued to expose the fallacy of the Douglas doctrine by demonstrating that when the proposition was reduced to its simplest form it meant merely that while the Dred Scott decision expressly gave any citizen the right to carry his slaves into a territory of the United States, under Douglas's "popular sovereignty" and "unfriendly legislation" the people of the same territory by vote could drive the slaves out of it again.

But Douglas's clever catch-phrases such as "Lincoln advocates . . . a war of sections," "popular sovereignty" is fair play, "niggers" are not the equal of white men, and the Supreme Court should be reverenced, served well as a shield to cover the weak points in his armor. His appeals played skillfully upon the emotions of his auditors. They recalled how he had dauntlessly defied President Buchanan and the slave oligarchy over the Lecompton constitution, which he had fought to its death. They admired him for his refusal to surrender his convictions of duty. They sympathized with him because the national Democratic Administration was carrying on a relentless war against him. Now they refused to repudiate him in favor of his Sangamon County rival, who was appealing to their intelligence rather than to their emotions.

More time was needed before the great moral truths Lincoln was uttering could sink into their hearts.

Douglas enunciated bad law when he asserted that no matter how the Supreme Court should decide, the people of a territory by their local legislation could still allow or prohibit slavery within its boundaries. Lincoln's interpretation of the Dred Scott decision was sounder. Yet tens of thousands of voters in Illinois approved Senator Douglas's principles as thoroughly in accord with democratic practices of a people's right to self-determination on questions of local concern. Lincoln, in denouncing the Dred Scott decision as bad law which should not become binding upon the political conscience of the people, spoke not as a lawyer owing obeisance to a mandate of the Supreme Court, but as a prophet.

In issues where moral rights were concerned, Lincoln surpassed his rival. But not even the most ardent supporters of the Springfield lawyer were entirely pleased with his tactics during the campaign.

In August, 1858, Theodore Parker, Herndon's Abolitionist friend, wrote: "I look with great interest on the contest in your State, and read the speeches, the noble speeches, of Mr. Lincoln with enthusiasm."

However, shortly after the first of the joint debates, where Douglas characterized Lincoln's failure to give a direct answer to the question whether or not he approved each article of the 1854 platform of the Republican Party—including the unconditional repeal of the Fugitive Slave Law, the restriction of slavery to those States in which it exists, and opposition to the admission of any more slave States into the Union—as "a miserable quibble to avoid the main issue," Parker's admiration cooled down perceptibly, for he wrote again: "In the Ottawa meeting, to judge from the *Tribune* report, I thought Douglas had the best of it. He questioned Mr. Lincoln on the great matters of slavery, and put the most radical questions . . . before the people. Mr. Lincoln did not meet the issue. He made a technical evasion."

Both Lincoln and Douglas were guilty of numerous evasions. Both spent much time in endeavoring to escape seemingly inescapable conclusions advanced by the opposition. Lincoln was often unresponsive, and, like Douglas, indulged in unjustified personal criticism.

Repeatedly, Douglas pointed to the inconsistency in Lincoln's refusal to accept the Dred Scott decision as a rule of political action and his willingness to comply with the moral obligation of obeying the law of the Constitution.

"Well," said Douglas, "if you are not going to resist the decision, if you obey it, and do not intend to array mob law against the constituted authorities, then, according to your own statement, you will be a perjured man if you do not vote to establish slavery in these territories."

And Lincoln could not extricate himself from the horns of this uncomfortable dilemma.

Again Douglas accused Lincoln of inconsistency by pointing to his attitude toward the negro. A dispassionate reading of Lincoln's speeches fail to substantiate this charge. He did diplomatically shift the emphasis of his arguments according to the varying character of his audiences. In districts with pronounced anti-slavery leanings, Lincoln stressed the moral wrong of slavery, but when he spoke in places like Charleston in the southern part of the State, he assured his auditors that he was not in favor of bringing about the social and political equality of the white and black races. Lincoln was an astute and practical politician who well realized that, after all, votes alone determine the outcome of an election.

All in all, the campaign was, as Parker wrote, "admirable education for the masses," and rightfully attracted national attention.

Myriad legends have arisen which depict Lincoln as the hero and Douglas as the villain of this epoch-making political drama; they declared that Lincoln had all the better of the verbal combat and literally wiped the platform with his rival. This is far from the truth. As in calm retrospect we re-read the speeches of these great political antagonists and attempt to choose the victor, we realize no absolute decision can be made.

Judged by immediate results, Douglas won. But by consequences more remote, the triumph was Lincoln's.

Lincoln went down to defeat in this memorable campaign. His candidates for the legislature polled approximately one hundred and ninety thousand votes as against one hundred and seventy six thousand for Douglas's men. But thanks to the district apportionment then existing in Illinois, the Democrats captured fifty-four places in the legislature to forty-six for the Lincolnites.

But what a glorious defeat it was! Douglas retained his seat in the Senate, but his Freeport "heresy" alienated the South from him forever. As the potential leader of a reunited democracy he was hopelessly destroyed. Lincoln in the meantime had become a national figure.

Well and eloquently did Judah P. Benjamin summarize the result when in arraigning Douglas as a traitor to the Southern cause because of his Freeport speech, he declared:

"We accuse him for this—that having bargained with us upon a point upon which we were at issue, that it should be considered a judicial point; that he would abide the decision; that he would act under the decision, and consider it a doctrine of the party; that having said that to us here in the Senate, he went home, and under the stress of a local election, his knees gave way; his whole person trembled. His adversary stood upon principle and was beaten; and lo, he is the candidate of a mighty party for the Presidency of the United States. The Senator from Illinois faltered. He got the price for which he faltered; but the grand prize for his ambition today slips from his grasp because of his faltering in the former contest, and his success in the canvass for the Senate purchased for an ignoble price, has cost him the loss of the Presidency of the United States.''

The inevitable split in the Democratic ranks—presaged by Douglas's Freeport doctrine—became a reality when the party assembled in national convention May 3, 1860, at Charleston, South Carolina, to elect its presidential candidate. Douglas, the strongest man in the party, still fighting for his principles, was the choice of the Northern wing; but the relentless leaders of the South, trembling at his "heresy," rejected him. Douglas was too honest and sincere to palter with his principles. He would not compromise or straddle the issue. Principle was dearer to him than even his great ambition.

The Democratic convention broke up into two irreconcilable factions; the Northern Democrats nominated Douglas, and the Southern faction John C. Breckinridge.

Lawyer Lincoln's deadly attacks against the Dred Scott decision and his masterful "cross-examination" at Freeport had developed its most potent consequence. They had made a senator, and unmade a president. They were yet to make a president.

XXI. LINCOLN'S FELLOW LAWYERS PROCURE HIS NOMINATION

ALTHOUGH the campaign of 1858 enhanced Lincoln's political fortunes, his personal finances suffered severely. For approximately six months he had absented himself from his law business, and deprived himself of all means of earning a livelihood, while paying all his own expenses of the canvass.

"I have been on expenses so long, without earning anything," he wrote his friend Norman B. Judd, chairman of the Republican State Committee, "that I am absolutely without money now for even household expenses. Still if you can put in $250 for me towards discharging the debt of the committee, I will allow it when you and I settle the private matter between us. This, with what I have already paid, with an outstanding note of mine, will exceed my subscription of $500. This, too, is exclusive of my ordinary expenses during the campaign, all of which, being added to my loss of time and business, bears pretty heavily upon one no better off than I am. But as I had the post of honor, it is not for me to be over-nice."[1]

[1] Lincoln to Judd, November 16, 1858; *Works*, V, 93.

271

Many lawyers of Lincoln's day and of today enter politics in order to gain publicity, attract important clients, and, in general, to build up their law practice. But in Lincoln's case, political activities resulted in just the reverse. During his two-year term in Congress he lost nearly his entire law practice. So now, again, the Douglas campaign curtailed his professional activities to such a degree as to leave him with practically no immediate income.

But though the campaign did set him back financially, he was glad he had made the race. "It gave me a hearing on the great durable question of the age, which I could have had in no other way," he wrote to A. G. Henry shortly after the unsuccessful election; "and though I now sink out of view, and shall be forgotten, I believe I have made some marks, which will tell for the cause of civil liberty long after I am gone."

Disappointed and exhausted, he returned to his dingy law office in Springfield to work off his debt and recoup his losses. This meant undivided attention to his profession. Clients had complained of the neglect of their business entrusted to him. S. C. Davis and Company, wholesale merchants of St. Louis, were dissatisfied over the failure of Lincoln & Herndon to collect some accounts sent them. Depressed by the loss of the senatorial campaign, the usually complacent and easy-going Lincoln was in no mood for complaints. He wrote this client that if they wished, he would surrender the matter to some other lawyer.

"My mind is made up—I will have no more to do with this class of business," he added. "I can do business in court, but I cannot, and will not follow executions all over the world."

Lincoln again applied himself assiduously to his profession. The following months were busy ones and enabled him to some extent to replenish his depleted finances. He carried a number of appeals to the Supreme Court in 1859, and during that time he also tried many important cases, including the sensational Peachy Harrison murder case.

He tried hard to concentrate upon his law work, but the many demands constantly made upon him by his party caused him to lose patience with some cases that were proving exasperating. To Jonathan Haines he wrote: "I have done nothing further with the Rugg case. How Dickey keeps that matter hanging along I do not comprehend. I do believe it would be better all around to let me surrender both your cases to some lawyer at Chicago. I really cannot give them proper attention.''

Another bothersome case which Lincoln desired to surrender at this time was Charles Ambos's claim against J. A. Barret. Twelve days after his offer to give up the Rugg case he wrote to Ambos: "I would now very gladly surrender charge of the case to any one you would designate, without charging anything for the much trouble I have already had.''

When another client complained to Whitney regarding Lincoln's apparent neglect of a case to which they were attending jointly, Whitney asked Lincoln to placate him. "Let him howl!'' Lincoln replied with exasperation.

Though busied again with his professional duties, Lincoln did not "sink out of view.'' On the contrary, he had become a permanent figure in national politics. From many parts of the country came invitations for lectures and addresses. Anxious to earn some ready money, he declined most of them.

In refusing an invitation of Hawkin Taylor of Keokuk, Iowa, to deliver an address there, Lincoln wrote him: "I have no thought of being there. It is bad to be poor. I shall go to the wall for bread and meat, if I neglect my business this year as well as last.''

But he could not long resist the call of his party. When Douglas spoke several times for the Democrats of Ohio in the 1859 campaign for governor, Lincoln eagerly accepted invitations to reply. At Columbus and Cincinnati he delivered noteworthy addresses which added to his growing reputation. In response to urgent solicitations he also made a number of speeches at different points in Kansas. These too were enthusiastically approved.

And then one day in February of 1860, unostentatiously as though starting upon a trip around the circuit, he departed for New York for his great triumph at Cooper Institute. In the celebrated address delivered here, Lincoln the courtroom pleader, whom the *New York Times* described as "a lawyer with some local reputation in Illinois,'' was at his best. Without any attempt at flowery rhetoric or flighty oratory or play upon emotions, but with lawyer-like arguments and invincible logic, simply, calmly, and dispassionately he presented the case against slavery. Masterfully he arrayed his facts and historical and legal data concerning the controversy. His hearers were people of intelligence—"a great audience, including all the noted men—all the learned and cultured—of his party in New York: editors, clergymen, statesmen, lawyers, merchants, critics." To them he argued his cause as he had often done before the Supreme Court of Illinois. He appealed to their reason rather than their emotions. He had devoted a great deal of time to research and preparation. And now, like a lawyer in court well fortified with briefs and precedents, he took up in proper order each and every argument the Southern leaders were making against the North at the time.

He chose as his text a statement Douglas had uttered at Columbus: "Our fathers, when they framed the government under which we live, understood this question just as well, and even better than we do now." He endorsed this pronouncement, but proceeded to prove that a majority of the "thirty-nine" who signed the Constitution were opposed to Douglas's doctrine of local control of slavery. On the contrary, he argued, the "fathers" favored federal control. They had marked slavery, he said, as "an evil not to be extended, but to be tolerated and protected only because of and so far as its actual presence among us makes that toleration and protection a necessity."

With impregnable arguments he answered the Southern complaints against the North: the alleged sectionalism of the North; John Brown's insurrection among the slaves; the threat of disunion because the North refused to construe disputed constitutional points according to the Southern viewpoint; and the refusal of the Republicans to abide by the Dred Scott decision. To each charge his reply was convincing, logical, and fortified by facts and remarkable accuracy of detail.

Again he assailed the reasoning on which the Dred Scott pronouncement was based, and emphasized that "the bare majority of the judges 'in the case' disagree with one another in the reasons for making it." Furthermore, the decision was "mainly based upon a mistaken statement of fact—the statement . . . that the right of property in a slave is distinctly and expressly affirmed in the Constitution.'' This being a false premise, he was hopeful that the Supreme Court would yet reverse the disputed decision.''[1]

All in all, the address was generally acclaimed as one of the most scholarly, effective, and convincing discourses of an argumentative nature heard in all that turbulent era of stirring political events. This masterful address contributed much toward making Lincoln a national figure and one of the leaders in the supreme crisis of our history.

None realized this startling fact better than his fellow lawyers of the Illinois bar. One evening during the early part of 1860 a number of Lincoln's associates of the circuit, who had come to Springfield to appear before the Supreme Court, assembled in caucus in the office of Secretary of State O. M. Hatch, and planned the first concerted effort that eventually landed the presidential nomination for Lincoln. Besides Hatch, there were Herndon, Norman B. Judd, Jackson Grimshaw, delegate to the Bloomington convention and a member of the State Central Committee in 1856, Leonard Swett, Ward H. Lamon, Ebenezer Peck, Nehemiah Bushnell, and Jesse K. Dubois.

"We all expressed a personal preference for Mr. Lincoln as the Illinois candidate for the Presidency," Grimshaw related, "and asked him if his name might be used at once in connection with the nomination and election. With his characteristic modesty he doubted whether he could get the nomination even if he wished it, and asked until the next morning to answer us if we thought it proper to do so to place him in the field."[2]

Soon Judd, Orville H. Browning, Gustave Koerner, Judge David Davis, Judge Logan, and Oliver L. Davis, who were to become delegates to the Chicago Convention, joined forces with Swett, Lawrence Weldon, John M. Palmer, former Democrat who was to become a pro-Lincoln elector in 1860, Richard Oglesby, Samuel C. Parks, Lamon, Herndon, J. W. Somers, a Republican

[1] *Works*, V, 294–309.
[2] Herndon and Weik, *Lincoln*, II, 163; C. A. Church, *History of the Republican Party in Illinois*, pp. 73–74; Lamon, *Lincoln*, p. 424.

organizer in Champaign County, Whitney, Joseph Gillespie, who presided at the Decatur Convention, Archibald Williams, who was temporary chairman at Bloomington, James Conkling, delegate to the Bloomington Convention, John Rosette, lawyer who also edited the Springfield *Republican*, and a number of other faithful circuit associates, and all quietly and persistently set about to create "Lincoln for President" sentiment. They knew him well, believed in him, loved him as a friend and companion, admired his sterling qualities, and had faith in his fitness for the highest office in the land.

They were the first to realize that behind his homely wit and kindly jest, behind his utter unpretentiousness, lay a certain greatness—a brain of sweeping range and power, an intellect brilliant and profound, a fine legal conscience, and a will of flint. All this at a time when Lincoln was scarcely known beyond the prairies of his own State. His faithful friends were not discouraged by the fact that the press of the East scarcely ever mentioned his name as a possible candidate. With such men as Seward, Chase, Bates, McLean, Bell, Cameron, Fremont, Wade, and Banks available, how could it be expected that prudent and conservative men would give even a passing thought to a comparatively unknown Western lawyer with absolutely no record for executive statesmanship, whose only claim to recognition lay in the fact that he could present a good argument against the spread of slavery!

But his circuit companions were convinced that their friend could lead their party to victory—if only they could first "sell" him to the Republican convention. "The lawyers of our circuit went there," wrote Leonard Swett concerning the convention, "determined to leave no stone unturned, and really they, aided by some of our state officers and a half dozen men from various portions of the State, were the only tireless, sleepless, unwavering and ever vigilant friends he had."[1]

But of all the men working in Lincoln's behalf, none were more sincere, tireless, resourceful, and faithful than his constant boon companion of the Eighth Circuit—Judge David Davis. No man contributed more to the molding of Lincoln's career. Possessing

[1] Swett to Josiah Drummond of Maine, letter, May 27, 1860.

few traits in common, these two men had been attracted to each other by some inexplicable bonds of affection which continued through to Lincoln's death. Even after that, the Judge was to carry on the will of his friend as administrator of his estate.

From Judge Davis, more than any other person, Lincoln sought guidance and comfort in the perplexing days when he was still unknown beyond the judicial circuits of his State. The rugged, corpulent jurist probably more than any other individual influenced Lincoln's career, yet his influence was ever conservative and restraining. He was among the first to recognize Lincoln's ability and sterling qualities, and more than any other man he became responsible for Lincoln's winning the Republican nomination for President. "It is my belief," said Leonard Swett, "if all other causes had existed as they did exist, and Judge Davis had not lived, Mr. Lincoln would never have been nominated, and consequently, never would have been President of the United States."[1]

For this loyal friend laid aside his judicial robes to devote all his time to lining up the Illinois delegates at the Republican State Convention at Decatur, May 9 and 10, 1860, and then to taking charge of the Lincoln headquarters at the national convention at Chicago. Seated behind a large table in the rooms of the Illinois headquarters, he assumed leadership of his state delegation and resolutely set about to perform a seemingly impossible task. He put all of Lincoln's friends to work where they were most effective. Samuel C. Parks of Logan, a native of Vermont, he directed to organize a delegation to call on the delegates from that State. Leonard Swett he urged to visit his old friends from his home State of Maine. He made use of the powerful lungs of Richard Oglesby by placing him in charge of a strong-voiced brigade of shouters to attract the arriving delegates on behalf of Lincoln. Everyone he put to work; and all reported back to him so that at all times he knew the situation of every delegation. Here throughout the days of the sessions, and for many hours in the nights, at one o'clock in the morning caucuses, in the hotel rooms and lobbies, on the floor of the convention, with a few others he

[1] Leonard Swett, memorial address delivered before Illinois State Bar Association, January, 1887, 19 Chicago Legal News 206.

worked tirelessly on the delegations of the doubtful States—bargaining, promising cabinet posts, urging, persuading—doing everything expedient to promote the interests of the "rail" candidate.

Judge Davis waged a hard fight to frustrate the plans of Seward's followers to slip Lincoln into the Vice-Presidency. He was confident that his friend was fit for first place.

"Make no contracts that will bind me," Lincoln wrote to his campaign managers. But how could Lincoln, anxiously waiting in Springfield, miles distant from the actual scene of the stirring political battle, realize the gravity of the situation, Judge Davis argued. Lincoln's lawyer friends at the convention hall undoubtedly felt that they were now virtually lawyers in court better acquainted with the issues than their absent client, and therefore empowered to use discretion even to the disregard of the "client's" specific instructions. At any rate, Davis, Judd, Logan, Swett, Browning, and the others went ahead with their negotiations. They proved their political sagacity by convincing unpledged delegations that despite William H. Seward's great talents and splendid services in behalf of the anti-slavery cause, he could never carry the Middle West.

His declaration in a Senate debate that there is a higher law than the Constitution governing the Nation's stewardship of the public domain had associated him in the public mind with extreme Abolitionists who were openly flouting the Constitution. Lincoln, they argued, was free from all such elements of weakness. He was a conservative on the slavery question. His greatest strength lay in his obscurity. Honest Abe's staunch stand for the security of private and public property would make him a strong candidate in all sections. Judge Davis and the other lawyers had often observed how careful and frugal their Springfield associate had been in taking care of the property of others. They were certain he would now be a far less objectionable candidate than Seward, and could best unite all the factions of the party.

In the early hours of Friday morning, the day of the convention, Judge Davis and Leonard Swett met with two leading delegates from Pennsylvania, and when Lincoln's tireless friends returned to the Illinois headquarters, they could announce that

Pennsylvania's forty-eight votes were Lincoln's—if on the second ballot he showed increasing strength. Thus were won over unpledged and floating votes that ensured the happy result.[1]

The fact that Lincoln, during his career at the bar, had become acquainted with a number of leading lawyers practicing in Indiana, some of whom were now members of the delegation from that State, made it easier for Judge Davis to win them over to Lincoln's cause.

After Seward had been placed in nomination, Norman B. Judd arose and said, "I desire on behalf of the delegation from Illinois to put in nomination as a candidate for President of the United States, Abraham Lincoln of Illinois."

A deafening roar of approval broke forth from the throats of the Lincoln contingent. Lamon had seen to it that the huge auditorium was filled with Lincoln shouters. While the Seward delegation, two thousand strong, had been marching over the muddy streets of Chicago, Lamon had packed the Wigwam with leather-lunged Lincoln adherents, who had gained their entrance by means of bogus admission tickets supplied by the boisterous, swashbuckling Lamon.

Caleb B. Smith of Indiana, to whom Judge Davis had undoubtedly promised a post in the cabinet, seconded the nomination. Lincoln was no stranger to this Indiana lawyer. Practice on the Eighth Circuit of Illinois had often brought them together. Smith and Daniel W. Voorhees, another member of the Indiana Bar, had frequently "come over with a torrent of eloquence" to practice in the eastern counties of the circuit. Both had become well acquainted with the future President.

When the pandemonium that broke loose finally subsided, Lincoln's former law partner, Judge Logan, now the Springfield delegate, rose to his feet and shouted, "Mr. President, in order or out of order, I propose this convention and audience give three cheers for the man who is evidently their nominee." In Judge Logan's pocket reposed a letter written by Lincoln authorizing the withdrawal of his name whenever his friends believed such

[1] McClure, *Lincoln and Men of War Times*, pp. 23–29; Tarbell, *Life of Abraham Lincoln*, I, 342–57; Whitney, *Life on the Circuit*, p. 289.

action appropriate. After the balloting began there never arose the danger that this letter need to be used. Lincoln's jubilant circuit friends had done their work well.[1]

Leonard Swett recalls that when Lincoln's nomination had become a certainty, "when delegations were changing their votes, and everything was in the confusion of coming to Lincoln, when everybody was shouting, and in the hurrah of bedlam, Judge Davis threw his great arms around a friend and cried like a child."

With the convention over, Judge Davis paid the expenses of the Lincoln headquarters and then, accompanied by Leonard Swett, called on Thurlow Weed to plan for the coming election.

Once again Lincoln gave up his law practice. He had not tried a case since March 19, about two months before his great victory in the "Wigwam." This had been the so-called "sandbar" case involving the question of accretion and the title to an extensive stretch of land on the shore of Lake Michigan.

After becoming the standard-bearer of the Republican Party he made one more appearance in federal court—his very last. It was the Dawson vs. Ennis plow patent case, heard in the United States District Court on June 20, 1860. Thus ended his notable career at the bar.

The dingy little law office of Lincoln & Herndon was hardly large enough to serve as headquarters for the standard-bearer of the Republican Party, so at the invitation of Governor Wood, Lincoln established himself in a room in the State House. But often at evenings he would return to his own office to confer with friends and advisors, in greater privacy than the public headquarters afforded.

The opposition press called him a "third-rate country lawyer, poorer even than poor Pierce," who would be a "nullity" if elected. But it soon became evident that his masterful handling of the Dred Scott decision two years before and the adroit entrapment of Douglas at Freeport, with the resultant split in the Democratic Party, made the election of this "third-rate country lawyer" a foregone conclusion. The victory that came laid on

[1] McClure, *Lincoln and Men of War Times*, p. 23; Murat Halstead, *Conventions*, p. 154. Schurtz, *Reminiscences*, II, 175–86.

his shoulders the most fearful responsibility an American President has ever been called to bear.

As President-elect his became the painful duty of remaining inactive in Springfield to watch the slow dissolution of the Union. In January of 1861, Joseph Gillespie, his colleague of the Eighth Circuit, called on Lincoln. They talked of old times. The President-elect was worried by the startling events taking place in the South.

"Gillespie," he suddenly said, "I would willingly take out of my life a period in years equal to the two months which intervene between now and my inauguration to take the oath of office now."

"Why?" asked his old friend.

"Because every hour adds to the difficulties I am called to meet, and the present administration does nothing to check the tendency toward dissolution. I, who have been called to meet this awful responsibility, am compelled to remain here, doing nothing to avert it or lessen its force when it comes to me."

As the two were about to part Lincoln asked: "Joe, I suppose you will never forget that trial down in Montgomery County, where the lawyer associated with you gave away the whole case in his opening speech? I saw you signaling to him, but you couldn't stop him. Now, that's just the way with me and Buchanan. He is giving away the case, and I have nothing to say, and can't stop him."

Ambitious cabinet-makers and voraciously hungry office-seekers swarmed into Springfield from all corners of the land and gave the President-Elect no peace. Practically all of these callers were total strangers to him. To Gillespie he said, while they were reminiscing about old experiences, that he could select an excellent cabinet right from the ranks of his colleagues at the bar with whom he had traveled the Eighth Circuit. When Gillespie reminded him that some of these lawyers were Democrats, Lincoln replied, "But I would rather have Democrats whom I know than Republicans I don't know."

Lincoln did not forget his associates of the Illinois judicial circuits who had helped him achieve his coveted goal. Months later, when Swett visited President Lincoln in the White House to discuss the question of appointments, he reminded his former circuit companion that he owed his nomination to his high office largely to the efforts of his fellow lawyers of Illinois and chiefly to Judge David Davis. In urging President Lincoln to appoint Judge Davis to a vacancy in the United States Supreme Court, Swett reminded him: "If Judge Davis with his tact and force had not lived, and all other things had been as they were, I believe you would not now be sitting where you are."

"Yes, that is so," Lincoln answered thoughtfully, according to Swett's account of the meeting.

"Now it is a common law of mankind," the lawyer urged further, "that one raised into prominence is expected to recognize the force that lifts him. . . . Here is Judge Davis, whom you know to be in every respect qualified for this position, and you ought in justice to yourself and public expectation to give him this place."

Shortly after this conference the appointment of Judge Davis to the United States Supreme Court was announced.

Lincoln remembered his other friends of Illinois who had been loyal to him, by appointing Judd, Minister to Germany; Koerner, Minister to Spain; Parks, Associate Justice of the Supreme Court of Idaho; Weldon, United States District Attorney for the Southern District of Illinois; Lamon, Marshal of the District of Columbia, Cullom, member of the War Claims Commission at Cairo; Whitney, a paymaster of volunteers; Somers, a member of the Board of Review of the pension office; Grimshaw, Collector of Internal Revenue for the Quincy district; and Williams, United States District Judge for Kansas.

But now, with his inaugural rapidly approaching, he was pondering over the contents of his inaugural address. He asked Herndon to get some books he wished to consult. His law partner was amazed to observe that the list included only Henry Clay's great speech delivered in 1850, Andrew Jackson's proclamation against nullification, and a copy of the Constitution. Later he also asked for Webster's reply to Hayne, which Lincoln regarded as the finest specimen of American oratory. With only this scant material, he locked himself in a dingy upstairs back room above a store across the street from the State House, and worked on his memorable address until completed.

February 11 was the date fixed for his departure for Washington. A day or two prior to this, he devoted to settling up private business matters; and then on the afternoon before departure, he wearily climbed the unbanistered stairway leading up to his dingy law office for a last heart-to-heart talk with faithful Billy Herndon. There were some legal affairs in which the President-Elect still felt some interest.

"We ran over the books and arranged for the completion of all unsettled and unfinished matters," Herndon related. "In some cases he had certain requests to make, certain lines of procedure he wished me to observe."

With these arrangements completed, Lincoln threw himself upon the old horse-hair sofa, "which, after many years of service, had been moved against the wall for support." Silently he lay for a few moments gazing up to the ceiling, begrimed with smoke from a rusty wood-burning stove. He reclined in deep reflection. He was soon to leave forever this unpretentious scene of so many stirring events of his life. On this very couch he had lain hundreds of times in the past years in this very same favorite attitude, thinking over his law cases. Here he had often discussed and argued with Herndon and other lawyers and clients and callers the very same issues—slavery, abolition, state rights, secession—leading to the crisis he was now being called on to avert. On the green baize-covered pine table where he had prepared his briefs he had also written his epoch-making political addresses. Here in this stuffy office he had struggled on these many years, tasting of bitter failures, disappointments, and soul-crushing defeats—but also of deserved successes and that glorious and surprising ultimate victory.

Presently, with a sigh, Lincoln suddenly inquired, "Billy, how long have we been together?"

The junior partner replied, "Over sixteen years."

"We've never had a cross word during all that time, have we?"

"No indeed, we have not," answered Herndon emphatically.

There was a lump in Lincoln's throat. Billy had been so loyal, so unselfishly self-effacing in his behalf. And Lincoln had watched over his younger associate like a big brother. Herndon's weakness for liquor had impaired his usefulness to the firm in many respects, and his conduct had frequently been an embarrassment to his colleague, himself a total abstainer. But "he never chided, never censured, never criticized my conduct . . . never, save on one occasion, alluded to it," Herndon said. "That was the evening we were together in our office for the last time." Even then Lincoln did not lecture him. He merely told him that on several occasions in the past other lawyers had endeavored to supplant Herndon in the partnership, but that not even for a moment had he ever entertained the thought of deserting his friend for weak creatures who "hoped to secure a law practice by hanging to his coat-tail." Lincoln believed in Billy despite his shortcomings, and the grateful Herndon insisted that "in his treatment of me Mr. Lincoln was the most generous, forbearing, and charitable man I ever knew." No more was said on the subject. Instead, the President-Elect began to recall amusing incidents and adventures of his circuit-riding days.

The sun was setting and Lincoln hurriedly gathered a bundle of personal papers, when his eye caught the old "Lincoln & Herndon" signboard swinging on its rusty hinges at the foot of the stairway.

"Let it hang there undisturbed," he urged in a low voice, poignant with regret and sadness. "Give our clients to understand that the election of a President makes no change in the firm of Lincoln and Herndon. If I live I'm coming back some time, and then we'll go right on practicing law as if nothing had happened."[1]

Lincoln loved his profession. As long as that sign hung there he would feel that he was still the lawyer and belonged in Springfield.

He took one last lingering look at the old quarters, then slowly walked out. His professional career was over. He would never come back to this office again.

---

[1] Herndon and Weik, *Lincoln*, III, 482; Weik, *The Real Lincoln*, p. 298.

XXII. PRESIDENT LINCOLN'S LEGAL AND CONSTITUTIONAL PROBLEMS

As IF by a rub of Aladdin's lamp, Lincoln, the self-trained lawyer from the Illinois prairies, suddenly found himself shifted from his dingy provincial law office to the helm of a mighty Nation in its hour of greatest trial.

Congress was not in session when the hostilities began. Of necessity, therefore, this Springfield lawyer alone became responsible for the policy of the new Administration for maintaining the Constitution and preserving the Union. In his hands were concentrated all the powers of the Government in this unprecedented emergency.

The exigency demanded a lawyer. The great living issues which divided the Nation were secession and slavery—questions of law, of constitutionality, and of right and wrong. Like all forms of special privilege and injustice, the barbaric institution of slavery lay strongly entrenched behind a barbed-wire entanglement of constitutional restrictions, judicial precedents, and legal technicalities which had multiplied and grown more intricate year by year since the birth of the Republic.

The issue of slavery soon merged into the other constitutional

285

issue—the right of state secession, which, though heretofore present, had remained in the background. Was the Union of the States a perpetual, indissoluble, and indestructible unity, or was it merely a venerable treaty of alliance leaving each constituent State a sovereign body, with an indefeasible right to withdraw whenever it wished so to do? The War or Rebellion followed the unsuccessful and elaborate legal discussion concerning the right of States to secede from the Union. It was a conflict of two contrary doctrines of constitutional law—the pedantically legal views of state rights as opposed to the rights of the Union.

And as the war of rebellion continued, a notable succession of grave legal and constitutional problems demanded summary solution.

In addition to the immediate and pressing question of the constitutionality of the assumed right of the Southern States to secede from the Union, there was the question of the President's constitutional right to determine the existence of a "rebellion" and his legal right to wage a defensive war without direct authorization from Congress. There was the exigent legal dispute concerning the President's authority to suspend the privilege of the writ of habeas corpus at his discretion, and his right to place persons under arrest without warrant and without judicially showing the cause of detention.

The question immediately arose as to whether or not the President had the right to increase the regular army by calling for volunteers beyond the authorized total. And had he, because of the emergency, constitutional authority to spend money from the treasury of the United States without congressional appropriation?

He had to determine whether a proposed act of Congress directing the President to confiscate the property of persons engaged in rebellion, by actions *in rem*, is compatible with the Constitution.

He was constantly confronted with the legal disputes concerning the authority of Congress to interfere with slavery in the States.

Emancipation of slaves by compensating slave-owners for their property was his cherished doctrine. Could it legally be carried into effect?

Long did he ponder over his constitutional authority to proclaim the emancipation of slaves held in States in rebellion on the ground of military necessity.

There were the many problems growing out of the law of treason, the establishment of martial rule in regions of unobstructed civil justice, the legal liability of federal officers for wrongs committed in their official capacity during the war, and the question of the constitutionality of the indemnity act to relieve officers of such liability. There were the numerous unprecedented legal questions emanating from the conscription acts, the administration of justice in occupied districts, and the governing and "reconstruction" of conquered States.

At every turn new legal and constitutional questions presented themselves for urgent consideration.

To the solution of these grave and unparalleled problems, the Lawyer-President applied the broad principles of law and justice with which he had stored his fertile brain during the twenty-three years of practice in the courts of Illinois. So well had he learned these principles that, with one or two exceptions, his interpretations of these unprecedented questions were eventually sustained in the courts.

The emergency was without parallel, and lacked ready-made machinery to cope with it. Extraordinary measures hitherto unknown to a free people had to be devised. Powers not specifically provided for in the Constitution had to be exercised. Who but a leader well trained in the law could guide the dumbfounded Nation through the countless legal and constitutional perplexities created by the situation? Who but an advocate with a masterly grasp of controlling principles could untangle the legalistic technicalities of a Constitution pregnant with confusion, and by wise interpretation give to the Constitution an elasticity and adaptability to enable the Government to cope with the crisis?

As a lawyer Lincoln had been dealing with the rights of men before the law. Was not that the basic issue now—this conflict between right and wrong, slavery and freedom? "That is the real issue," Lincoln had said. "That is the issue that will continue in this country when these poor tongues of Judge Douglas and myself shall be silent. It is the eternal struggle between these principles—right and wrong—throughout the world." Lawyer-like, he urged, "Let us have faith that right makes might."

The effects of his legal training became visible at once, following his election as President. In his mode of reasoning on constitutional questions, in the acuteness of his replies, and in defining the issue he revealed himself as the lawyer. The caution with which he arrived at right conclusions, his almost unerring judgment and insight into character and motives, are traceable to this experience. In the rough-and-tumble of hundreds of court battles he had acquired the ability to untangle the most conflicting testimony and make difficult things clear to the humblest understanding. Unwittingly he had been preparing for the Presidency for many years.

His first Inaugural Address—conciliatory in tone and breathing the spirit of justice and kindness—presented a calm, lawyer-like, candid appeal to the entire country in behalf of law, order, and peace. It loomed a masterpiece of pleading and persuasiveness. In it the lawyer who so often in the past had endeavored to discourage litigation and to persuade litigious clients to compromise their differences with their adversaries, now as the Chief Magistrate of the Nation was pleading with his millions of new "clients" to refrain from quarreling and to remain friends.

To save the Union, not to destroy slavery, was the burden of this message. As a lawyer he realized that he had no lawful right to interfere with property rights in slaves. The existing laws, including the fugitive slave laws, would be strictly enforced, according to his solemn declaration. So at the very outset he sought to reassure the Southern people that so long as they themselves obeyed the Constitution and laws which protected slavery, his Administration could not under any circumstances disturb their rights therein.

As his long experience at the bar had taught him that every controversy of merit has two sides to it, so now as the impartial Magistrate of the whole Republic he could see that neither the North nor South was altogether right or altogether wrong in the present controversy. He realized that slavery was implied in the law of the land and sanctioned by the courts. He could even secure to the South their slave rights by explicit constitutional provision, although, by implication, slavery was already countenanced by that document.

He combated the argument of the Southern statesmen that secession was consistent with the Constitution, and therefore lawful and peaceful. "Where is the express law for it?" he demanded. As a lawyer he knew that nothing could be implied as law which leads to unjust or absurd consequences. Secession was not a basic popular right. It was not a lawful procedure within the Constitution. It was illegal, and all ordinances of secession were absolutely void. From this conclusion nothing could move him.

Again he is the lawyer, as he discusses the status of the American Union. It is not a mere compact to be broken at will, but a supreme law ordained and established by the people of the United States. The States had been cemented and blended into an indivisible mass for all time, he argued.

"I hold," he said, "that in contemplation of universal law and of the Constitution, the Union of these States is perpetual. Perpetuity is implied, if not expressed, in the fundamental law of all national governments. It is safe to assert that no government proper ever had a provision in its organic law for its own termination."

He combated the compact theory of the Union current in the South with this lawyer-like argument:

"Again, if the United States be not a government proper, but an association of States in the nature of contract merely, can it, as a contract, be peaceably unmade by less than all the parties who made it? One party to a contract may violate it—break it, so to speak; but does it not require all lawfully to rescind it?"

In other words, even if it were true that the Constitution had been conceived as a compact between the States, "in order to form a more perfect Union," the end designed by it had been attained and the contract was now an executed one. Restating the well-established principle of law that a contract could not be abrogated except by the mutual consent of all parties to it, he challenged the right of any State to withdraw from this so-called compact without the consent of all the other States.

"It follows from these views," he added, "that no State upon its own mere motion can lawfully get out of the Union; that resolves and ordinances to that effect are legally void; and that acts of violence, within any State or States, against the authority of the United States are insurrectionary or revolutionary, according to circumstances.

"I therefore consider that in view of the Constitution and the laws, the Union is unbroken; and to the extent of my ability I shall take care, as the Constitution itself expressly enjoins upon me, that the laws of the Union be faithfully executed in all the States."

No legal precedent existed by which the unforeseen and uncontrollable events endangering the existence of the Republic could be averted. There were no adjudicated authorities to guide the new President, fresh from his Springfield law office, in the unprecedented crisis. Should he seek to suppress the uprising by the civil power through the process of the courts with the military forces as the marshal's posse, and thus give the insurgents the status of ordinary criminals? Or would it be more expedient to recognize the rebels as belligerents and seek to subdue them with military force alone? This was his first legal problem as President.

A system of original construction of the articles of the Constitution had to be devised by him to meet the unparalleled circumstances demanding summary executive action. There was no time for reflection or timidity. Delay or recklessness would have been equally disastrous. So with the crushing responsibility of maintaining the integrity of the Union resting on his shoulders alone, he alone decided the Government's course of action in its struggle for life—in the same manner that years before he alone had planned his court battles when left to his own resources by his first partner, Stuart.

He was careful not to give the seceded States the dignity of belligerents and thus in effect virtually recognize their independence. Secession, he declared, was a nullity, and every act done pursuant to it was illegal. He declined to recognize the state organizations as elements of the uprising against the General Government. He defined the status of the rebellion primarily as an unlawful combination of individuals against the laws of the United States. He confined the legal character of the conflict to a mere domestic uprising by insurgents who owed allegiance to the Government they were seeking to overthrow and who were obstructing the execution of the laws by combinations too powerful to be suppressed by the ordinary course of judicial proceedings.

Far-reaching and momentous were the legal bearings of the President's decision in defining the legal character of the movement in the South as treasonable insurrection. Not only did it define our own Government's official attitude toward the Southern States, but also prevented foreign powers from recognizing the Confederacy as an independent nation.

There is a legal difference between war and insurrection, and the powers and duties of the President are different in each instance. In an insurrection captured rebels are amenable to the municipal laws for crimes and treason and need not be treated as prisoners of war. Captured crews of insurgent warships and privateers are punishable as pirates. Their property is subject to confiscation. Municipal law can be exercised in territory recaptured from the rebels. And the President has authority to suppress an insurrection, whereas only Congress can declare and carry on a war.

Between the bombardment of Fort Sumter on April 12 and the assembling of Congress July 4, 1861, President Lincoln assumed full responsibility for the means used in protecting the national cause against the rebellion. He called out the militia, enlarged the army and navy beyond existing legal limits, issued proclamations of blockade against the Southern ports, and suspended the privilege of the writ of habeas corpus.

When the legality of some of these acts was questioned, President Lincoln defended them by pointing out that they were necessary for the public safety. "These measures," he said in his message to Congress, "whether legal or not, were ventured upon under what appeared to be a popular demand and a public necessity; trusting . . . that Congress would readily ratify them. It is believed that nothing has been done beyond the constitutional competency of Congress."

Later our Supreme Court upheld the legality of Lincoln's policies by declaring, in effect, that the President had not initiated a war, but had only taken necessary measures of resisting a war forced upon the Government.

Lincoln's long experience in the practical application of legal and judicial principles became most useful to him with the outbreak of the conflict. As President, he at once became the fountainhead of military justice, with supreme power of review over the decisions of all military courts. Daily he had to deal with cases of persons accused of treason, conspiracy, obstructing the draft, and other wartime crimes. Under his authority special war courts were established in all regions under martial law, and these tribunals assumed both civil and criminal jurisdiction, including all "human acts and transactions capable of becoming subjects of judicial investigation."[1]

Lincoln's human sympathy, his lawyer-like caution, and his dislike of arbitrary rule enabled him to exercise this unprecedented judicial power with a blending of merciful and practical considerations. Though the rule of law was often ignored by overzealous subordinates who operated above the law and were immune from penalties for wrongs committed; and though men were often imprisoned outside of the law and independently of the civil courts, Lincoln's high professional regard for constitutional rights served as a constant restraint upon his aides, and modified and softened the harsh effects of the arbitrary wartime measures.

Motivated by the one overmastering desire to restore peace on the basis of a revived Union, President Lincoln never for a moment lost sight of the fact that sooner or later the cancer of slavery would have to be cut out from the body politic. But violent emancipation by confiscation found no favor in his legalistic mind. Beside the economic disruption that was sure to follow, he found no legal justification for interfering with the property rights of the slave-owners. He was too good a lawyer to disregard the legal importance of their vested interests and their rights to compensation.

[1] Judge Charles A. Peabody, "United States Provisional Court of Louisiana," American Historical Association, Annual Report for 1892, pp. 199–210.

"The liberation of the slaves is the destruction of property," he declared. Morally wrong though slavery was, he insisted that moral justice was no excuse for violations of the law. So long as slavery was fixed in the law of the land, countenanced by the Constitution, and sanctioned by the courts, it must be granted every constitutional safeguard. With lawyer-like caution and conservatism he sought the destruction of this hated institution by means compatible with law and the preservation of the Union. His oath of office was a vow to enforce the laws, not to break them.

In November, 1861, the Reverend George Gordon, President of Iberia College, Iberia, Ohio, was indicted in the Federal Court of the Northern District of Ohio for violation of the Fugitive Slave Law. Despite an aroused public opinion, he was convicted and sentenced to six months imprisonment and fined three hundred dollars. Indignant Abolitionists throughout the North at once petitioned President Lincoln to pardon the Reverend Gordon. Bitterly they assailed the constitutionality and morality of the law. They thought it strange that a Government engaged in a war for the suppression of a slave-holder's rebellion should enforce this odious slave act.

President Lincoln acceded to their pleas and pardoned the offender. But in the pardon he emphasized that executive clemency alone determined his action, as the conviction and sentence were legal. So long as the Fugitive Slave Law remained unrepealed, the Government would have to recognize its validity, he wrote.[1]

In his December 1, 1862, Message to Congress, President Lincoln recommended the amendment of the Constitution to the effect that compensation be awarded owners of slave property who would voluntarily emancipate their slaves. Voluntary emancipation by the States with compensation by the Nation was his earnest desire. He regarded this method as the most just, equitable, and legally sound as well as the most economical one.

He proposed to pay the Southern States four hundred million dollars—the cost of one hundred days of war—as compensation for their slaves on condition that those States return to the Union

[1] Randal and Ryan, *History of Ohio*, IV, 138.

and accept emancipation. But prejudice and passion stood in the
way and military emancipation became inevitable. Only after all
legal means had failed did Lincoln resort to emancipation by
proclamation, and then only on the ground of imperative military necessity.

The problem of emancipation of the slaves presented a number
of legal and constitutional questions that the Lawyer-President
had to decide. Never for a moment did they leave his thoughts
while he patiently awaited the opportune hour to strike. It was
clear that in time of peace and in the normal exercise of his
constitutional powers, the President had no authority to liberate
even a single slave. But now that the Southern slave-owners were
public enemies by reason of their rebellion against the Federal
Government, could he, under the Constitution, as Commander-
in-Chief of the army and navy, in the exercise of his war powers,
emancipate their slaves on grounds of military necessity? And
would a proclamation of emancipation lawfully result in the immediate unconditional and perpetual emancipation of all slaves
in the insurgent States? And thirdly, what would the legal status
of the slaves so liberated by military edict be upon the restoration
of peace? In other words, should by chance the Civil War end
with the insurgent States' returning to the Union, with the Federal
Constitution unchanged and the legal rights and relations of the
States under it substantially the same as before the war, would
the slaves emancipated by the President's proclamation still remain free in law and in fact? Or would they return to their
former status of slavery? How he answered these questions is
told in another chapter.[1]

When the western counties of Virginia constituted themselves
into a Unionist Government and sought admission into the Union
as the independent State of West Virginia, Congress approved
the petition. But when the "West Virginia bill" was presented
to President Lincoln, he manifested distress over its questionable
constitutionality. He immediately called the members of his Cabinet into consultation. To each he submitted these two questions:
Is the act constitutional? Is the act expedient?

[1] See Chapter XXV.

Seward, Stanton, and Chase answered affirmatively to both questions. But Bates, Blair, and Welles answered "No." Caleb B. Smith, Secretary of the Interior, had resigned and no successor had yet been named. Lincoln, therefore, had to decide for himself. In a long paper he presented his reasons why he regarded the act as both constitutional and expedient, and signed the bill.

Answering the claim that the organization claiming to be the State of Virginia, which consented to the partition of the Old Dominion, was nothing more than a provisional government composed almost entirely of loyal citizens beyond the mountains, he declared that no legal consideration is ever given to those who do not choose to vote. And especially in this case, no consideration need be paid to those who refrained from voting, for not only were they neglectful of their rights, but, moreover, they were in open rebellion against the Government.

"We cannot deny," he concluded, "that the body which consents to the admission of West Virginia is the Legislature of Virginia."[1]

The Thirty-seventh Congress at its second session enacted a law making rebellion a felony and fixing severe penalties for treason and rebellion. It directed the President to cause the confiscation of all the property of whatever kind belonging to persons engaged in, or aiding and abetting, the existing rebellion. The property so seized was to be condemned and sold by action *in rem* as enemy property, and the proceeds were to be used for the support of the army of the United States. After the passage of this act by Congress, it was sent to President Lincoln for approval. It then became known that he proposed to veto it because of constitutional scruples.

The proceedings *in rem* enabled the Executive to deprive men of their property without trial by jury and without trying and convicting the owners themselves. There were the provisions of the Constitution that "No bill of attainder . . . shall be passed"; "no person shall be . . . deprived of . . . property without due process of law; nor shall private property be taken for public use without just compensation"; and finally, "no attainder of treason

---

[1] Nicolay and Hay, *Abraham Lincoln: A History*, VI, 309–11.

shall work ... forfeiture except during the life of the person attainted.''

Was not this proceeding in effect but a punishment of treason by the forfeiture of a man's property without due process of law and in disregard of the constitutional inhibition limiting the forfeiture for treason to the life of the person attainted?

Among the leading proponents of the Confiscation Bill was Senator Sumner. In an address before Congress he declared that the Constitution is entirely inapplicable to the situation. For, said he, "The war powers of Congress are derived from the Constitution, but when once set in motion are without any restraint from the Constitution, so that what is done in pursuance of them is at the same time under the Constitution and outside the Constitution.... Sacred and inviolable, the Constitution is made for friends who acknowledge it, and not for enemies who disavow it; and it is made for a state of peace and not for the fearful exigencies of war."[1]

President Lincoln, however, disagreed with the view that the Constitution was inapplicable to the situation. He insisted that the constitutional restrictions be respected. His legalistic mind objected to confiscation in any form. He especially objected to that provision of the act which forever extinguished guilty persons' title to real estate. He regarded this feature as a violation of the attainder clause of the Constitution. He prepared an elaborate veto message. In it he pointed out that "for the causes of treason and the ingredients of treason not amounting to the full crime" the proposed confiscation law declared forfeitures extending beyond the lives of the offenders. This, he maintained, would be unconstitutional. Once again he was the lawyer with keen insight into legal points as he pointed out additional objections to the bill. By proceedings *in rem* the proposed law would confiscate property "without a conviction of the supposed criminal, or a personal hearing given him in any proceeding," he argued. He disliked this feature. It was his firm conviction that

1 *Congressional Globe*, Thirty-Seventh Congress, Second Session, June 27, 1862.

owners accused under the Confiscation Act should be given a personal hearing.

When Congress learned of the President's intended veto, his objections were ascertained and an explanatory resolution was quickly adopted to comply with his views. The most important provision of this resolution emphasized that the punishment and proceedings under the act should not be construed as to work a forfeiture of the property of the offender beyond his natural life.[1]

Although the modified bill as approved by the President did not provide for a personal hearing for the owner of affected property, the severe measures of the law were never carried into practical execution to any large extent, and to the end of the war were but lightly applied by Lincoln's administration.

When the constitutionality of the conscription laws was strenuously disputed, Lincoln's emphatic views, in the absence of a Supreme Court decision, became the prevailing legal opinion on the subject. He wrote:

"They tell us the law is unconstitutional. It is the first instance, I believe, in which the power of Congress to do a thing has ever been questioned in a case when the power is given by the Constitution in express terms. Whether a power can be implied when it is not expressed has often been the subject of controversy; but this is the first case in which the degree of effrontery has been ventured upon, of denying a power which is plainly and distinctly written down in the Constitution. . . . The case simply is, the Constitution provides that the Congress shall have power to raise and support armies, and by this act the Congress has exercised the power to raise and support armies. This is the whole of it. . . . The Constitution gives Congress the power, but it does not prescribe the mode or expressly declare who shall prescribe it. In such case Congress must prescribe the mode, or relinquish the power. There is no alternative. . . . If the Constitution had prescribed a mode, Congress could and must follow the mode; but, as it is, the mode necessarily goes to Congress, with the power expressly given. The power is given fully, completely,

[1] Dunning, "The Constitution in the Civil War," *Political Science Quarterly*, I, 163; *United States Statutes at Large*, XII, 627; *Works*, VII, 280–86.

unconditionally. It is not a power to raise armies if State authorities consent, nor if the men to compose the armies are entirely willing; but it is a power to raise and support armies . . . without an 'if.' "[1]

Although in 1862 there existed no federal statute specifically authorizing a military draft, various States conducted a draft during that year, solely upon a presidential order. Thus the first attempt in our history to raise federal troops by conscription was a presidential draft. The legality of this act was seriously questioned, but Lincoln the lawyer relied upon two well-known United States Supreme Court cases[2] to support his profound conviction that the Executive is the exclusive judge of the existence of a rebellion or insurrection and of the necessity of calling out the militia.

Abraham Lincoln was the most striking instance of the lawyer-statesman. His every important state paper is marked by his training as a lawyer. Even the immortal Gettysburg Address, embodying "the ripened wisdom of legal and political and human experience," was but his homage to justice.

At practically every step menacing legal obstacles confronted the Lawyer-President as he sought to perform a task even more difficult than that of Washington. No President had had greater need of a thorough knowledge of law. Fortunately, Lincoln knew the Constitution well. Almost a worshipper of that instrument, he endeavored ever to solve the general governmental problems in a legal way compatible with the Constitution. That his interpretation of some of the questions, hitherto unadjudicated, was at variance with the theories of others was inevitable. As only an accomplished lawyer could, he tackled the unprecedented legal and constitutional problems that confronted him. He met them all with courage and firmness, with logic, wisdom, and prudence. As a result, with hardly any exceptions, his judgments were eventually ratified by the courts.

---

[1] *Works, VII, 49–51.*
[2] Martin vs. Mott (12 Wheaton 19) and Luther vs. Borden (7 Howard 1).

XXIII. INTERNATIONAL LAW

WITHIN a few weeks following his inauguration, President Lincoln found himself in the midst of the first of a series of international legal controversies which more than once were to bring this Nation to the very brink of a foreign war. But thanks to his characteristic caution and astuteness and understanding of the basic principles of international law and justice, an outbreak of foreign hostilities was averted and the Union saved from irremediable disaster.

In his law-student days at New Salem, Lincoln had browsed through chapters of his providentially found Blackstone's *Commentaries* dealing with the law of nations—principles of law concerning: ambassadors, piracy, high treason, and the like. He had not the slightest idea then that he would ever make practical use of this brief academic study. Now it was standing him in good stead.

In international law President Lincoln's theory of the unlawfulness of secession was accepted, and no foreign power ever recognized the Confederate States as a lawful government.

Although the Federal Administration itself could not and did not constitutionally take cognizance of the Confederate States as a foreign power, nor could other nations recognize them as sovereign and independent without furnishing good cause of war to the United States, the magnitude of the struggle soon compelled all to treat the Southern Republic as a belligerent under the principles of international law.

Despite President Lincoln's contentions that war did not exist in the international sense and that the struggle was strictly a local insurrection which did not concern the rest of the world, in actual practice the Federal Government's conduct of the conflict of necessity became that of a public war rather than of a mere rebellion against its municipal laws.

Unintentially, President Lincoln himself made an acknowledgment to the nations of the world that a state of war did exist. On April 19, 1861, "in pursuance of the law of nations," he issued a proclamation of blockade of Southern ports and ordered the search and seizure of any ship entering or leaving blockaded ports. From the standpoint of constitutional and international law, a blockade is a recognized incident of actual warfare. Thus, inadvertently, the President proclaimed to the world the existence of war in the international sense.

When shortly afterwards England, in an effort to protect her commerce, issued a formal proclamation enjoining strict neutrality upon her subjects, great indignation against that nation swept over the Northern States. This declaration of neutrality, which incidentally was followed by similar proclamations from France, Spain, the Netherlands, and other great powers, was in conformity with a perfectly legal practice in international law.[1] But as its effect was an acknowledgment of the South as a belligerent power, it was considered throughout the North as an unfriendly act and the first step to ultimate recognition of the independence of the Confederacy.

In international law there was no foundation in fact or reason for these fears. A declaration of neutrality did not commit the powers to a recognition of the independence of the Southern States. It meant merely the granting to them of belligerent rights whereby their flag would receive recognition on the high seas and their ships when in neutral ports would be entitled to the same privileges as those of the North. This concession, which in effect placed the Confederate States on an equality with the

[1] Moore, *International Law Digest*, I, 184–93.

Union as to belligerent rights, was naturally galling to the North. It clashed sharply with Lincoln's theory that the secessionists were ordinary insurgents and traitors amenable to the municipal laws of the land. And yet it was Lincoln's own act—his proclamation of blockade, a power exercisable only in time of war—which, without formally acknowledging it, virtually conceded belligerent rights to the South.

Lincoln's proclamation would have treated captured confederate naval officers and seamen as pirates amenable to the death penalty under municipal law. International law, however, forbids the punishment, as pirates of those who operate at sea under the authority of an organized responsible government. Attempts early in the war to treat captured Southern naval officers as pirates were frustrated when Jefferson Davis threatened retaliations upon Northern captives. In the interest of humanity and to prevent the cruelties of reprisals, such belligerent rights as belonged, under the law of nations, to armies of independent governments engaged in war against each other were conceded by the Union to the seceded States. In brief, the Federal Government was compelled by necessity to treat the Confederacy as a belligerent power without formally recognizing it as such.

In practice, however, Lincoln's administration assumed the perfectly tenable position in international law of exercising both belligerent and sovereign rights over the South, employing, for example, belligerent powers of blockading Southern ports and sovereign powers of prosecuting insurgents for treason. Though recognizing the Southern States as public armed enemies, the Administration never for a moment ceased to treat them as members of the Union and their inhabitants as its own citizens. This position was later affirmed by the Supreme Court of the United States.[1]

Although sober afterthought recognized the legality in international law of England's neutrality proclamation, for weeks following its pronouncement unbridled indignation was voiced against that Government throughout the North.

This intense feeling of bitterness reached a climax when Lord

---

[1] Prize Cases, 2 Black, 665; Ford vs. Surget, 97 U.S. 594; Moore, *International Law Digest*, 1, 190; Woolsey, *International Law*, edition of 1878, p. 304.

John Russell, the British Secretary for Foreign Affairs, informed the United States Minister that he would unofficially receive the commissioners of the Confederacy who had arrived in London. Upon hearing this, Secretary of State Seward, an able diplomat but now extremely strained and excited, angrily penned a dispatch to be forwarded to the British Government through Charles Francis Adams, the American Minister at the Court of St. James. It was not merely a remonstrance; it was a challenge.[1]

In blunt, indignant language, the note protested against England's policy of raising the Southern States to the position and privilege of a belligerent power. Categorically it threatened that nation with war if she should recognize the Confederacy.

This dispatch was but an echo of Secretary Seward's amazing "Thoughts for the President's Consideration," which less than sixty days earlier he had submitted to Lincoln. In this astounding document, Seward had proposed to provoke a gigantic foreign war to heal the domestic disunion. "I would demand explanations from Spain and France categorically at once," read his recommendation. "I would seek explanations from Great Britain and Russia. . . . And if satisfactory explanations are not received from Spain and France, would convene Congress and declare war against them."

Quixotically he had hoped that a foreign war would unite the alienated sections and rally them again as comrades in a common defense against a common foe.

Now he was again inviting a foreign conflict—a war against both England and France, as these two powers were acting together in American affairs. Had the original draft of the note been sent, it appears certain that friendly relations between England and the United States would have been immediately broken off and war would have become inevitable.

Fortunately Secretary Seward submitted his intemperate dispatch to President Lincoln before sending it to Minister Adams.

The wary, cool-headed Western lawyer, endowed with a caution and circumspection gained from hundreds of legal battles, realized at a glance that the dispatch would prove most offensive

---

[1] Adams, *Great Britain and the American Civil War*, I, 126.

to Great Britain and serve as an invitation for intervention on behalf of the Southern Confederacy.

Without any previous diplomatic experience, but skilled in the writing of thousands of legal documents, the Lawyer-President, by a few master touches of his pen and with the language of a life-long conciliator, promptly revised Seward's offending message and paved the way for the re-cementing of peaceful relations between Great Britain and the United States.

Lincoln's long practice of writing legal instruments and briefs had proved invaluable as a check against rambling thought and redundant speech. The textbooks of the science, replete with formulas, definitions, axioms, and principles rigid as the multiplication table, discouraged the misuse of words or logic. They encouraged brevity and conciseness in thought and expression and prompted Lincoln ever to seek the accurate word and exact phrase.

So when Secretary Seward in his dispatch to Minister Adams termed certain acts of England as "wrongful," the President, prompted by his training as a lawyer, changed it to "hurtful," for to a legal practitioner a "wrongful" act implies an intention to do harm, whereas, in "hurtful" no such intention or willfulness can be attributed.

Seward referred to certain explanations made by the English Government. Lincoln reminded his minister that "It does not appear that such explanations were demanded." Therefore he wrote in the margin, "Leave out." An implied threat—"The laws of nations afford us an adequate and proper remedy, and we shall avail ourselves of it"—Lincoln ordered stricken out. "If that nation will now repeat the same great crime," wrote the Secretary of State; and the cautious President toned "crime" down to "error."

Seward wrote: "When this act of intervention is distinctly performed, we from that hour shall cease to be friends and become once more, as we have twice before been forced to be, enemies of Great Britain." The President endeavored to modify this threat, but finally gave up the attempt and obliterated the entire sentence. He struck out additional offensive and irritating sentences and phrases and softened and modified others. Without changing the substance he transformed the whole spirit of the note, and made friendly negotiations easier instead of more difficult.

As a lawyer he had early adopted the rule that it is good policy never to plead what you need not, lest you oblige yourself to prove what you cannot. He had acquired the attribute possessed by all great lawyers of saying nothing when there is nothing to be said, or rather, of not saying that which had better be left unsaid. These qualities, acquired on the Illinois judicial circuits, had now aided him in avoiding a disastrous war with Great Britain.

Serious international legal controversies also arose by reason of the President's suspension of the privilege of the writ of habeas corpus. For whenever subjects of foreign governments were arrested and held without the privilege of the writ, they appealed to their ministers for aid. On several occasions, when Englishmen were imprisoned and denied the right of habeas corpus, Great Britain attempted to discuss diplomatically the legality of the President's extraordinary action. But the Administration steadfastly refused to enter into any such discussion, holding the matter to be purely one of domestic concern.

At a most critical juncture in this strained relationship between England and the United States there suddenly arose a new controversy which again threatened a violent rupture in the diplomatic affairs of the two nations. Again serious questions of international law had to be decided; and again the caution and astuteness of President Lincoln—this time aided by the tact of Secretary Seward—saved the United States from embroilment in a disastrous war with Great Britain.

Former Senators James M. Mason of Virginia and John Slidell of Louisiana had boarded the British mail-steamer *Trent* at Havana, en route to England and France respectively, there to act as emissaries of the Southern Confederacy. Watchful Captain Charles Wilkes of the United States Navy seized the *Trent*, forcibly removed Mason and Slidell and their secretaries, and permitted the vessel to proceed on her way.

The North went wild with joy at the capture of the Confederate envoys, and Secretary of the Navy Welles even telegraphed his congratulations to the indiscreet naval officer, praising him for the great public service he had rendered. Secretary of War Stanton applauded the exploit, and Congress passed a resolution of thanks to Captain Wilkes. Never had the hostility toward England become more violent and demonstrative.

But in England an uncontrollable wave of indignation swept over the island kingdom. The British Cabinet was hastily summoned, and amid great excitement denounced Captain Wilkes's exploit as a violation of international laws of neutrality and an affront to the British flag. The immediate release of the Confederate emissaries and reparations were demanded in no uncertain terms. Refusal to comply with these demands made war inevitable.

The controversy placed President Lincoln in a most difficult position, one in which a less resolute leader would surely have failed. His legal training enabled him at once to comprehend the grave and indefensible aspect of the affair. He was quick to see that Captain Wilkes's act constituted a flagrant reversal of the very principles and practices for which the United States had always contended, and that it was more like the former British practice of extracting seamen out of neutral vessels upon the high seas. Now Great Britain was demanding a right which for more than half a century she had arrogantly denied others, and for the defense of which the United States had fought the War of 1812.

In international law there is no process by which a nation may extract from a neutral ship on the high seas a hostile ambassador or persons charged with treason or any other crime. If Captain Wilkes had followed the procedure of bringing the *Trent* into a Northern port, and there having a prize court adjudge Mason and Slidell to be the bearers of enemy dispatches, he would have been within the law. Then the rebel envoys, being citizens charged with treason, would have been amenable to the laws of the United States. The American naval officer's conduct, however, clearly violated well-established international usage and subjected his Government, although it had not authorized the act, to the well-founded protests of the offended British nation.[1]

Shortly after the news of the stopping of the *Trent* had been brought to President Lincoln's attention, he walked into the office of Attorney-General Bates, and according to Titian J. Coffey, the Assistant Attorney General, said to that cabinet officer: "I am

[1] Woolsey, *International Law*, ed. of 1878, p. 334.

not getting much sleep out of that exploit of Wilkes's, and I suppose we must look up the law of the case. I am not much of a prize lawyer, but it seems to me pretty clear that if Wilkes saw fit to make that capture on the high seas he had no right to turn his quarterdeck into a prize court."[1]

On the other hand, the current political difficulties, the temper of public sentiment, and the injudicious advice of more than one member of Lincoln's cabinet made a peremptory compliance with the British demands most difficult. The press was teeming with comments on the legal points involved and with citations from the leading authorities on international law to justify the mooted exploit of Captain Wilkes.[2]

But the wary Lawyer-President was not carried away by the public clamor. As a lawyer he had learned that there are two sides to every controversy of merit, both of which have to be known to understand either. He had learned to study his adversary's case as well as his own, and recognized the strength as well as the weakness of the opposition. In his study of the *Trent* affair he came to the conclusion that international law and justice were on the side of the British. Though publicly he said not a word concerning the controversy, to visitors who called at the White House he freely admitted his doubts regarding the legality of Wilkes's act, and expressed his fears that the traitors would "prove to be white elephants."

"We must stick to American principles concerning the rights of neutrals," President Lincoln declared. "We fought Great Britain for insisting, by theory and practice, on the right to do precisely what Captain Wilkes has done. If Great Britain shall now protest against the act, and demand their release, we must give them up, apologize for the act as a violation of our doctrines, and thus forever bind

[1] Titian J. Coffey in Rice, *Reminiscences*, p. 245.

[2] Caleb Cushing, former Attorney-General of the United States, and one of the ablest lawyers of the time, wrote that Mason and Slidell were contraband of war and liable to seizure and that Captain Wilkes's act was legal. William Beach Lawrence, outstanding authority on international law, wrote that Captain Wilkes had acted legally and that no difficulty with England need be apprehended as a result.

her over to keep the peace in relation to neutrals, and so acknowledge that she has been wrong for sixty years."[1]

The critical condition of affairs at home and the necessity of maintaining a united North caused President Lincoln to act with even more than his accustomed deliberation. With his habitual desire to conciliate whenever possible, Lincoln entertained the notion of proposing arbitration of the dispute. Perhaps the letters of John Bright, the British liberal, had suggested this plan. Bright had written:

"If opinions on your side and ours vary and are not reconciled—I mean legal opinions—then I think your government may fairly say it is a question for impartial arbitration, to which they are willing to submit the case; and further, that, in accordance with all their past course, they are willing to agree to such amendments of maritime or international law as England, France and Russia may consent to . . . I think you may do this with perfect honor."[2]

Secretary Seward in the meantime was writing a reply to Great Britain. The President said to him: "You will go on, of course, preparing your answer, which as I understand it will state the reasons why they ought to be given up. Now, I have a mind to try my hand at stating the reasons why they ought not to be given up. We will compare the points on each side."[3]

From considerations that the United States did not have a good case, Lincoln did not press his proposal of arbitration. His cool judgment enabled him to rise above the prejudice of public passion clamoring for the summary punishment of the rebel agents. His decision was not to sacrifice principle for temporary gratification.

Breasting public sentiment, the President joined with Secretary Seward in ordering the release of Mason and Slidell.

The Secretary of State penned an exhaustive and temperate review of the case in which he justified Captain Wilkes's seizure of the Confederate envoys and their dispatches as contraband of war; but he admitted that the American naval officer had erred

[1] Nicolay and Hay, *Works*, V, 26.
[2] Pierce, *Sumner Papers* (MS.); Nicolay and Hay, *Abraham Lincoln*, V, 32.
[3] Adams, *Great Britain and the American Civil War*, I, 324.

in not bringing the vessel itself before a prize court for determination of her status. In surrendering Mason and Slidell to British custody, Seward emphasized that the United States was actually enforcing "an old honored and cherished American cause" and was doing "to the British nation just what we have always insisted all nations ought to do to us."[1]

It was "gall and wormwood," as Secretary Chase expressed it, to release the hated rebels, but it was accomplished adroitly, without arousing popular dissatisfaction at home and without humiliation abroad. Another troublesome foreign complication was thus peacefully and tactfully disposed of, and a valid excuse for England and France to countenance the Southern Confederacy was quickly removed.

The affair of the *Trent* has become one of the classics of international law, as it succeeded in committing Great Britain to the side of neutral rights upon the seas. Incidentally it brought to the imperious Seward the realization that the President intended to control policy, and instilled in him a profounder respect for Lincoln's customarily sound judgment.

Supporters of Secretary Seward have ascribed to him full credit for the favorable outcome of the *Trent* dispute, depicting Lincoln's role as more or less incidental. But remembering Seward's anti-British policy, his desire for a foreign war, and his own admission contained in a letter to his wife following Lincoln's reply to his insolent "Thoughts for the President's Consideration," that "Executive force and vigor are rare qualities; the President is the best of us," it is far more likely that it was chiefly the wise and restraining influence of Lincoln which resulted in the happy consummation of the affair.

Lincoln himself later claimed personal credit for this achievement. In one of those confidences so rare to his nature he said to an acquaintance, "Seward knows that I am his master." And by way of explanation he went on to relate how he had compelled his Secretary of State to yield to Great Britain in the *Trent* dispute.

Lincoln—so habitually modest and humble—would never have claimed credit for the achievement of another.

---

[1] Seward, *Diplomatic History of the War of the Union*, pp. 295–309.

XXIV. PRESIDENT LINCOLN
AND CHIEF JUSTICE TANEY

A FEW minutes after Chief Justice Roger Brooke Taney administered the oath of office to President-Elect Lincoln, on that blustery day in March, 1861, the new Chief Executive made the venerable head of the Supreme Court wince when, during the course of his inaugural address, he said:

"If the policy of government upon vital questions affecting the welfare of the whole people is to be irrevocably fixed by decisions of the Supreme Court, the instant they are made, the people will have ceased to be their own rulers, having to that extent practically resigned their government into the hands of that tribunal."

Here was justification for his attacks against Chief Justice Taney's decision in the Dred Scott case. But he intended no new assault upon the court or the judges, said President Lincoln.

"I do not forget the position assumed by some," he asserted, "that constitutional questions are to be decided by the Supreme Court; nor do I deny that such decisions must be binding, in any case, upon the parties to a suit, as to the object of that suit, while they are also entitled to very high respect and consideration in all parallel cases by all other departments of the Government.

And, while it is obviously possible that such decision may be erroneous in any given case, still the evil effect following it, being limited to that particular case, with the chance that it may be overruled and never become a precedent for other cases, can better be borne than could the evils of a different practice.''

Yet the President clearly left the impression that he did not regard it as nigh unto sacrilege to refuse to hold every decision of that court as the ultimate of wisdom.

Less than three months later, President Lincoln and Chief Justice Taney came to grips in one of the most memorable constitutional law battles in American history.

It arose over the President's suspension of the writ of habeas corpus following the attack upon Fort Sumter. No other phase of Lincoln's war policy was to be more vehemently criticized and more strenuously defended than this extraordinary act. And though this legal battle raged on throughout the war, the controversy remains a mooted question until this day.

John Merryman, a prominent citizen of Baltimore, was suddenly arrested by the military on May 25, 1861, for allegedly aiding the enemy. He was charged with treason and imprisoned in Fort McHenry. A copy of the order or warrant under which Merryman was arrested was demanded by his counsel, but was refused. Thereupon a writ of habeas corpus was applied for.

Chief Justice Taney happened to be in Baltimore at the time, residing with his son-in-law. Going to the Federal circuit court of that city, he took jurisdiction of the case, and in chambers issued a writ ordering General Cadwalader, the commanding officer, to produce the prisoner in the Baltimore court.

The general refused to obey the writ on the ground that President Lincoln had authorized him to suspend the writ for public safety. Immediately the Chief Justice issued an attachment against the military officer for contempt, but the marshal who sought to serve it was refused admission to the fort. Judge Taney explained to the marshal that he could summon to his aid the *posse comitatus*, but realizing the hopelessness and inadequacy of such a move, excused the exercise of this power.

Fearlessly expressing his condemnation of the suspension of

the great writ, the frail old jurist, deeply grieved, quietly left the court to ponder over his next step. Within a few days he returned; and although he predicted that his stand would soon bring about his own imprisonment in the very fortress that confined Merryman, the dauntless Chief Justice, unaided and alone, calmly set about to write his famous opinion in the case of Ex parte Merryman and to do his duty as he understood it.

In phrases terse that breathed the spirit of Magna Charta and stirred the blood of freemen, the venerable jurist, unshaken in will, indomitable, and unafraid, pronounced his opinion.

"A military officer residing in Pennsylvania issues an order to arrest a citizen of Maryland upon vague and indefinite charges, without any proof, so far as appears," began his recital of the facts. "Under this order, his house is entered in the night, he is seized as a prisoner, conveyed to Fort McHenry and there kept in close confinement, and when a habeas corpus is served on the commanding officer requiring him to produce the prisoner before a Justice of the Supreme Court, in order that he may examine into the legality of the imprisonment, the answer of the officer is, that he is authorized by the President to suspend the writ of habeas corpus at his discretion, and, in the exercise of that discretion, suspends it in this case, and, on that ground, refuses obedience to the writ."

Defiantly he flung down the gauntlet to the Nation's Executive. "The President has exercised a power which he does not possess under the Constitution," declared the intrepid jurist. Only by act of Congress can the writ of habeas corpus be suspended. With trenchant logic and an array of authorities he supported his position. He cited the section of the Constitution which governed the situation: "The privilege of the writ of habeas corpus shall not be suspended, unless when in cases of rebellion or invasion the public safety may require it." (Art. I, Sec. 9, Clause 2.) True, he admitted, the clause is silent as to who shall exercise the privilege in a case of rebellion, but precedent and authority confined the determination of the necessity as a legislative function. Besides, the Chief Justice pointed out, there was no need of Merryman's arrest by the military power at a time when the

Federal courts of Maryland were known to be open and their proceedings unobstructed so as to have permitted him the usual trial by jury. The overriding of judicial process in loyal parts of the country the Chief Justice denounced as military usurpation. Under such a state of affairs, he contended, "the people of the United States are no longer living under a government of laws; but every citizen holds life, liberty, and property at the will and pleasure of the army officer in whose military district he may happen to be found."

Unflinchingly he proclaimed the status of the judiciary as the defender of the rights of the citizen in war as well as peace. He ordered the proceedings to be laid before President Lincoln, but the Executive refused to argue the case with the Chief Justice and ignored the opinion completely.[1]

The feeble old jurist had boldly performed his duty and was ready to stand by the consequences. But though he anticipated imprisonment in Fort McHenry, he suffered nothing at the hands of that large and magnanimous man who was carrying on his slender shoulders the crushing load of an unprecedented civil conflict.

A whirlwind of abuse similar to the storm of criticism that greeted his Dred Scott edict and his later notable Ableman vs. Booth decision upholding the constitutionality of the hated Fugitive Slave Law[2] now followed Taney's Ex parte Merryman pronouncement. The eighty-four-year-old jurist, feeble in body but with a mental power which seemed to defy decay, was now accused of taking sides with the traitors by "throwing around them the sheltering protection of the ermine." He was using his great "authority and position to the advantage of those who are armed against the Union." He was serving treason and embarrassing and injuring the Government by giving aid and comfort to the enemy. So read some of the published accusations.[3]

---

[1] The Ex parte Merryman opinion was not the decision of the Supreme Court, but rather the individual opinion of Chief Justice Taney sitting as a circuit judge. It is reported as a circuit court decision. 17 Federal Cases 144.

[2] 26 How. 26.

[3] New York *Evening Post*, May 29, and June 4, 1861.

But these views were not universal, even among Republicans, and the Chief Justice found many staunch supporters for his valiant stand for personal liberty.

Equally vehement denunciation was aimed against the President. He shared in the vilest criticism and he was assailed as a tyrant and an usurper. His act of suspending the writ of habeas corpus was branded by many as an unjustified violation of the Constitution. "It is eminently proper," said the Baltimore *American*, "that a government which is fighting to maintain the integrity of the Constitution should interpose no arbitrary action to suspend or interfere with rights plainly guaranteed under it, if it would have the support and countenance of its citizens."

But the President had acted in accordance with the principle that in time of public peril so grave and imminent as to allow for no delay the necessities of the emergency were supreme, and that he as Commander-in-Chief of the military was justified in suspending the great writ when the salvation of the State demanded it.

Thus was started one of the most famous controversies in our constitutional history. Clearly the section of the Constitution which provides that "The privilege of the writ of habeas corpus shall not be suspended, unless when in cases of rebellion or invasion the public safety may require it," contemplates that the vital privilege may be suspended in the emergency of rebellion and invasion, for the preservation of the public safety. But who is to determine when such an exigency exists? Does that power belong to Congress or to the Chief Executive, or is it a concurrent power?

President Lincoln, in his Message to Congress, argued that the imperative demands of the unforseen emergency had left no choice in the matter.

"The whole of the laws which I was sworn to take care that they be faithfully executed were being resisted, and failing to be executed, in nearly one-third of the States," he explained. "Must I have allowed them to finally fail of execution, even had it been perfectly clear that by the use of the means necessary to their execution some single law, made in such extreme tenderness of the citizen's liberty, that practically it relieves more of the guilty than the innocent, should, to a very limited extent, be violated? To state the question more directly, are all the laws but one to go unexecuted, and the Government itself go to pieces, lest that one be violated? Even in such a case I should consider my official oath broken, if I should allow the Government to be overthrown, when I might think that disregarding the single law would tend to preserve it. But in this case I was not, in my own judgment, driven to this ground.''[1]

He staunchly justified his act even though its legality and propriety were questioned. And yet at no time would he concede that it was a violation of the Constitution. "In my opinion," said he, "I violated no law."

"The provision of the Constitution that the writ of habeas corpus shall not be suspended unless, when in case of rebellion or invasion, the public safety may require it, is equivalent to a provision—is a provision that such privileges may be suspended when, in cases of rebellion or invasion, the public safety does require it," he declared. "I decided that we have a case of rebellion and that the public safety does require the qualified suspension of the writ of habeas corpus, which I authorized to be made.

"Now, it is insisted that Congress, and not the Executive, is vested with the power. But the Constitution itself is silent as to which is to exercise the power, and as the provision was plainly made for a dangerous emergency, I cannot bring myself to believe that the framers of that instrument intended that, in every case, the danger should run its course until Congress could be called together, the very assembling of which might be prevented, as was intended in this case, by the rebellion.''

His imperative duty as Chief Executive to preserve the integrity of the Government, a duty on whose performance the very life of the Nation depended, had determined his course in the matter. This was his practical answer to the scholarly opinion of the Chief Justice. Congress applauded his conduct and immediately passed a law ratifying the principle on which he had acted.

[1] *Works*, VI, 309; Elliot, *Biographical Story of the Constitution*, p. 225.

Later in a letter the President reiterated his position in these words:

"The Constitution contemplates the question (the suspension of the habeas corpus) as likely to occur for decision, but it does not expressly declare who is to decide it. Be necessary implication, when rebellion or invasion comes, the decision is to be made from time to time, and I think the man whom for the time the people have, under the Constitution, made the Commander-in-Chief of their army and navy, is the man who holds the power and bears the responsibility of making it. If he uses the power justly the people will probably justify him; if he abuses it, he is in their hands to be dealt with by all the modes they have reserved to themselves in the Constitution."[1]

Chief Justice Taney had cited legal precedents and authorities that seemingly clashed with the position of the President. He maintained that Tucker's *Blackstone* and Story's *Commentaries* indicated that Congress alone can suspend the writ of habeas corpus and that the United States Supreme Court through Chief Justice Marshall in the case of Ex parte Bollman and Swartwout (4 Cranch 75) had indicated a similar opinion. But actually the Supreme Court had never definitely made a conclusive pronouncement with reference to the fundamental point as to whether the suspending power rests with the President or with Congress. The Bollman case had no direct bearing upon this controversy. It had merely decided that if at any time the public safety should require the suspension of the powers vested by the Judiciary Act of 1789, giving the United States courts the authority to issue the writ of habeas corpus, it is for the legislature and not for the courts to say so.[2] So at the time President Lincoln assumed the power to suspend the great writ, there was no clear-cut principle of undisputed legal authority in all American jurisprudence to gainsay the legality of his act.

[1] Letter to M. Birchard and others, June 29, 1863; *Works*, II, 361; IX, 3–4.

[2] In the case of Ex parte Bollman and Swartwout, 4 Cranch 75, Chief Justice Marshall said, in an obiter dictum: "If at any time the public safety require the suspension of the writ of habeas corpus, it is for the legislature to say so. The question depends on political considerations of which the legislature is to decide."

Nor was Lincoln without legal support to sustain his position. In an elaborate opinion Attorney-General Bates maintained that in pursuance of the President's obligation to execute the laws, he must be accorded the widest discretion as to the means. Since it was within his powers as Commander-in-Chief to use military force to suppress the rebellion all incidents of warlike action must be included.

He pointed out further that it was not within the province of the Judiciary, a co-ordinate and not a superior branch of the Government, to interfere with the Executive in the exercise of these powers. Therefore, he concluded, as a temporary and extraordinary measure, in an emergency, the President has the authority to order a suspension of the privilege, and he is under no obligation to obey a writ of the court regarding the matter. He is answerable before the high court of impeachment for any breach of this great trust and before no other tribunal.[1]

The President found additional chief defenders in Horace Binney, an eminent lawyer, and Chief Justice Joel Parker of New Hampshire. As in the case of the Attorney General's opinion, their arguments, too, were based almost solely upon the technical circumstances and necessities of the present emergency rather than upon established precedent.[2]

The impotency of the Judiciary as against the Executive amid the smoke of battle and roar of cannons immediately became apparent. Congress neglected to take any action on the matter. The result was a temporary dictatorship with practically all the powers of the Government concentrated in the hands of a single man—the former lawyer from Sangamon County. In his hands lay the control over the life, liberty, and property of millions of persons—a power rarely wielded by any ruler in history. By degrees the suspension of the writ of habeas corpus was extended all over the country. From Maine to California men were seized as public enemies, imprisoned without being furnished the information of the charge against them, and refused the service of the great writ. Military trial and military censorship violative of

[1] McPherson, *Rebellion*, p. 158.
[2] Nicolay and Hay, *Works*, VIII, pp. 30–31.

the principles advanced by Taney—but urged by the President and his Secretary of War as justified by the conditions—followed in the wake.

War, it was clear, to a large extent meant the negation of civil rights. Frightful injustice was often done. But how could it be helped in the mad cataclysm into which the Government had been plunged? Abuses of individual civil liberties had to be endured with fortitude at a time when bullets rather than indictments were the means of enforcing submission to the laws.[1]

A storm of malignant abuse, obloquy, and vituperation that not even the much maligned Taney had known now assailed the President. Tyrant, usurper, and oppressor, he was called.[2]

How grotesque it now appears that a man who during all his life had identified himself with the preservation of free institutions, and had ever manifested a most sincere reverence for liberty and law, should be charged with aiming at arbitrary power. He sanctioned military arrests, it is true, but only because he conscientiously believed them to be a power granted to the Commander-in-Chief by the Constitution and that military necessity required them for the public safety. Scrupulously he sought constitutional justification for every act.

President Lincoln regretted the stern necessity of his acts. Reluctantly he adopted the measures requiring the suspension of the citizen's safeguards against arbitrary arrest or any other established American principle. But he eloquently justified his position as compatible with his constitutional powers and absolutely essential for the preservation of the Union.

To those who angrily reminded him that the safeguards of the writ of habeas corpus and trial by jury "were secured substantially to the English people after years of protracted civil war and were adopted into our Constitution at the close of the Revolution," President Lincoln calmly replied:

---

[1] Thorpe, *Constitutional History of the United States*, III, 517; Rhoades, *History of the United States from the Compromise of 1850*, IV, 222; *American Historical Review*, XXIV, 626; W. A. Dunning, "The Constitution in the Civil War," *Political Science Quarterly*, I, 163.

[2] Samuel Tyler, *Memoir of Roger Brooke Taney*, pp. 422 ff.

"Would not the demonstration be better if it could have been truly said that these safeguards had been adopted and applied *during* the civil war and *during* our revolution, instead of after the one and at the close of the other? I too am devotedly for them after civil war and before civil war, and at all times 'except when in cases of rebellion or invasion the public safety may require their suspension.' "

Chief Justice Taney died October 12, 1864, a broken-hearted, maligned, and ostracized man. President Lincoln fell victim to the assassin's bullet about six months later. So neither of these actors in this grim legal drama could hear the ringing words of the very tribunal over which the aged jurist had so long presided, by which it completely vindicated the constitutional doctrines pronounced by Chief Justice Taney in Ex parte Merryman, and condemned the President's exercise of martial law in regions outside of the theater of the war as highly illegal and indefensible.

Two years after the mortal remains of the martyred Executive had been interred in the earth of his beloved Springfield, the Supreme Court of the United States, now composed largely of Republicans and presided over by Chief Justice Chase, who had been elevated to that position by Lincoln at Taney's death, in the case of Ex parte Milligan held that the Executive had no constitutional authority to establish military tribunals in States where the civil courts were open. "The Constitution is not suspended during war," was the gist of this great pronouncement delivered by Lincoln's own closest friend, David Davis, then a justice of the Supreme Court by appointment by his former Illinois circuit companion.

"The Constitution of the United States," said Justice Davis, "is a law for rulers and people equally in war and peace, and covers with the shield of its protection all classes of men at all times and under all circumstances. No doctrine involving more pernicious consequences was ever invented by the wit of man than that any of its provisions can be suspended during any of the great exigencies of government. Such a doctrine leads to anarchy and despotism. . . . Martial rule can never exist where the courts are open, and in the proper and unobstructed exercise of their jurisdiction. It is also confined to the locality of actual war.''

This pronouncement of Justice Davis has become one of the bulwarks of American liberty.

It is to be observed, however, that the Milligan case[1] does not declare against Lincoln's theory of the President's right to suspend the writ of habeas corpus. The question of the suspension of the great writ is not dealt with at all in this case. The sole point Judge Davis made was that Milligan, arrested in Indiana, remote from the theater of war, on a charge of conspiracy against the Government, was unlawfully tried by a military commission at Indianapolis where the civil courts were functioning. It was conceded, however, that in conquered territory and in districts in and contiguous to the theater of war martial law and trials by military commissions were proper and lawful.

It is to be observed further that the Milligan case was decided after the war, with the rebellion crushed and the public safety assured. Yet when two years previously, during the midst of the hostilities, an analogous case came before the Supreme Court, that high tribunal sided with the Administration by pronouncing an opinion just the reverse of the Milligan decision. This was in the Vallandigham case, decided in February of 1864.

Clement L. Vallandigham, an influential and outspoken anti-war agitator, was arrested for declaring disloyal opinions with the object of weakening the power of the Government. General Burnside, in command of the ''Department of the Ohio,'' caused a military commission to be convened to try the accused. But Vallandigham protested against the proceeding, declaring that the ''alleged offense'' with which he was charged was unknown to the Constitution and the laws. He demanded his constitutional guarantees of due process of law, including indictment and trial by jury. The military commission, however, disregarded the protest, heard the evidence, and found him guilty as charged and

[1] Ex parte Milligan, 4 Wall. 120, and dissent by Chief Justice Chase, which Colonel William Winthrop (*Military Law*, II, 38) regards as the ''sounder and more reasonable'' view.

ordered him imprisoned during the war. His petition for a writ of habeas corpus was refused by the United States District Court at Cincinnati, and the case was brought up to the Supreme Court for review of the sentence of the military commission. But the Supreme Court ruled that such a commission was not a court within the meaning of the Judiciary Act of 1789, where-from federal tribunals derived their appellate jurisdiction, and its acts, therefore, were not reviewable by the Supreme Court.

Though there exist some technical differences between the Vallandigham and Milligan cases, yet both substantially dealt with the same problems: the legality of military commissions when used for the trial of citizens in non-military areas, and the rights of civil courts to set aside the proceedings of such commissions. The conflicting opinions that emanated from the two hearings before the Supreme Court clearly indicate how the alarming exigencies of war had affected judicial decisions. While the war was in progress and the public safety endangered, the Supreme Court in the Vallandigham case refused to interfere with the proceedings of a military commission; but with the return of peace and the necessity of such commissions ended, that highest of courts in no unmistakable terms denounced the illegality of their proceedings.

Men now shudder with horror at some of the wartime policies of President Lincoln—his suspension of the privilege of the writ of habeas corpus, the exercise of martial law, spending money without congressional appropriation and enlarging the army and navy beyond the limits fixed by law, the dictatorial position assumed by him, and the concentration of nearly all the powers of the Government in his own hands. What irony of fate that so gentle a spirit and so sympathetic and kindly a nature should be forced by the stern logic of events to become so absolute a dictator! Though imperative necessity compelled him to exercise powers never before assumed by a President, he honestly and profoundly believed his every act—Justice Taney's opinion notwithstanding—to be compatible with and justified by the Constitution. Even under the most trying circumstances he endeavored to remain within the constitutional limitations of his office.

No measure, however important or expedient, ever received his official sanction unless in his opinion it was in agreement with the fundamental law of the land. It was inevitable that under such unprecedented and turbulent circumstances his interpretation of the limitations imposed by the Constitution—made apparently for a state of peace and not for the fearful exigencies of war—should be severely criticized. It was inevitable that in an upheaval like a civil war the distinction between executive and legislative functions should become uncertain. The powers assumed by the President and the prerogatives claimed by him were naturally not in keeping with the normal tenor of American law. Though Congress alone had the authority to enact the necessary measures intended to weaken the enemy, the will of the President as Commander-in-Chief was supreme wherever troops were stationed. Wielding unlimited powers of martial law, through the establishment of military commissions and "special war courts" to try civilians, the modest Westerner became through circumstances an absolute dictator such as this Republic had never before nor has since known. And yet if he were a dictator, it must be admitted that he was a benevolent dictator. This fervent disciple of freedom who would not be a slave, could not be a tyrant. Not for personal gratification did this great democrat and exponent of government by the people wield his nearly limitless arbitrary powers, but for the salvation of the State.

He took the people into his confidence and argued with great care to justify the use of every extraordinary power. He was anxious that the masses from whom he had sprung and to whom he hoped to return should understand that if he crossed the constitutional limitations of his office, he did so only because the salvation of the State demanded it. He was careful to mark his exceptional measures as imperative emergencies justified only by the demands of the war, so that they would never become peacetime precedents.

His one paramount desire at all times was to save the Union. By means believed by him to be constitutional, all circumstances considered, he sought to maintain the Constitution inviolate. He sought to do so with as little deviation from the strict letter of the Constitution as possible. But there was something far more grievous in his opinion than a possible deviation from the strict letter of the Constitution. It was worse and far more irretrievable to lose the Government for which the Constitution was made. "Was it possible to lose the nation and yet preserve the Constitution?" he asked. "I could not feel that, to the best of my ability, I had even tried to preserve the Constitution if, to save slavery or any minor matter, I should permit the wreck of the Government, country, and Constitution altogether."

He would risk the violation of a minor law to prevent the whole fabric of the law from going to ruin. "Often a limb," he said, "must be amputated to save a life; but a life is never wisely given to save a limb."

Perhaps his construction of the Constitution respecting the President's authority to suspend the writ of habeas corpus would now be considered wrong and Taney's right. Perhaps in a strictly legal sense this exercise of power would now be construed as having been usurped. But he was not insincere in contending that his acts were justified legally as well as morally.

"If I be wrong on this question of constitutional power," he said, "my error lies in believing that certain proceedings are constitutional when, in cases of rebellion or invasion, the public safety requires them, which would not be constitutional when, in absence of rebellion or invasion, the public safety does not require them; in other words, that the Constitution is not in its application in all respects the same in cases of rebellion and invasion involving the public safety, as it is in times of profound peace and public security. The Constitution itself makes the distinction, and I can no more be persuaded that the Government can constitutionally take no strong measures in time of rebellion, because it can be shown that the same could not be lawfully taken in time of peace, than I can be persuaded that a particular drug is not good medicine for a sick man because it can be shown to not be good food for a well one."

His interpretation of the Constitution, like Hamilton's, was "qualified and controlled" by considerations of "convenience," "reason," and "natural justice."

He was too resourceful a lawyer not to be able to find in the Constitution, at least by implication, provisions for its own preservation.

The dictatorial position assumed by him was responsible for two most important results instrumental in bringing about ultimate victory for the Northern cause: the preservation of the Capital, and the maintenance of Union sentiment in the wavering border States. Though stern necessity compelled him to give wide latitude to his interpretation of the Executive's constitutional wartime powers, it is gratifying to recall that as soon as the preservation of the Capital was assured and the border States made safe for the Union cause, the administration of the Government returned once more to the accustomed methods of departmental co-ordination.

The silence of the Constitution which enabled him to give broad interpretations to the President's wartime powers as to enable him to adopt summary measures was indeed fortunate, as events proved. For what careful student of the times can assert that the Nation could have been preserved without the exercise of just such discretionary powers? And though the Constitution was strained and though he wielded dictatorial powers unparalleled in our Nation's history, yet when his task was completed, as Carl Schurz has said, he left "essentially intact our free institutions in all things that concern the rights and liberties of the citizen."

Woodrow Wilson, our last wartime President, well summarized the situation when he said: "Mr. Lincoln did all things with a wakeful conscience, and certainly without love of personal power for its own sake; seeing substantial justice done, too, whenever he could. But the Constitution was sadly strained nevertheless."

Fortunate indeed was the American Nation that during the stormiest and most perilous crisis in its history two such forceful characters as Lincoln and Taney headed the executive and judicial departments of the Government. Fortunate it was that during that period of confusion and irregularity—in civil administration, in legislation, and in constitutional interpretation—the President was a resourceful lawyer and lover of the Constitution, who though possibly performing extra-constitutional acts was motivated only by the desire to save, not destroy, free institutions; who while moving above the law moved in the plane of a benevolent statecraft; who could relinquish his dictatorial powers as soon as the peril was passed, and be the first to work for the restoration of a normally functioning Government.

Fortunate for the Nation that amid the roar of cannon and clash of contending arms, amid the clouds of confusion, turmoil and uncertainty, the assumption of dictatorial powers by the President and the inevitable wide-spread negation of civil rights, the intrepid old Chief Justice, indifferent to public opinion, unafraid of the superior power of the Commander-in-Chief of the armed forces, alone and unaided, attempted to exert a check upon the Chief Executive and uphold the supremacy of the Constitution and civil authority.

Congress acquiesced in the President's usurpation of its functions, but the venerable Chief Justice would not permit such arbitrary stretches of power to pass without a vigorous protest.

Serene and unafraid, though engulfed in the seething torrent of sectional animosities, partisan fury, and overzealous and ungovernable patriotism, he performed his duty as he saw it and stood ready to suffer, whatever the consequences might be. Never had a high public official braved public opinion more boldly in the performance of a duty. Immovable in the onrushing flood, it ruthlessly swept over him. With the fortitude of the bravest soldier he bore his wounds and went to his grave, a true martyr in the battle for constitutional government.

Now that the clouds of sectional passion and strife have been swept away, and that in the enjoyment of a national unity we can appreciate with calmer retrospect the acts of Chief Justice Taney, how different than that of his contemporaries must be our opinion of this jurist? Whatever else may be said of the reasoning he employed in the Dred Scott decision and the scope of that pronouncement and its fatal error, that it could determine the great political controversy involved, who now can question his conspicuous legal ability, lofty ideals of the judicial function, independence of character, personal integrity and sincerity, and deep-seated conviction that he was rendering a patriotic service by attempting a final settlement of the slavery question and thus averting the impending civil war?

What sublimer act can be found in all the annals of the Anglo-Saxon judiciary than this feeble old magistrate's defiance of the President, as he valiantly attempted to uphold the supremacy of the Constitution and civil authority in the midst of arms?

Taney failed and fell, crushed by the ruthless demands of the conflict, but he performed his duty, true to the noblest traditions of his office and his profession.

The speedy vindication of his principles by the Supreme Court decision in the Milligan case is a fitting recognition of his noble service and invincible spirit.

But while a grateful Republic has virtually deified the simple Western lawyer who saved it from disintegration, it has yet to render the full measure of justice to the memory of the indomitable Chief Justice Taney.[1]

---

[1] Chief Justice Taney was never forgiven by implacable anti-slavery Republicans for his Dred Scott pronouncement. When he died in 1864, Charles Sumner, on the floor of the United States Senate, protested against paying him the customary honors accorded to deceased members of the Supreme Court. (James G. Blaine, *Twenty Years of Congress*, I, 135–36.) "I object," said Senator Sumner, "that an emancipated country should make a bust to the author of the Dred Scott decision. . . . The name of Taney is to be hooted down the page of history" (Thirty-Eighth Congress, Second Session, February 23, 1865, pp. 1012 ff.)

XXV. LINCOLN'S CONTRIBUTIONS TO THE CONSTITUTION

To LINCOLN, the self-trained lawyer, history must assign a place on a level with Washington, Hamilton, Marshall, and Webster as an outstanding figure in the creation, interpreting and expounding of the Constitution. As Washington, the presiding officer of the constitutional convention, furnished the inspiration and leadership at its creation, and Hamilton the necessary influence through the *Federalist* for its ratification; as Marshall, for thirty-four years the Nation's Chief Justice, was its great interpreter, defining its character and breathing into it life and vitality, and Webster, its great expounder standing on the Constitution as his one and only platform, to define the issue and keep the disunionists at bay pending the coming of just such a figure as Lincoln, so must history ascribe to this lowly-born prairie lawyer the title of the preserver and humanizer of the Constitution.

William Howard Taft, the only man in American history to serve as President of the Republic and as Chief Justice of the United States Supreme Court, has stated that no man ever lived who would have made an abler Chief Justice of the Nation's highest judicial tribunal than Abraham Lincoln.

President Lincoln manifested a power of clear reasoning and grasp of basic principles that make it safe to conjecture that had he been placed in the position of John Marshall, he would have made as great a contribution in constitutional interpretation. Who could doubt that had he lived through the turbulent days of reconstruction he would have proved himself the greatest constitutional lawyer of the nineteenth century, and that many of the mistakes and horrors of that shameful period would never have become part of America's history.

To Lincoln was given the colossal task amid fratricidal strife, chaos, and sectional bitterness, to save the Constitution from its disunionist enemies as well as from its over-zealous and impatient Abolitionist friends. To him fell the duty of reviving the stricken Nation and breathing into its fundamental law new life and new strength. The degree with which he succeeded in this epoch-making undertaking is his crowning glory and everlasting monument to fame.

Lincoln inherited a crumbling Government and a Constitution made impotent by the slavery-subservient and vacillating Buchanan. When in December, 1860, South Carolina had insisted on her right to secede, President Buchanan in his message to Congress declared that such a right was "wholly inconsistent with the history as well as the character of the Federal Constitution." "This government," he maintained, "is a great and powerful government, invested with all the attributes of sovereignty over the special subjects to which its authority extends." But while concluding a State retained no constitutional right to secede, he disclaimed any power to bring force to bear to suppress insurrection in such a State, "where," he maintained, "no judicial authority exists to issue process, and where there is no marshal to execute it, and where, even if there were such an officer, the entire population would constitute one solid combination to resist him." He could find no power in the Constitution to enable Congress to coerce into submission a State that is attempting to withdraw, or has actually withdrawn, from the Union. In other words, he believed that though no State had the right to secede, still the National Government could not prevent a State from seceding. He then adopted the time-honored method of meeting the emergency by dodging the issue, by eulogizing the Constitution, affirming the supremacy of the National Government in its sphere and at the same time emphasizing the reservation of rights of the States. Desirous of avoiding bloodshed, he hoped against hope that the difficulty would yet be settled by negotiation, and that the Union, now disintegrating, would be patched together again by an old-time compromise. His very weakness, vacillation, and fear to take an aggressive step were paradoxically all that prevented a number of additional hesitating States from seceding before Lincoln finally took up the helm of the storm-tossed ship of state.[1]

Lincoln's first Inaugural Address, that marvelously touching and pathetic appeal for peace and the Union, had been unwavering on the question of the extension of slavery. Uncompromising as it was on the proposition of slavery's restrictions, it asserted just as definitely that there must be no encroachment upon its existence within the States where it was already established. "I have no purpose, directly or indirectly, to interfere with the institution of slavery where it exists," he declared, repeating the words of a previous speech. "I believe I have no lawful right to do so and I have no inclination to do so." And although the entire address was extremely moderate in tone and a passionate plea for conciliation, and pronounced no policy different from his predecessor's, it was the first utterance that definitely and unequivocally defined the status of the Union from a legal aspect.

There was no dodging of the issue. The Union of the States was perpetual and indissoluble, Lincoln declared. No State could lawfully withdraw from the Union, for never had a provision for its own destruction been embodied in the organic law of any government. He held the Constitution to be a contract that could not be rescinded without the consent of all. Not only historically and legally was the Union indissoluble, but also "physically speaking, we cannot separate," he insisted. He minced no words when he declared, "Plainly, the central idea of secession is the

---

[1] W.A. Dunning, "The Constitution in the Civil War," *Political Science Quarterly*, I, 163.

essence of anarchy.'' There could be no such thing as lawful secession. Such an act could be characterized only as revolution or rebellion. The seceding States were still in the Union, he asserted, and could not get out without successfully resorting to revolution or rebellion.

His supreme desire was peace. But with the outbreak of hostilities, Lincoln the pacificator threw all his mind and all his strength into the battle—a battle for the life of the Union and the preservation of the Constitution. The situation in which the President found the Government lacked all precedent. With force the enemies of the Union would bring about its destruction; with force he realized he must now battle for its preservation. His July 4, 1861, Message to the Congress was a striking contrast to his first inaugural address. Gone was the offer of concession and compromise; gone the pleading, conciliatory tone. Replacing it came, instead, a clear, unequivocal, and aggressive trumpet-call for a war to the finish for national supremacy and the integrity of the Union. The issue involved, declared Lincoln, ''embraces more than the fate of the United States. It presents to the whole family of man the question whether a constitutional government of the people by the same people, can or cannot maintain its integrity against its own domestic foes. . . . Must a government of necessity be too strong for the liberties of its people or too weak to maintain its own existence?''[1]

The secessionists had raised the issue, and unflinchingly he met their challenge.

Lincoln combated the sophism of the Secessionists who maintained that any State of the Union, consistently with the Constitution, might lawfully and peacefully withdraw from the Union without the consent of the Union or of any other State.

Such Southern leaders as Alexander H. Stephens and Jefferson Davis argued ably that the States never parted with their sovereignty when they voluntarily entered the Union. Nor could sovereignty be surrendered by mere implication, they contended. To them, the expression ''We the people of the United States'' meant the people of the individual States. The ''supreme law

[1] *Works*, VI, 304.

clause" of the Constitution, they maintained, did not make the United States sovereign over the States. Although the people of the States bestowed the supreme governmental power upon a general government as their agent, nevertheless they neither limited nor surrendered the sovereignty inherent in themselves. On the contrary, the spokesmen for the South emphasized, some of the States like Virginia, New York, and Rhode Island even reserved the right of withdrawal from the Union when they ratified the Constitution. Moreover, what is the Constitution, they argued, but a "compact" between the States and binding upon the confederated parties only so long as all the States live up to the terms of the compact? Some of the confederates having violated the compact, the others were relieved from all further obligations.[1]

The trouble lay in the fact that the limitation of State sovereignty never had been settled by the Constitution. That instrument, the child of compromise and concession, had left unsettled this grave issue: Was the United States a mere federation of sovereign States, or did the States derive their sovereignty from that of the Nation? The question had been evaded and obscured. Perhaps some of the original States would never have come into the Union had it been definitely determined that they could not go out when they felt just cause to do so. At least the equivocal language of the Constitution now gave the leaders of the Southern Confederacy an arguable case for secession.

But to Lincoln, the Constitutional lawyer, all their contentions were mere sophism. A State in becoming a member of the Union enters into an indissoluble relation and becomes an organic part of the Nation, he answered with invincible legal reasoning. How could disunion be consistent with the Constitution? Where was the law that expressly or by implication sanctioned it? How could any government, founded upon such principles of disintegration, endure? Secession was unconstitutional. It could mean only treason and civil war.

The sophism of the secessionists, Lincoln declared, derived much, perhaps the whole, of its currency from the assumption

[1] Alexander H. Stephens, *A Constitutional View of the War Between the States*, I, pp. 68, 80–83, 138, 491, 495–510.

that there was some omnipotent and sacred supremacy pertaining to the individual State of the Federal Union. "The States have neither more nor less power than that reserved to them in the Union by the Constitution—no one of them ever having been a State out of the Union," he pointed out. "The original ones passed into the Union even *before* they cast off their British colonial dependence; and each of the new ones came into the Union directly from a condition of dependence, excepting Texas, and even Texas, in its temporary independence, was never designated a State. . . . The express plighting of faith by each and all of the original thirteen, in the Articles of Confederation . . . that the Union should be perpetual, was most conclusive."

He decried the South's claim to "state sovereignty."

"What is a 'sovereignty' in the political sense of the term," he demanded. Would it be far wrong to define it "a political community without a political superior"? Tested by this, no one of the States, except Texas, ever was a sovereignty; and even Texas gave up the character on coming into the Union, by which act she acknowledged the Constitution of the United States, and the laws and treaties of the United States made in pursuance of the Constitution, to be for her the supreme law of the land.

"The States have their status in the Union, and they have no other legal status. If they break from this, they can only do so against law and by revolution. The Union, not themselves, separately, procured their independence and their liberty. By conquest or purchase, the Union gave each of them whatever of independence and liberty it has. The Union is older than any of the States, and, in fact, it created them as States. Originally some independent colonies made the Union, and, in turn, the Union threw off their old dependence for them, and made them States, such as they are. Not one of them ever had a State constitution independent of the Union."[1]

Therefore, how can secession be consistent with the Constitution and lawful and peaceful, demanded Lincoln.

He emphasized that the Constitution specifically provided that "the United States shall guarantee to every State in this Union

[1] *Works*, VI, 315.

a republican form of government." What was to prevent any seceding State from adopting other than a republican form of government? Therefore, he concluded, to insure the maintenance of the guaranteed form of government, the Federal Government, of necessity, must have the right to prevent the secession of the States, for "when an end is lawful and obligatory, the indispensable means to it are also lawful and obligatory."

Such were the arguments of the constitutional lawyer.

One section of the country believed that slavery was right and sought to extend it, while the other maintained it was wrong and demanded its restriction and eventually its extermination. This, President Lincoln knew to be the basic substantial dispute. But in this Message to Congress not once does he mention slavery. There is now but one issue—the supremacy of the Constitution and the preservation of the Union with all the dignity, equality, and rights of the several States unimpaired. The Nation is the sovereign. The States are local organizations and subordinate to the Nation. The General Government, an all-inclusive sovereignty, represents the Nation and is limited in no way by the State governments but only by the Federal Constitution.

Here was the statement of his case for nationalism—the one, the paramount, the supreme issue of the day. No one had ever given such clear expression to the national idea. The Civil War would be fought not for the overthrow of slavery but for the destruction of the principle of disunion. Once and for all time it must be determined whether the Government of the people of the United States should be a national, unbreakable, permanent Union or a Confederacy easily dismembered and always in danger of being disrupted by any unjust, imaginary, or trivial grievance of any constituent State. Once and forever the question "Can a State constitutionally withdraw from the Union?" must be answered.

Impatient Abolitionists, however, refused to accept Lincoln's theory that the supremacy of the Constitution and the preservation of the Union were the only and the paramount issues. They demanded the immediate emancipation of the slaves. Those who had been Lincoln's friends and supporters now criticized and censured him with the vehemence of his bitterest enemies.

Almost from the very outset of his inauguration, Abolitionists had importuned him to bring about the immediate destruction of slavery by emancipation. Lincoln hated slavery with every fiber in his being; he fervently wished that all men everywhere might be free; he had been the outspoken antagonist of the slave-power. But despite his personal inclinations as a private citizen, now as an elected officer with powers and duties prescribed by a fixed Constitution whose provisions he had sworn to obey, his personal feelings had to be sacrificed for his sworn obligation. It was his duty to uphold the Union and the laws. The barbaric institution was a part of the law of the land countenanced by the Constitution and sanctioned by the courts. It had existed even before the Constitution itself and had been accepted by the creators of that great instrument as an unavoidable evil. Congress, he believed, had no right to interfere with slavery in the States where it existed. He feared lest he should invade the slightest constitutional right of the slave-owners. Morally wrong though slavery was, moral justice, in his opinion, did not countenance the violation of the law which tolerated the institution. It did, however, clearly indicate the direction in which the law should be changed.

Respect for the law and veneration for the Constitution are stamped upon Lincoln's every public act. The destruction of slavery, he insisted, must come about only by means compatible with the Constitution. He realized, too, that slavery had become so much a part of the South that immediate abolition or emancipation would bring economic chaos to the Nation and certain disruption of the Union. He realized that the Abolitionists' rash disregard of the constitutional rights of the slave States tended only to drive more States out of the Union and make the disruption permanent.

With all his sympathy for the downtrodden slave, with all his opposition to the extension of slavery, he took the anomalous position of supporting, defending, and preserving the Constitution, which forbade interference with this institution. So when the spirit of disunion ran wild, when sectionalism, bitterness, and partisan strife were at fever heat, when impatient extreme Abolitionists and rabid Secessionists were aiming a blow at the heart of the Nation, he never lost sight of the cardinal importance of preserving our constitutional form of government.

As the experienced lawyer keeps the issue on trial continually before the court and jury, so now Lincoln would not, under any pretext, permit the one, vital, overwhelming issue of the preservation of the Union to be obscured by any other. Radical Abolitionists—many of whom even welcomed disunion because the Union sanctioned slavery—attributed the President's failure to liberate the slaves immediately by a military edict to his weakness and unsteadiness of purpose.

Horace Greeley, imperious New York editor, bitterly attacked the President for failing to take immediate steps for abolishing slavery by some sweeping proclamation of emancipation. With all the humility of a private citizen, the President who had acquired a power that never before had been wielded by a ruler of this Nation forgot the might and dignity of his office and penned a reply to Greeley.

It was a reiteration of his whole creed, so far as emancipation and the preservation of the Union were concerned. His personal wish, he declared, was that all men everywhere could be free. But now his paramount object in this struggle was "to save the Union, and not either to save or destroy slavery." It was a remarkable pleading—the embodiment of legal expression—clear, pointed, concise, and undemurrable, and it answered Greeley's case out of court.

But though the President subordinated the question of the overthrow of slavery to the more important and paramount issue, eventual emancipation never for a moment left his mind.

Calmly he awaited the fullness of time for accomplishing the great undertaking. Through all those soul-torturing struggles of the first two years he was reading the signs of the times, calmly waiting, patiently waiting, for the propitious moment when circumstances would permit the fulfillment of his devout wish that all men everywhere might be free. But he sought its accomplishment while adhering strictly to legal and constitutional methods.

Bravely he bore the criticism of impatient friends and the hostility and calumny of open and avowed enemies. He had registered an oath in heaven to preserve, protect, and defend the Constitution. The rights of the individual States in regard to their slave property must remain inviolate until the safety of the Union demanded their forfeiture in favor of the higher obligation. He alone was to be the judge of when that exigency had arrived. His alone was to be the awful responsibility. As a lawyer he believed in the inviolability of property rights. He opposed the confiscation of property without due process of law. He earnestly sought to avoid the sudden and violent destruction of slavery. In vain he urged compensated emancipation.[1]

He waited until slavery's extinction became an imperative duty—until further temporizing would prove disastrous to the cause of the Union. Convinced that the propitious moment was at hand, without further hesitation, without consultation, simply, undramatically, he struck the death-blow to slavery.

He issued the preliminary edict of freedom on the twenty-second day of September, 1862, just after the battle of Antietam. "I made a solemn vow before God, that if General Lee was driven back from Pennsylvania, I would crown the result by a declaration of freedom to the slaves," he told Secretary Chase. The preliminary Emancipation Proclamation called on the rebellious States to return to their allegiance before January 1, otherwise the slaves within their borders would be declared freemen. So on New Year's Day of 1863, none of the States having returned, the final Proclamation was issued.[2]

By virtue of his power as Commander-in-Chief, the President ordered that all persons held in slavery in the designated States should be thence forward free, and that the Government, including the military and naval authorities thereof, "will recognize and maintain the freedom of said persons." Upon this momentous and most beneficent military decree of history, and by him "believed to be an act of justice, warranted by the Constitution," he invoked "the considerate judgment of mankind and the gracious favour of Almighty God."[3]

[1] *Works*, VII, 172–73.
[2] "Diary of Salmon P. Chase, July 21, 1862 to October 12, 1862," in American Historical Association *Report*, 1902, pp. 87–88.
[3] *Works*, VII, 36–49.

The Proclamation did not in itself abolish slavery. It was made applicable only to those States or part of States in open rebellion. But with its pronouncement "that the Executive Government of the United States, including the military and naval authorities thereof, will recognize and maintain the freedom of said persons," the mortal wound to the hated institution, as events proved, had been inflicted, and its absolute extinction through the length and breadth of the land became only a matter of time.

The Proclamation of Emancipation, which takes rank with the Declaration of Independence as the second great charter of American freedom and yields in importance to no other event in modern history, is the simply written, brief, lucid, and concise document of a lawyer. Mighty and vast as were its consequences, Lincoln prepared it without consultation with or the knowledge of the Cabinet. With the self-reliance with which he as a novice lawyer in the early days as Stuart's partner had written the legal papers for the cases that had come to their office, he now drafted this immortal edict. Strong, simple, and clear was its reasoning.

By virtue of his power as Commander-in-Chief of the army and navy in time of actual armed rebellion against the authority of the Government, and as a fit and necessary war measure for suppressing said rebellion, he justified his act. It had no sanction as a constitutional provision. Congress had not approved it as a statute and no court had pronounced it as a binding rule of law.

In normal times he was convinced that the President could not interfere with slavery in the States, nor had he legal power to liberate a single slave. But now, with the Nation engaged in a life-and-death struggle with public enemies, he was just as convinced that his wartime powers authorized him to use against the rebels every expedient countenanced by public law. Among these powers was the confiscation of the enemy's slaves.

In the past, as a lawyer, he had relied but little upon the mouldering volumes of ancient precedents in trying his cases in the courts. He had argued them on original principles of common sense, logic, reasoning, and natural justice. And now in this unparalleled exigency, with the fate of a Nation at stake, he would rely on no outworn precedents to guide his course. The issues of the present conflict alone were the determining factors in governing his actions, and he hoped that they alone would govern the future judges of courts in their interpretation of the validity of this beneficent edict.

In all probability, had the legality of the Proclamation ever been tested in an actual court case, it would have been upheld as a proper exercise of the President's powers as Commander-in-Chief of the armed forces, and as freeing in law those slaves who obtained actual freedom in consequence of the edict.

Physically the Proclamation could liberate only those slaves of Southern owners in rebellion who actually came into the Union lines. It was physically inoperative as to those who were beyond the reach of the federal authority. Moreover, it was urged that under the international law of postliminy, by which persons or things taken by the enemy are restored to their former state when they come again under the power of the nation to which they formerly belonged, the slaves so liberated would automatically return to their original status. It was also pointed out that the edict would have no effect upon the children of slaves born in the future. Many doubted the efficacy of the Proclamation altogether, for what was there in it that would have prevented the future re-establishment of slavery in the South after the return of peace?

President Lincoln never claimed any legal force for his Proclamation other than as it constituted an act of war based on imperative necessity and helpful in a military way to the Union cause. He was frank to admit its legal weakness and its insufficiency as a permanent means of destroying slavery. But it was a step in the right direction from which he would never retreat.

He was determined never to retract or modify this edict. Not one slave liberated under its provisions must ever be returned to bondage.

"If the people should, by whatever mode or means make it an executive duty to re-enslave such persons, another and not I must be their instrument to perform it," he declared.[1]

If the Emancipation Proclamation, as a permanent and univer-

---

[1] Message to Congress, December 6, 1864.

sal remedy for the evil, was futile, then the next step was to change the Constitution itself to confer upon Congress express power to enlarge the field of personal liberty and restore to the four million human beings the God-given right of freedom so long denied them. This could be accomplished by confirming President Lincoln's beneficent edict of freedom by embodying the Proclamation of Emancipation in the organic law of the land by constitutional amendment. The Proclamation had at least theoretically destroyed slavery in the rebellious States. Now it remained for a constitutional amendment to make its effects practical and permanent, not only in those regions but also in States not included in the proclamation. Such an amendment would not only destroy the legal existence of the cursed institution, but would forever prohibit its re-establishment.

Lincoln's earlier attitude toward the general proposition of amending the Constitution had undergone a great change.

As a congressman in 1847, he had expressed his view that the Constitution is unalterable. "No slight occasion should tempt us to touch it," he had said. "It can scarcely be made better than it is."

Then, as President during the unprecedented Civil War, he found his powers to cope with the emergency limited by strict interpretation of certain provisions of the instrument. He was fearful lest he violate this "Higher Power." "I hope I may say nothing in opposition to the spirit of the Constitution," was his prayer. But the unparalleled exigencies confronting the Nation fighting for its life caused him to interpret the Constitution from the new viewpoint of military necessity, lest the Constitution itself, and the government created by it, perish. This attitude made possible the Emancipation Proclamation.

Toward the end of his career he no longer regarded the Constitution as an unalterable code of laws, but as an instrument for uplifting humanity. His advocacy of the Thirteenth Amendment followed naturally as a sacred duty.

"A question might be raised as to whether the Proclamation was legally valid," said the President in urging the immediate passage of the proposed amendment. "It might be added that it aided only those who came into our lines, and that it was inoperative as to those who did not give themselves up; or that it would have no effect upon the children of the slaves born hereafter; in fact, it could be urged that it did not meet the evil. But this amendment is a king's cure for all evils. It winds the whole thing up.''[1]

In 1864, a measure to submit a constitutional amendment abolishing slavery came before the Thirty-Eighth Congress. Lincoln's friend from Illinois, Senator Trumbull, reported the Thirteenth Amendment from the Committee on the Judiciary and led the fight in its behalf in the Senate. "This amendment adopted," he declared, "not only does slavery cease, but it can never be reestablished by State authority, or in any other way than by again amending the constitution." By a large majority it was approved by the Senate; but in the House the necessary two-thirds vote could not be obtained.[2]

However, when Congress reconvened after Lincoln's re-election, the President, in his Message, pointed out that the victory of his party clearly demonstrated that it was the will of the majority that the amendment be ratified. Therefore, "May we not agree that the sooner the better?"[3]

On January 6, 1865, the debate on the question was reopened. Powerful, eloquent, and elaborate speeches covering both sides of the proposition were made. On the last day of January a vote was finally reached, the roll-call proceeded, and amid the deepest excitement, enthusiasm, and fervid rejoicing the Speaker of the House declared the amendment approved.[4]

To a body of citizens who marched to the Executive Mansion the night following the passage of the measure, to congratulate the President, Lincoln in his characteristic homely fashion declared the "great job" was completed. "The occasion," said he,

---

[1] Raymond, *Life and State Papers of Abraham Lincoln*, p. 646.

[2] *Congressional Globe*, 38th Cong., 1st Sess., pp. 19 *et seq.*

[3] Annual message to Congress, December 6, 1864; *Works*, XI, 612–13.

[4] Joseph H. Barrett, *Life of Abraham Lincoln*, p. 685; John Sherman, *Recollections*, pp. 277 *et seq.*; Blaine, *Twenty Years*, I, 504, *et seq.*; *Congressional Globe*, 38th Cong., 2d Sess., pp. 138, 531.

"is one of congratulation to the country, and to the whole world. But there is yet a task before us—to go forward and have consummated by the votes of the States that which Congress so nobly began yesterday." The necessary ratification by twenty-seven of the thirty-six States was not to be accomplished until December 18, 1865, months after the madman's bullet had laid Lincoln low, but the "great job" was virtually finished. His cherished hope that all men, everywhere, might be free would soon be made good by law.

The extinction of slavery in America and the rededication of this Government to the doctrine of the equality of all men before the law as put into permanent form by the Thirteenth Amendment is Lincoln's crowning written contribution to the Constitution. That amendment reduced to law, as it were, Lincoln's life and Lincoln's creed.

But even more potent than this, though not in the form of a written law, is his great unwritten contribution—a sort of quasi-amendment that definitely settled for all time the constitutional status of the Union. By annihilating the assumed right of State secession and with it the whole doctrine of State sovereignty in all of its ramifications, he preserved the very existence of the Constitution. He thus not only removed the one pregnant source of endless confusion and acrimonious controversy at the very base of our system, but also established forever the integrity, indissolubility, perpetuit, and supremacy of the Union on constitutional foundations that can never be moved.

Always had the threat of secession been lurking about. Furtively it had skulked in the Kentucky and Virginia resolutions of 1789–99. When the Louisiana Purchase of 1803 vastly increased slave territory, and again in 1913 when New England opposition to the war with England culminated in the Hartford Convention, there had been wild talk of a separate Northern republic. "Texas or disunion," was heard throughout the South in 1843–44. On two other occasions prior to 1860 South Carolina had solemnly affirmed that it had a right to secede. "Elect Fremont and the South leaves the Union," was the threat during the campaign of 1856; and four years later it was "Elect Lincoln and the South will secede"! The constant menace hanging over the Union like a Damoclean sword had finally become a living, flaming reality with the outbreak of the Civil War. But the issue had been so defined by Lincoln that when the conflict was over the menace to the integrity of Union was also forever ended.

No longer could the Union be considered by the States as an arbitrary and artificial alliance established among them to be broken at will, but on the contrary, a Union sprung from the common origin, the mutual sympathies, the kindred principles and the similar interests of the American people, and now proved to be indissoluble and indestructible.

Abraham Lincoln had assumed the reins of the crumbling Government with four million human beings doomed to lifelong slavery and oppression. At Gettysburg, in deathless words, he had expressed his cherished hope for a "new Nation conceived in liberty and dedicated to the proposition that all men are created equal." Before he laid down his crushing burdens the spark of life had been breathed into the seemingly forgotten principle that all men are created equal, and the shackles fell from the limbs of the bondsman.

And as he unbound the slave, he bound the Nation. He had found the United States a federation of self-styled sovereign commonwealths infused with intense state consciousness and deep local prejudice, and inculcated with the doctrine of the supreme authority of the State as compared with the Union. He left them with a new sense of nationality and with the Nation's supremacy over the State forever at rest.

He had come upon the scene with the people blind to the potential greatness of a unified Nation. He left the States a single political people, a sovereign Nation exalting the Union with a heritage of perpetuity based on freedom and justice to all. "These" United States through Lincoln's efforts became "The" United States.

It was but fitting and natural that the Supreme Court of the United States should give constitutional interpretation and definite written form to President Lincoln's great achievement in these words: "The Union of the States never was a purely artificial and arbitrary relation. It began among the Colonies, . . . was confirmed and strengthened by the necessities of war, and received definite form . . . from the Articles of Confederation. By these the Union was solemnly declared to 'be perpetual.' And when these Articles were found inadequate the Constitution was ordained 'to form a more perfect Union.' It is difficult to convey the idea of indissoluble unity more clearly than by these words. What can be indissoluble if a perpetual Union, made more perfect, is not?

"The Constitution . . . looks to an indestructible Union composed of indestructible States."[1]

At first written only in the hearts of his grateful countrymen, Lincoln's triumphant doctrine now virtually assumed the effect of a constitutional amendment.

And so this crowning achievement of preserving the very existence of the Constitution by wiping out the assumed right of state secession and the mistaken doctrine of state sovereignty, the maintenance of the Union of the States as an indissoluble, indestructible, and perpetual relation, and the making of the American Government a sovereign Nation of enduring unity, a single people with one flag and one destiny, must remain along with the Thirteenth Amendment as Abraham Lincoln's monumental contributions to the Constitution.

---

[1] Texas vs. White, 7 Wall. 700; Knox vs. Lee, 12 Wall. 557; Keith vs. Clark, 97 U.S. 454.

XXVI. LINCOLN CLEARS THE TITLE DEED TO DEMOCRACY

AN AGGRESSIVE minority, constantly harassing President Lincoln and planning for his downfall at the polls, caused the sentiment to prevail in England that the North was dissatisfied with Lincoln's policies and desired a change.

London *Punch* in its issue of September 24, 1864, near the end of the presidential campaign of that year, pictures President Lincoln as a lawyer sitting at a table in his law office with his client, Mrs. North, a fine lady of affluence, seated at his right. Apparently she is not pleased with the services of the counselor who has represented her in a legal way for four years. Attorney Lincoln's countenance is marked with dejection and distress as the client ruthlessly addresses him in these words: "You see, Mr. Lincoln, we have failed utterly in our course of action; I want peace, and so if you cannot effect an amicable arrangement, I must put the case in other hands."

Punch, reflecting the sentiment that General McClellan would soon replace Attorney Lincoln as President of the United States, did not understand or appreciate the grip which the Springfield lawyer held upon the affections of the masses of his Nation.

Democrats were predicting that Lincoln would soon be back

343

in Springfield to resume his law practice, and were facetiously passing out "business cards" reading as the card reproduced on page 331.

A. LINCOLN
ATTORNEY AND COUNSELLOR AT LAW

Springfield, Ill.

To Whom it May Concern:

My old customers and others are no doubt aware of the terrible time I have had in crossing the stream, and will be glad to know that I will be back on the same side from which I started on or before the 4th of March, next, when I will be ready to Swap Horses, Dispense Law, Make Jokes, Split Rails, perform other matters in a Small Way.

As it turned out, General McClellan carried but three States in the ensuing election.

In unfading words the successful President's second Inaugural Address spoke this prayer of a repentant Nation "that this mighty scourge of war may speedily pass away."

And now with the conflagration practically ended, reconstruction—the second phase of the problem imposed by secession—was confronting the President. Again he lacked constitutional authority or legal precedent for guidance. Never before in history had just such a problem arisen. Often in the past, insurgent populations had been subjugated and national sovereignties preserved. But here was a different situation. Here arose the unprecedented problem of restoring into a national entity a number of organic political units, each possessing a republican form of government and claiming the inherent right to secede and to form new political groupings at will. But with this right denied and defeated by the outcome of the Civil War, just what was the status of the erring States? Were they in the Union or out? Did they still form with the loyal States an "Indestructible Union of Indestructible States," or was the constitutional connection between these units forever broken, leaving the States which had unsuccessfully attempted secession in the status of conquered territories?

This unparalleled situation called for an original solution. The legal and constitutional interpretations applicable to the theories of reconstruction would necessarily be varied and conflicting. Again there was need for the exercise of the broad principles of law and justice with which the twenty-three years of practice at the bar had endowed Abraham Lincoln. Again there was need of wise exercise of the large discretionary powers of his high office and a sane interpretation of the Constitution to give it elasticity and adaptability to cope with the unprecedented emergency.

As early as December 8, 1863, President Lincoln, amid a multitude of conflicting counsels and partisan prejudices, made known his own views regarding reconstruction.

He issued a proclamation based on his pardoning powers, extending amnesty to all, with the exception of certain classes, who should take a prescribed oath of allegiance to the Government of the United States. The proclamation further provided that whenever as many as one tenth of the number of voters in 1860 should thus recover the franchise in any State which had been the scene of rebellion, they might organize a state government with a constitution providing for the abolition of slavery. The President would then recognize such government as the legal government of the State, although—and he made this plain—Congress would have to decide for itself the question of admission of representatives from the State. This proclamation resulted in the organization and recognition of such governments in Tennessee, Louisiana, and Arkansas.

All along he had claimed that the Union was legally indestructible and the ordinances of secession enacted by the Southern States a mere nullity. Therefore, from the strictly legal standpoint, they had never been out of the Union, for if these States could not secede they could not become foreign. Of course their constitutional governments had been destroyed. But now that hostilities had ceased and their citizens were ready to fulfill all constitutional obligations and to re-establish governments republican in form and loyal to the Union, why should not the General

Government lend its advice and aid and even armed forces to enable the loyal citizens of the States in their efforts to re-establish loyal governments?[1]

Charles Sumner, B. F. Wade, Henry Winter Davis, Thaddeus Stevens, and other leaders of Congress disagreed violently with Lincoln's theory that reconstruction was an executive function. They regarded it as a legislative problem to be solved by congressional act and constitutional amendment. In general, they would have Congress deal with the rebellious districts not as "States" of the Union but as territories which had lost the form, powers, and functions of "state" governments during the rebellion and were now neither out of the Union nor in the Union, but under the control of the Central Government as territories inhabited by a population disorganized as to local government. Congress could impose whatever requirements it saw fit as conditions precedent to their readmission to full membership in the Union.[2]

Lincoln believed that his theory of reconstruction was more in consonance with the general constitutional theory upon which the North had waged war, but he did not care to press this view. He refused to commit himself to an exclusive and inflexible plan of reconstruction. He was not inclined to quibble over details respecting the legal and constitutional status of the seceded States if the end he was seeking could be as well attained in another way.[3]

In his last public address, April 11, 1865, in commenting upon the mooted question whether the seceded States were in the Union or out of it, President Lincoln refused to quibble over technicalities. He was too cautious to commit himself to an unnecessary legal position. As he had always done in his practice on the Eighth Circuit, he brushed away the husk and went to the kernel of the case. The vital issue now was no pedantic controversy, he insisted.

---

[1] Willoughby, *American Constitutional System*, pp. 85–98; John W. Burgess, *Reconstruction and the Constitution*, pp. 8–30; Charles H. McCarthy, *Lincoln's Plan of Reconstruction*, pp. 190–95; James Schouler, *History of the United States under the Constitution*, VI, 532–35; *Works*, II, 444; IX, 219–22.

[2] *Congressional Globe*, Thirty-Eighth Congress, First Session, February 15, 1864, p. 668.

[3] *Works*, II, 454.

"That question," he declared, referring to the technical status of the lately rebellious commonwealths, "is bad as the basis of controversy, and good for nothing at all—a merely pernicious abstraction. We all agree that the seceded States, so called, are out of their proper practical relation to the Union, and that the sole object of the Government, civil and military, in regard to those States is to again get them into that proper practical relation."

The great object was to bring the Southern States back to their former original standing in a "spirit of conciliation, friendship, and forbearance which should characterize a generous and forgiving people." So the President added:

"I believe that it is not only possible, but in fact easier to do this without deciding or even considering whether these States have ever been out of the Union, than with it. Finding themselves safely at home, it would be utterly immaterial whether they had ever been abroad. Let us join in doing the acts necessary to restoring the proper relations between these States and the Union, and each forever after innocently indulge in his opinion whether in doing the acts he brought the States from without into the Union, or only gave them proper assistance, they never having been out of it."

Lincoln's view regarding reconstruction, to the effect that the constitutional existence of the States perdured through the rebellion, was eventually sustained by the judiciary. "Circumstances had disarranged their relations with the Federal Government, but with the correction of the disturbance the former conditions could be resumed."[1]

Good Friday, April 14, 1865, was Cabinet day for President Lincoln. Now that Congress was adjourned he believed he could better discuss with his advisors the momentous problem of reconstruction without hindrance from the "disturbing element in the legislative body." "If we are wise and discreet we shall reanimate the States and get their governments in successful operation

---

[1] Hosmer, *Outcome of the Civil War (American Nation Series*, vol. XXI), p. 138; Dunning, *Essays on the Civil War*, p. 72; *Prize Cases*, 2 Black 668; Case of Venice, 2 Wallace 278. Texas vs. White, 7 Wallace 700.

with order prevailing and the Union re-established'' before Congress reconvenes, he told his ministers.

Four years of trial by fire had left Lincoln weary, gray of visage, heavy-eyed—his face furrowed with lines of care. Trained to a profession of peace but plunged by circumstances into the vortex of a bloody fratricidal war, he found now in its virtual termination a happiness he had never before experienced.

Others were demanding "persecution" and "bloody work" as punishment for the rebels, but in the heart of this man was no room for resentment or revenge against the bleeding and humiliated South. The same tenderness that had prompted the circuit-riding lawyer to dismount from his horse to replace in their nest some baby birds fallen to the muddy roadside would now stop all display of vengeance toward his fellow countrymen of the exhausted South.

"No one need expect me," President Lincoln asserted, "to take any part in hanging or killing these men, even the worst of them. Frighten them out of the country, open the gates, let down the bars, scare them off. . . . We must extinguish our resentment if we expect harmony and Union," he pleaded with his Cabinet. The vindictive and uncharitable Lincoln, who as a young lawyer strove ruthlessly to crush James Adams when convinced that this Springfield politician had cheated the widow Mary Anderson, had long since passed into the humanitarian of the second inaugural.

The President dismissed his cabinet. With a heart lighter than at any time since he entered the White House, he walked upstairs for a long talk with his son Robert, recently returned from the front after serving as a member of General Grant's staff.

The President was proud of Robert. The father could boast of less than twelve months of actual schooling. Throughout his life he had felt deeply the need of literary attainments, and he had determined that his son should not be lacking at least in that particular. Robert was now a Harvard graduate and the President was very happy. Of course he, too, could now boast of college degrees—two honorary degrees of Doctor of Laws, conferred by Knox College at Galesburg, Illinois, in 1860 and by the College of New Jersey, afterwards known as Princeton University, in

1864. They were granted in recognition of his noble services for his Nation. The once bookless boy was taking his place with the masters of his native tongue. His writings were being recognized as patterns of classic diction. The self-trained backwoods lawyer had risen to a plane of the immortals of constitutional interpretation. His broad views, the versatility and acumen of his argument, his insight into the ruling principles of statecraft, and the eloquence of his pleading had proved well his qualifications for the great undertaking to which he had consecrated his life.

But he had resolved that his son should not lack the early opportunities he himself had missed. In 1859, he decided that Robert should go to Cambridge. And though disappointment came to him when Robert failed in every subject of the Harvard entrance examinations except one, and was refused admission, the Springfield lawyer willingly spent a sizable portion of his annual income to enroll his son in Phillips Academy at Exeter, New Hampshire, one of the best preparatory schools in the land. Here Robert studied for his admission to Harvard.

The younger Lincoln would relate laughingly in later years that but for his failure at the Harvard entrance examinations, his father never would have become the President of the United States. He would then explain that his father's desire to visit him at Exeter to interview his teachers regarding the progress he was making in his studies was chiefly responsible for Abraham Lincoln's acceptance of the invitation to speak at Plymouth Church in Brooklyn. The place for the address was changed to Copper Union, and here the Springfield lawyer delivered that most momentous speech of his career.

Upon Robert's graduation from Harvard in 1864, he became an aide-de-camp to General Grant. He returned to Washington with the General, and his proud father was delighted with the young captain's comments about the campaign. The elder Lincoln now was anxious that Robert should turn his attention to his future career. He favored Robert's return to Harvard Law School and preparation for the bar. Lincoln had never read a law book through in all his life. He himself had said so. But Robert's opportunities were different, and he would become a far greater lawyer than his famous father. This was Abraham's devout wish.

"If you become a lawyer you will probably make more money at it than I ever did," he told his son, "but you won't have half the fun."

Longingly he was thinking of the bygone exhilarating days on the circuit. Some day he would return to his Springfield law office. Perhaps Robert would become a partner. . . .

Late that afternoon President Lincoln went out for a ride with Mrs. Lincoln. The crushing weight seemed lifted from his shoulders. The characteristic look of unutterable grief was gone from his eyes. An indescribable expression of serene joy now marked his countenance—"as if conscious that the great purpose of his life had been achieved."

"Mary," he said during the course of the drive, "we have had a hard time of it since we came to Washington; but the war is over, and with God's blessing we may hope for four years of peace and happiness, and then we will go back to Illinois, and pass the rest of our lives in quiet. We have laid by some money, and during this term we will try and save up more, but shall not have enough to support us. We will go back to Illinois, and I will open a law office at Springfield or Chicago, and practice law, and at least do enough to help give us a livelihood."[1]

He was going back again to join Herndon in their humble Springfield law office when the duties of the Presidency should be over. Henry Winter Davis, Reverdy Johnson, William Pitt Fessenden, Edwin M. Stanton, William H. Seward, and a host of other great lawyers were on the stage, and Lincoln had risen superior to them all in the realm of constitutional interpretation. But the Lincoln & Herndon sign still hung at the foot of the stairway leading to their dingy office, and he would keep his promise to Billy to return.

Only a few weeks previously a letter from Herndon had been delivered to the President. It contained a check for one hundred and thirteen dollars, Lincoln's share of collections made from

---

[1] Statement of Mary Lincoln to Isaac Arnold, in Arnold, *Abraham Lincoln*, p. 429; Nicolay, *Short Life of Abraham Lincoln*, p. 532; Lamon, *Recollections*, pp. 119–20; F. B. Carpenter, *Inner Life of Abraham Lincoln; Six Months at the White House*, p. 293; Tarbell, *Life of Abraham Lincoln*, II, 235.

outstanding fees of the old firm. Fifteen dollars more would be forthcoming, Billy promised. He thought his famous partner would be interested in knowing how he was faring back in Springfield, so he added: "I am toddling on tolerably well, just making ends meet, but that is enough for me or any man in this world at this time. Above all, I am a sober man, and will keep so the balance of my days."[1]

The preserver of the Union and liberator of the slaves was ready to step back into the ranks as soon as his term was over. "If I live," he had promised Herndon, "I'm coming back some time, and then we'll go right on practicing law as if nothing had ever happened."

"If I live! . . ."

But in the evening Abraham Lincoln went to Ford's Theater— and to his martyrdom.

A sorrowing Nation bore Abraham Lincoln to his beloved Springfield. Judge David Davis and Ward Hill Lamon, who so often in the past had traveled with him around the judicial circuit, now escorted his remains from Washington.

Springfield, draped in mourning, broken-hearted but proud in her grief, took back her famous son. In endless streams came men and women to pay their last tribute to a neighbor and friend. To them Abraham Lincoln was still the genial lawyer and re-sourceful political debater. With heavy hearts they bore him past the scenes of his early struggles. The Lincoln & Herndon shingle swung mournfully in front of the old law office. "Old Bob," the once-sturdy horse which for years had carried Lawyer Lincoln over the muddy roads as he made his lonely trips around the circuit, now walked slowly behind the hearse of his dead master as the imposing funeral procession wound its way to the tomb. In the bosom of the familiar prairie, gay with Maytime blossoms, Abraham Lincoln was laid to rest.

His work was done. The one-time humble lawyer had saved the cause of popular government. He had cleared the title to the deed to democracy!

---

[1] W. H. Herndon to Lincoln, Springfield, February 11, 1865; Davis MSS.

INDEX

353